T0355420

THE

EASTERN CHURCH

IN THE

SPIRITUAL

MARKETPLACE

THE
Eastern Church
IN THE
Spiritual
Marketplace

American Conversions to

Orthodox Christianity

AMY SLAGLE

NIU PRESS

DeKalb

Library of Congress Cataloging-in-Publication Data
Slagle, Amy.
The Eastern Church in the spiritual marketplace: American conversions to Orthodox
Christianity / Amy Slagle.
    p.   cm.
Includes bibliographical references (P.   ) and index.
ISBN 978-0-87580-670-9 (pbk.)
1. Orthodox Eastern converts—United States. 2. United States—
Religious life and customs. I. Title.
BX390.S63 2011
248.2'4088281973—dc23
2011016761

Parts of chapters 3 and 4 of the present work appeared previously as an article in *Religion and American Culture* 20, no. 2 (Summer 2010): 233–57. Copyright by University of California Press. Used here with permission.

For my parents—Robert and Nancy—and my niece, Kathryn

Contents

THE
EASTERN CHURCH
IN THE
SPIRITUAL
MARKETPLACE

Introduction

A self-assured stay-at-home mother of two in her midthirties, Karen in many respects epitomized domestic and religious rootedness.[1] She was also the first person I interviewed as I began ethnographic research into the processes and motivations of contemporary American conversions to Eastern Orthodox Christianity first in Pittsburgh, Pennsylvania, in 2005–2006 and then in Jackson, Mississippi, in the spring of 2009. As we sipped tea in her cozy living room filled with family pictures, toys, books, and Orthodox icons, Karen's infant daughter sat contentedly nearby in her carrier and the family's friendly basset hound periodically lumbered in and out of the room. Although Karen had moved away to attend college on the East Coast, she had returned to her native Pittsburgh in the late 1990s with her husband to complete a doctorate in architectural engineering and to start a family. Raised within a solidly Roman Catholic home, she recalled a warm childhood filled with Christmas Eve midnight masses and the kitchen bustling of her beloved Slovak-born grandmother. A dedicated Christian, Karen was active in her parish, St. Michael's Orthodox Church, where she had been received into the faith in 2003, and attended services each Sunday with her (still Protestant) husband and (now Orthodox) small daughters.

However, beneath the placid connectedness to family and church that seemingly defined the contours of Karen's life lay a youth marked by deep spiritual restlessness. In the course of our afternoon conversation Karen, a self-styled "seeker of truth," related her nearly fifteen-year "personal journey" in search of its ecclesial embodiment. Drifting away from her childhood Catholicism during her freshman year of college, Karen began attending a Pentecostal church upon the urging of a classmate, an initial move that prompted her to investigate other churches over time. Dissatisfied with one after another, Karen made her way through a variety of non-denominational, evangelical mega-churches, with multimedia worship services and rock music catering to Gen-Xers, to arrive eventually at high-church Anglicanism, with its staid traditionalism and glimmerings of Chestertonian "romance," years later. This latter setting proved to be the last of Karen's Protestant life before she embraced Orthodox Christianity, a faith with which she had had periodic contact through friends in graduate school.

In discussing what fueled her religious search, Karen pointed to the confusion she felt when confronted by the vast array of competing theologies, forms of worship, and ecclesial polities abounding within contemporary Christianity. She explained:

> I just started getting theology books and there would be a man who wrote this book and he'd talk about his theology and my question would be, "Well, that's his opinion or is that truth?" Because then I'd have another book on the same topic and it would give different information. So if you want to say something on prayer, you could have a thousand different opinions. This is how you pray and this is how you pray and this is how you pray and they're different. So, how do I know how to pray? And this is the church. No, no, no, they're wrong. This is what the church is. Well, either they're contradicting each other or one of them's right or they're all wrong. . . . It just seems strange to me, all these people having different opinions.

Such a state of affairs deeply disturbed Karen, who considered "truth," even in her youth, as singular and unchanging. Although, in her words, she "did not have the name pluralism" at the time to describe this multiplicity of practice and interpretation, it appeared to her as preeminently wrong. Now endowed with such a name, Karen declared from her present standpoint as an Orthodox Christian, "Pluralism just does not work within Christianity although many people try to make it work that way. It doesn't work. That's an invention. Pluralism is not Christianity, in my opinion."

Distasteful or not, it was precisely this trenchant religious pluralism that allowed Karen's personal journey to materialize and proceed to its conclusion within Orthodox Christianity. Like so many contemporary Americans, Karen had become a full participant in what scholars today refer to as the spiritual marketplace of expanding religious diversity and individual choice-making that has marked the post–World War II American religious landscape. As one early theorist of the workings of the religious marketplace, Peter Berger, argues in *The Sacred Canopy*, the once venerable, premodern religious monopolies providing "the ultimate legitimation for individual and collective life" in centuries past have fragmented into a plurality of competing worldviews and religious options available for individual choosing. Pointing to the example of American denominationalism, Berger describes how religions, now "competitive marketing agencies," vie for a clientele that increasingly considers religion to be a private affair undertaken for the meeting of psychological needs and fulfillments rather than as a source of social cohesiveness.[2]

In this vein, Philip Hammond has identified the 1960s as the decade in which "the values of free choice and the experimentation of the religious marketplace" became normative for many Americans. The willingness of Americans to trade denominational loyalty, often grounded in familial, ethnic, social, or economic constraint, for more individualized, novel, and eclectic religious expressions can be gauged by comparing two well-known assessments of American religious life divided by the increased diversity and individualism fomented in the 1960s. While Will Herberg, on the one hand, characterized 1950s America to be neatly composed of "Protestant, Catholic, Jew," Robert Bellah, on the other, was left to wonder, with no small amount of sarcasm by the mid-1980s, whether there might not be "over 220 million American religions," a circumstance he much lamented in his discussion of the nurse Sheila Larson and her self-formulated and described religion of "Sheilaism." Whereas lifelong ecclesial or religious affiliations were once the expectation in many corners of society, Americans, like Karen, feel little inhibition about investigating different churches and formally crossing religious boundaries at will. According to a 2009 survey conducted by the Pew Research Center's Forum on Religion and the Public Life, approximately half of adult Americans have changed their religious affiliation at least once in their lifetimes, with the majority of these persons, like Karen, leaving their childhood faiths by age 24.[3]

Despite concerns expressed on the part of Peter Berger (at least in his early scholarship), Robert Bellah, and others that the spiritual marketplace signaled the demise of traditional religious communities, other sociologists have noted the robustness of religious movements, especially those of a more conservative ilk, in bringing new members into their folds and contributing to contemporary discourses. As early as 1972, sociologist Dean M. Kelley posed the question, "Why are conservative churches growing?" in his famous book of the same title. He argues that stricter religious groups demanding higher degrees of behavioral conformity and adherence are often much more success-ful in attracting and maintaining modern converts than their more liberal and lenient counterparts. He further concludes that the moral and behavioral strictness conservative churches offer fosters a sense of togetherness with the chosen community and apartness from the outside world that many individuals find compelling.[4]

A number of studies, especially those authored from the perspec-tive of rational choice theory, have also posited the relative strength and growth potential of conservative churches in the United States. Laurence R. Iannaccone, for example, has maintained that the relative strictness of a religious community is in direct proportion to the commitment its members demonstrate towards it. In short, the theological and behavioral strictness of conservative churches increases commitment in weeding out religious free-riders and ce-menting social cohesiveness among a group's members. Roger Finke has offered a similar argument in equating the late twentieth-century decline in the numbers of women entering Roman Catholic religious orders to an easing of restrictions regarding dress and other behav-iors following the Second Vatican Council of the 1960s. Even more broadly, rather than observing a general disintegration of religious groups and expression in the over two centuries of America's exis-tence, Rodney Stark and Roger Finke have provocatively argued that twenty-first-century Americans are *more* inclined to attend church and actively participate in religious communities than their colonial counterparts. Furthermore, in the midst of this historical "church-ing of America," conservative churches have generally been more successful than those falling along the liberal Protestant mainline in attracting and maintaining members. Beyond the rational choice ap-proach and on a more popular level, Colleen Carroll too has recently documented the attraction that conservative Christianity holds for young adults.[5]

Thus, in addition to sharing with others of her generation a penchant to investigate and experiment with religious options, Karen, like many Americans, was also drawn to the moral certitude and singularity of conservative Christianity. Encountering Orthodoxy through social contacts and over the course of her extensive readings, Karen felt a particular affinity with the early church fathers, whose teachings, in her view, aligned precisely with those of contemporary Orthodox Christianity. She declared, "I came [to Orthodoxy] because the doctrines that I read of the [church] fathers didn't match up with *any* other church on the planet. And I believe if Christ truly taught his disciples these things or this is what the *church* led by the Holy Spirit believed then and what it believes now. . . . The closer you get your doctrines to match those of the early church, the closer you're going to get to the truth." For Karen, the discovery of this "truth" ensured that she would no longer inhabit the hinterlands of uncertainty, for as she noted, "Finally it [Orthodox Christianity] answered all of my questions. I was just stunned. I couldn't believe it. In fact, I would have converted a lot earlier but I think I was waiting for my husband to convert along with me" (at the time of our interview, Karen's husband remained a staunch Protestant).

While Karen's conversion to Orthodoxy may be considered a direct reaction against the relativism, individualism, and consumerism of American religious life, in many ways it more adequately reflects what Jean and John Comaroff describe as the "long conversation" of religious change and transformation as disparate cultural elements and formulae that come to be used and transmuted in the course of individuals' lives.[6] Karen's investigation and embrace of Orthodox Christianity is not a simple exchange of generalized American for Eastern Orthodox beliefs, idioms, and ways of acting in the world—a simple exchange of the "modern" for the "traditional"—but a subtle blending and melding together of elements from these quite distinct sources. For Karen, the subjective self remained the primary seat of religious authority and enactment, even in her humble yielding to the moral and spiritual guidance of an "ancient" Christianity. She readily embraced the religious autonomy and choice-making the spiritual marketplace afforded her. Not only did Karen choose the sources that guided her to the Orthodox faith according to personal preference and taste (as she said, "I just got books that seemed interesting"), but she also trusted her own ability to interpret these texts and to question the doctrinal verity of her Protestant pastors in light of their teachings.

At the same time, Karen's eventual conversion to Orthodox Christianity cannot be mechanistically attributed to the marketplace alone, for the doctrinal, ritual, and communal offerings of the Eastern Church too play a vital role in attracting individuals and furnishing a rich cachet of strategies for constructing post-conversion identities within the Orthodox Church. From its historical claims as the church of the early apostles and its emphasis on unchanging truth and tradition to the sensory appeal of its liturgical forms, the Orthodox Church provides Karen and her fellow converts novel ways of thinking about and enacting their lives. While these Orthodox cultural tools are often portrayed as the very antithesis of the American spiritual marketplace, convert acceptance and utilization of both illustrate their fundamental entwinement. Furthermore, this interplay resonates far beyond the experiences of individual converts to shape the perspectives of clerics and lifelong church members in local Orthodox parish life. Just as conversion itself does not represent an either/or scenario of moving from the spiritual marketplace to Orthodox ecclesial stability, so too have local Orthodox parishes in the United States deeply imbibed the language and methods of the marketplace in ways long overlooked by its typical characterization as a conservative, "ethnic" Christianity set apart from the profound transformations witnessed in post–World War II American religious life. The influences of these cultural contexts on contemporary conversions within American Orthodox communities stand as a central theme of this book.

Eastern Orthodoxy and American Culture

In spite of Karen's and many other converts' recent discovery of and enthusiasm for the Orthodox Church and the overall robustness of conservative religions and movements, Orthodox Christianity typically receives little more than an honorable mention in most traditional histories of religion in America.[7] First brought to North America at the end of the eighteenth century by Russian missionaries intent on spreading their faith to the indigenous peoples of Alaska, Eastern Orthodoxy, throughout most of the twentieth century, was regarded as something of an immigrant religion, tied to the various groups from eastern and southeastern Europe and the Middle East that came and settled in the United States at the turn of the last century.[8] By the late twentieth century, about a million of Orthodox Christianity's 180–216 million members worldwide (estimates vary) resided in the United

States.[9] Characterized by one convert whom I interviewed as a seemingly "stuffy, old church that doesn't have any fun at all," Orthodox Christianity emerged as an increasingly viable religious option for many Americans in the wake of a series of well-documented and high-profile conversions of evangelical Protestants and persons of other religious confessions beginning in the mid-1980s.[10]

Since that time, the church has become especially attractive to educated, upper-middle-class Americans with a number of prominent academic and media figures, such as the eminent church historian the late Jaroslav Pelikan, the scholar of African American religions Albert Raboteau, and the Pittsburgh Steelers team member Troy Polumalu, among others, becoming Orthodox in recent years. Pointedly drawn to the church for theological and/or liturgical reasons after years of active religious seeking and questing, many of these converts have set upon the self-proclaimed task of spreading Orthodoxy to America at large through active evangelism and the establishment of mission parishes in areas of the United States with little historical Orthodox presence such as the Deep South.[11] Integral to these efforts has been the expansion of print and electronic materials dedicated to the sharing of converts' stories and the educating of interested inquirers into the liturgical and doctrinal intricacies of the Orthodox faith.

While Eastern Orthodoxy has received less ethnographic and scholarly attention than other conservative religions in the United States, including Orthodox Judaism and fundamentalist/evangelical Protestantism, scholars have begun to explore the impacts modern processes of globalization and pluralism have wrought upon Orthodox Christianity in the United States and elsewhere. A common verdict of many of these studies is that Orthodoxy remains highly resistant to marketplace influence and change.[12] In his ongoing demographic overview of American Orthodoxy, Alexei D. Krindatch, for example, maintains, "Today, in spite of the fact that American society is richly endowed with multiple venues for public dialogue and cultural exchange, the Eastern Christians remain to a significant extent in self-isolated communities. Even gradual disappearance of the urban ethnic neighborhoods did not change this situation." Observing the worldwide interplay of Orthodoxy with the forces of late modernity, Victor Roudometof and Alexander Agadjanian write in their introduction to the essay collection *Eastern Orthodoxy in a Global Age*, "The *dominant mode* of Eastern Orthodox responses to globality has been self-protective and communitarian (rather than self-adjusting and individualistic)."[13]

According to sociologist Elizabeth H. Prodromou, the "institutional culture" of American Orthodox churches, including the "hierarchy, clergy, and laity," has remained suspicious of the "market metaphor" and, therefore, "slow to develop the kinds of strategic vision and operational mechanisms required for religious competition in the public sphere." She rightly posits that the "internal pluralization" of Orthodox churches, as evidenced in conversions, interfaith marriages, and the gradual replacement of original Old World immigrants with their American descendents, may precipitate a serious self-reevaluation and redefining of the Orthodox Church's place within American culture. Yet, how and to what effects religious pluralism impacts Orthodox Christianity have yet to be fully understood, for as Prodromou concludes, "Analysis of the [Orthodox] response to these questions is the material for a rich research agenda that is ready for implementation."[14]

I consider this book on the language and enactment of choice among American converts to the Orthodox Church a modest way of advancing this "rich research agenda." Religious pluralism and individualism are not hypothetical circumstances, awaiting hierarchical acknowledgment and engagement once the scales of ethnicity supposedly fall from official eyes, but are habitualized and taken for granted among the participants of Orthodox parish life. Ethnographic research in actual Orthodox communities, where the words and actions of religious participants are taken seriously and faithfully recorded, affords us a new way of measuring and understanding the extent to which Orthodox Christianity has become enmeshed with American cultures. While the Orthodox Church may not yet occupy the center of the American public square, in a sense the American public square has come to occupy its own space within local communities. A reading of Orthodoxy's official "institutional culture," its official pronouncements and theological formulae alone, simply may not reflect these developments and habits. Therefore, this study offers another, long-overlooked, vantage point from which to understand Orthodox Christianity in the United States.

A few studies documenting and analyzing American conversions to Orthodoxy exist as well. Among them are the 1997 article by Paisios Bukowy Whitesides, "Ethnics and Evangelicals: Theological Tensions within American Orthodoxy," in which are discussed opposing hermeneutics, cut along essentialized "iconic"/"textual" lines and represented by ethnic Orthodox Christians and evangelical Protestant converts. As the article's subtitle suggests, these hermeneutic approaches are believed to create tensions in the formulation and expression of Eastern Orthodox theology in the United States today. While Whitesides examines the theological impact of conversions, Phillip Charles Lucas has investigated the history and religious evolution of a 1960s esoteric group, the Holy Order of MANS, members of which converted to Orthodox Christianity in the late 1980s. While focused upon issues of religious transformation and conversion of import to my own research, Lucas's book, *The Odyssey of a New Religion*, is more solidly devoted to the changing place of MANS as a New Religious Movement from the 1960s to 1980s than to the subsequent experiences of its members as converts to Orthodoxy. From this work, Lucas authored an article, "*Enfants Terribles*: The Challenges of Sectarian Converts to Ethnic Orthodox Churches in the United States," in which he describes and provides analysis of the challenges that conversions to Orthodoxy, including those of former MANS members, pose for ethnic communities.[15]

Two additional studies of converts to Eastern Orthodoxy have been conducted, contextualizing this group within modern American culture. First, H.B. Cavalcanti and H. Paul Chalfant interviewed the American converts of a Boston Orthodox parish to determine the extent to which collective religious life drives and gives expression to personal belief. In their valuable study, these researchers note the "interactive" nature of these conversions in their social context and the ways in which the "private belief systems find communal support" in the course of Orthodox parish life. Second, Richard P. Cimino interviewed 30 young adults between the ages of 23 and 35 years of age who had embraced (through conversion and reversion) "traditional Christianity" in its Roman Catholic, Reformed Protestant, and Eastern Orthodox guises. His results, especially in regard to the motives young people cite for participating in "traditional Christianity," will stand as an important point of comparison to my own examination of conversion motives and meanings of Orthodox Christianity detailed in chapter four.[16]

This book differs from these important methodological and theoretical forebears in a number of respects. First, I have attempted to understand and present conversion to Orthodox Christianity from the perspectives of diverse social actors in parish life. While the emphasis is placed on the experiences of converts entering the Orthodox Church for theological and/or liturgical reasons, they are not the entire focus of this book since I also take into account the perspectives of intermarriage converts, clerics (including a Pittsburgh-area bishop), and lifelong church members. Second, this book moves beyond one parish or demographic group (young adults) to include women and men of diverse backgrounds, ages, Orthodox jurisdictions, and regions of the United States. Third, I am interested in what Orthodoxy and its embrace signifies not only to individual converts but to local communities as a whole. What does it mean to be a convert in local Orthodox parish life? If converts are perceived as distinct in their communities, what is it that distinguishes them from and among other religious insiders? What do these intra-parish views tell us about the relative place of Orthodox Christianity in American life? No other study of Orthodox converts takes into account this more generalized context.

Finally, as already indicated, this book reflects the relatively recent and ever more pervasive trend to focus on what is variously described as "lived," "living," and "everyday" religion. I have entered a tiny, rather circumspect part of the vast religious landscape about us, the terrain of Orthodox Christian converts in Pittsburgh and Jackson, to report on how the grand macro-processes of conversion, marketplace seeking and choice-making as well as embrace of an ancient, heavily ritual- ized and ethnic form of Christianity exist and are made manifest on the micro-level of individual lives and relationships. Scholars such as David Hall, Robert Orsi, and Nancy T. Ammerman have embraced the category of "lived" or "everyday" religion as a way of breaking through the fundamental dichotomization of religious experiences between those of "ordinary" nonelites and institutional officialdom, a dichotomy engrained in the notion of "popular religion" itself. "Lived" religion, as an analytical category, allows researchers to consider the religious ideas and actions of what Nancy Ammerman refers to as "nonexperts" in relationship to and within official religious institutions and theological frames of reference.[17]

In keeping with my intent to stay as close as possible to the words and actions of study informants, I have found elements of practice theory, especially as formulated in the work of Ann Swidler, particularly use- ful for understanding the "on the ground" enactment of conversion in Orthodox parishes. Drawing upon the work of Pierre Bourdieu, Ann Swidler has argued that culture is best conceptualized as a "toolkit," "repertoire," or "bag of tricks" of context-specific resources available in a way similar to those employed by an artist or musician. In Swidler's view, cultural repertoires provide "discrete skills, habits, and orienta- tions" for mastery and reproduction in a variety of settings. Some "cultural orientations" may become so habitualized that they are largely unconscious, while others require massive amounts of effort and atten- tion to master.[18]

Thus, while acknowledging the importance of choice and the marketplace metaphor as wielded in the abovementioned studies grounded in rational choice theory, I more impressionistically here survey the ways in which choice and choice-making are articulated in conversion narratives and are observed within the framework of parish social interaction. The marketplace and its choice-making engines are not the sole determinants of conversions to Orthodoxy or American religious life more generally, but simply one among many possible toolkits to be utilized in the organizing of experience. Furthermore, the marketplace is not an assumed context on my part, imposed from without upon informants' narratives, but a field, conveyed by informants themselves, that provides a powerful set of habits, strategies, and assumptions for meaning-making in converts' post-conversion lives. I contextualize these conversions within the spiritual marketplace because informants in Pittsburgh and Jackson themselves readily wield the concepts, language, and methodologies of the marketplace in their narratives.

Fundamentally, these narratives yield richly detailed accounts of the mechanics of conversion as an epistemological endeavor, as a Bakhtinian "knowledge through struggle," or as Gauri Viswanathan maintains, a "knowledge-producing" activity, whereby processes of negotiation and strategizing affect processes of cultural and religious change.[19] Conversion does not happen to the converts of this study, it is something they *do*. Converts engage in extensive campaigns of investigating different worldview options and religious practices through formal study, private reading, and comparison. They become critically self-aware in evaluating their own needs, desires, and beliefs vis-à-vis the religious options available for experimentation or adoption. At the same time, converts must learn and acquire the skills and beliefs of Orthodox Christianity, a religious system known for its doctrinal and ritual intricacies that are often quite foreign to the assumptions and sensibilities that converts unconsciously wielded before and after their respective entries to the church.

This book, therefore, is about the ways in which Orthodox converts as well as the priests and lifelong parishioners of their respective communities draw upon the two competing repertoires of the American spiritual marketplace and Eastern Orthodox belief and practice to make sense of and enact conversion as well as construct ongoing post-conversion identities within the church. While, as the ethnographic data make clear, the term "conversion" is defined in a number of ways among my informants, "convert" as commonly used in ordinary parish life and in contemporary American Orthodox literature refers specifically to individuals who come to accept membership in the Orthodox Church in adolescence or adulthood. The same terminology is used regardless of the specific motivations cited for this change in religious affiliation, whether for reasons of marriage or out of doctrinal or liturgical concerns.

All the convert informants selected for this book underwent the adult initiatory rites of baptism and/or chrismation or confession. Since there is no uniform, churchwide protocol for which rituals should be administered to adult converts, the precise manner of reception varies among jurisdictions, dioceses, and parishes. While all Orthodox Church members must be baptized, the baptisms of most other Christian confessions are considered valid. Therefore, the already baptized are usually brought into Orthodoxy through chrismation, a sacrament involving the anointing of a newly baptized person (either an infant or an adult) with chrism or holy oil. This ritual is analogous to the sacrament of confirmation performed in other Christian churches. Meanwhile, Roman and Byzantine Catholics are occasionally brought into Orthodoxy through confession alone.[20]

Overview of Chapters

The ways in which converts draw upon the vocabularies and concepts of the American spiritual marketplace and Orthodox Christianity will be treated in a roughly chronological fashion from informants' pre-conversion seeking and choice-making to post-conversion uses of ritual and ethnicity long after entry to the Orthodox Church has occurred.

Chapter one introduces Eastern Orthodoxy as a religious system as well as the primary field sites of St. Michael's and Ascension (Pittsburgh) and St. Seraphim's (Jackson) where I met and conversed with the informants whose stories rest at the heart of this book. An overview of methodological issues will be treated in this chapter as well.

Chapter two explores the ways in which modern American religious diversity and seeking influence the pre-conversion biographies of informants, especially as individuals begin to compare and experiment with different worldview options in young adulthood. In addition to examining the experiences of seeker converts drawn to Orthodoxy for theological and/or liturgical reasons, the ways in which intermarriage converts and clerics respond to this overarching context will receive our attention.

Chapter three affords an important overview of Orthodox catechesis as implemented in the selected field sites. Here, issues of commitment, the primary tie binding persons to religious communities in the spiritual marketplace, take on crucial importance as would-be converts are woven into the fabric of Orthodox communities. The ways in which intermarriage converts are catechized and socialized into parish life will also be discussed along with the strong relationships often forged between clerics and converts over the course of catechetical counseling and instruction.

Chapter four will more concertedly focus on the complex issues of conversion motives and informant perceptions of the Orthodox Church. Orthodox Christianity as a rich storehouse of conceptual material for informants to make sense of their religious lives will receive our attention. Yet, even in their embrace of Orthodox tradition, converts retain generalized American assumptions that religion should promote interior growth, fulfillment, and psychological comfort. The ways in which these come to be interwoven within the collected narratives will be an important point of discussion.

In addition to theological and historical understandings, ritual and liturgy remain key elements of Orthodoxy's "toolkit" of strategies for converts to identify with and stand as individuals within the Orthodox Church. Chapter five, therefore, will explore the ways that informants appropriate Orthodox ritual in their pre-conversion lives as well as act as "ritual critics" within their adopted communities. This chapter will conclude with a brief treatment of the religious boundary crossing Orthodox Church members engage as they participate in the rituals of other religious confessions, a phenomenon that heretofore has received little attention.

Chapter six attends to ethnicity as a potent ground for informant post-conversion experimentation and identity construction within the church. Rather than standing as a necessary obstacle to convert participation in parish life, expressions of ethnicity too can serve as important resources for converts in Orthodox communities. How ethnic lifelong church members regard issues of conversion in their parishes will also be briefly addressed.

Finally, chapter seven is dedicated to a brief discussion of thematic differences and emphases discerned in the narratives of the informants from St. Seraphim's in Jackson, Mississippi. Possible regional differences between this southern parish and its northern counterparts will be noted.

CHAPTER *One*

Introduction to the

Eastern Orthodox World

Converts to Eastern Orthodoxy are fond of referring to their new-found faith as one of the "best-kept secrets" in America, given its continued obscurity on the American religious landscape. In his widely read conversion narrative, *Becoming Orthodox*, the former Campus Crusade evangelist-cum-Orthodox priest Fr. Peter Gillquist documents how he and a cadre of fellow evangelical Protestants undertook a nearly two-decade search for the "church of the New Testament." Gillquist admits that at the outset of their intense studies into the worship, governance, and doctrines of early Christianity, this group of seminary- and college-trained pastors and evangelists had little knowledge of the Orthodox Church. In this regard, Orthodoxy only appeared on their collective investigative horizons years later. Musing upon the difficulties he and his colleagues encountered in finding and embracing Orthodoxy, Gillquist lamented from post-conversion hindsight, "We Orthodox do perhaps the worst job of any religious body in America of communicating with those outside the Church. This [the Orthodox Church] is the best-kept secret on the continent, to our shame."[1]

Gillquist and his colleagues are certainly not alone in characterizing their discovery of Orthodox Christianity as something of a revelation. American converts to Orthodoxy in Pittsburgh and Jackson, most of whom had attended college with some individuals possessing extensive travel experiences, frequently claimed to have only learned of the existence of the Orthodox faith well into adulthood. Informants with an early familiarity with Orthodoxy frequently assumed it was a religion that shunned converts. Thus, it is not surprising that many study informants were exasperated with Orthodoxy's apparent religious and cultural invisibility. One young man in Pittsburgh responded from his own experience, "It's important to get the faith out there to people who may have never even heard of the Orthodox faith. And some people say the Orthodox faith is the best-kept secret in America—and America is strongly blessed to have that faith. I've felt that we've got to start sharing the secret with other people and it's kind of sad because if it's good we got to make it available to people." Meanwhile, a woman in Jackson similarly observed, "I think when you hear that statement, that 'the Orthodox church is the best-kept secret.' I think that is so true. I think it's becoming a little bit better. But I do believe that we could have a bigger impact on our community in some shape, form, or fashion. I don't know what it would be. But, I believe, maybe we should try."

The general lack of knowledge and awareness of Orthodoxy found among many Americans is all the more unfortunate given scholarly and popular tendencies to portray this historically and culturally complex and multifarious religion in unidimensional ways. Despite its ongoing dynamism as exemplified precisely in the phenomenon of increased American conversions, Eastern Orthodoxy has long been the object of what Paul Valliere refers to as a kind of "Christian orientalism." According to these alternate readings, Orthodoxy comes to be cast either as a rigid, backward form of Christianity, caught in the rote repetition of ethnic folk customs and ancient rituals and doctrines, or as a mystical, otherworldly church offering a vast array of spiritual exotica and physical beauty but little in the way of practical reflection on legal, political, or social issues of critical import to modern lives. As John Anthony McGuckin points out, the fact that Orthodox Christians continue to be so rarely encountered "'in the flesh,' in the ordinary experience of most Western Christians," certainly contributes to the orientalist, subaltern characterizations of Orthodoxy as "romantically exotic," a religion existing outside of regular historical time in either a perpetual past or a perpetual transcendence.[2]

Thus, in order to provide a wider framework for understanding the experiences of the increasing numbers of Americans who have come to discover and embrace what in the West continues to be an obscure variety of the Christian faith, this chapter briefly charts the overarching ecclesial and local parochial worlds to which the informants featured in this book are converting. After an initial discussion of the distinguishing hallmarks of Orthodox Christianity as a religious system, especially when compared to Roman Catholicism and Protestantism, I will turn my attention to laying out the specific historical and social terrains of the parishes that converts in Pittsburgh and Jackson have come to call home. The conclusion of this chapter will contain a brief note on methodological issues related to my ethnographic fieldwork.

Eastern Orthodoxy—A General Overview

Numerically the second largest Christian body in the world after Roman Catholicism, Orthodox Christianity stands as a truly global religion today, well established in areas of eastern Europe, the Middle East, and Africa as well as, more recently, western Europe, east Asia, Oceania, and the Americas. Representing one of the three main branches of Christianity along with Protestantism and Roman Catholicism, Orthodoxy shares with its Western kin a general doctrinal core grounded in belief in the Incarnation and the Trinity that came to be articulated in the fundamental creeds of early Christianity (such as the Nicene-Constantinopolitan of the fourth century) and developed in a series of church councils that dotted the first thousand years of Christian history. Although the adherents of these different varieties of Christianity conceptualize the structures and constituents of the "church" in various ways, nearly all consider it the continuation of Christ's work on earth and often trace or liken their own to that described in the New Testament.[3]

While the Eastern Orthodox generally identify themselves as Christians in the simplest and most unvarnished of senses in looking back to the earliest apostles and Christ himself as the concrete establishers of their church, they do possess a unique historical and cultural grounding in what became known as the Eastern Roman or Byzantine Empire, which spanned the fourth to the fifteenth centuries and counted the great city of Constantinople its political and spiritual center. Despite the fact that Eastern Orthodoxy in twentieth-century America has generally been regarded as a religion lacking a clear missionary ethos, the Byzantine Christians wielded missionization and conversion as potent foreign policy tools bringing otherwise hostile neighbors peaceably into their sphere of influence. Over the centuries, the Bulgarians, Serbs, and Russians among other peoples embraced Orthodox Christianity, thus comprising what historian Dimitri Obolensky referred to as the "Byzantine Commonwealth." Long after the Ottoman Turks captured Constantinople in 1453 and the Balkans came under Islamic rule, Orthodoxy continued to thrive and develop in Russia, which cloaked itself in the mantle of Byzantine imperial language and symbolism and styled its Moscow as a "Third Rome" succeeding the "New Rome" of Constantinople itself.[4]

In many respects, this historical trajectory accounts for what appears to many Americans as among the more puzzling features of the Orthodox Church, its organizational segmentation into independently governed jurisdictions largely divided along national and geographical lines (Greek, Serbian, Bulgarian, and so forth). In addition to the four ancient patriarchates of Constantinople, Alexandria, Antioch, and Jerusalem, cities that held a place of honor in early Christendom (along with Rome, which became the seat of Roman Catholicism) and continue to do so within the Orthodox world, there are currently eleven self-governing or autocephalous churches located in Russia, Romania, Serbia, Greece, Bulgaria, Georgia, Cyprus, Poland, Albania, the Czech Republic, and Slovakia as well as St. Catherine's Monastery on Mt. Sinai. Autocephalous churches have their own independent bishops and hierarchies. Meanwhile, Finland, China, and Japan are self-governing in many respects but are not fully autocephalous.[5] Two of my primary field sites, St. Michael's and St. Seraphim's, belong to the Orthodox Church in America (OCA). The original Russian Archdiocese in North America granted autocephaly by the Moscow Patriarchate in 1970, the OCA has not been officially recognized as self-governing by the majority of jurisdictions. Significantly, this multiplicity of national Orthodox churches, including the OCA, is doctrinally and liturgically united, its members sharing full communion with one another.

What eventually became the Eastern Orthodox and Roman Catholic churches have been in formal schism since the eleventh century (in an event known as the Great Schism) with Orthodoxy never officially reconciling itself with the many Protestant denominations that have emerged over the centuries in the aftermath of the Reformation.[6] As Timothy Ware points out in his classic study, *The Orthodox Church*, Westerners tend to focus on Roman Catholicism and Protestantism as "opposite extremes," while Orthodox Christians are more likely to consider them "as two sides of the same coin" given the depth of their shared historical experience vis-à-vis that of the Orthodox world.[7] Roman Catholics and Protestants stand as direct heirs to Scholasticism, the Renaissance, the Reformation (along with its Catholic response, the Counter-Reformation), and the Enlightenment, events and movements that barely or only indirectly impacted traditionally Orthodox lands. At the same time, Roman Catholic and Protestant theologians often drew upon the same thinkers such as Augustine (4th–5th century), Anselm (11th century), and Thomas Aquinas (13th century) in their active dialogues with one another over the centuries. These figures have held little significance for Orthodox theology in much the same way that many of the great church fathers of the Orthodox East, including Maximus the Confessor (6th–7th century), John of Damascus (7th–8th century), and Gregory Palamas (14th century) among others remained, for centuries, virtually unknown in the West.[8]

Indeed, the differences between East and West are so pronounced that observers often describe Orthodoxy as "speaking" a different theological language from its Western counterparts, for as one convert in Pittsburgh remarked, "It's just like you need a translator when you're speaking from a Western versus an Orthodox perspective. I mean, the Church needs to be defined. You can't even say, the 'church.' You can't even say, 'Christian.' You can't even say 'salvation' and mean the same thing. We're all speaking a different language." Similarly, Timothy Ware maintains that, while Catholics and Protestants may disagree over fundamental issues, they are essentially asking the same questions. Meanwhile, in Orthodoxy, "it is not merely the answers that are different—the questions themselves are not the same as in the west."[9]

Among the many issues about which Orthodox Christians have come to "speak" differently over the centuries, the nature and constituents of church authority have been among the more acute and longlasting in fomenting the divisions between the Eastern and Western churches. Indeed, one of the fundamental issues precipitating the Great Schism was Western claims that the bishop of Rome (the pope) could exercise authority over other bishops. Orthodox Christians have consistently rejected this proposition. Although the Orthodox Church possesses a hierarchical structure (composed of deacons, priests, and bishops) similar to that found within Roman Catholicism, Orthodox theologians often employ characteristically Pauline imagery in drawing an analogy between the church and a living body composed of many interrelated and interworking parts. The patriarchs of the ancient sees, of which the Ecumenical Patriarch in Constantinople is identified as the "first among equals" among the brotherhood of bishops, are not the singular leaders of the Orthodox faith. In effect, the Orthodox Church has no centralized earthly authority since "each local church under its single bishop is the full and entire Church of Christ."[10]

Thus, according to this view, the fullness or catholicity of the church resides in the coming together of the many to form the one, rather than the ecclesial authority of a single figure over or apart from others. The collective, conciliar witness of the church—whether in the brotherhood of bishops gathering to discuss the nature of Christ in formal councils or the assemblage of the faithful each Sunday for the Eucharistic celebration—embodies this fundamental "unity in diversity" variously denoted in Orthodox literatures by the Greek term *koinonia* and in Russian as *sobornost*.[11] Familiar with churches that in one way or another valorize the individual, in either the person of the Roman Catholic pope or the singular Protestant lay person with her open Bible as the nexus and focus of authority, many would-be converts find the notion of conciliarity a startlingly novel way to conceptualize and understand the church.

In addition to the spatial component of *koinonia* or *sobornost* whereby bishops and local churches work together and come to a consensus, at least ideally, across communities, however ethnically or geographically defined, Tradition embodies the temporal dimension of conciliarity. Indeed, few Christians today appeal to Tradition with the consistency and zeal of most modern Orthodox theologians, clerics, and lay persons. As Paul Valliere notes, Orthodox theologians, like Fr. Georges Florovsky (1893–1979) and Vladimir Lossky (1903–1958), who fled to the West in the aftermath of the Russian Revolution, were especially keen to stress the historical continuity of their church in emphasizing Tradition, as articulated in the church fathers, as the sine qua non of the Orthodox faith. Developing their theological frameworks for the first time in predominantly non-Orthodox environments, these thinkers endeavored to return to what they considered the "roots" of Orthodox Tradition, the abovementioned church fathers, rather than to draw upon Western philosophical trends, such as German idealism, as had those of the "Russian school" represented by figures such as Vladimir Solovyov (1853–1900), Fr. Pavel Florensky (1882–1937?), Nicolai Berdyaev (1874–1948), and Fr. Sergei Bulgakov (1871–1944). Although interested in the theological singularity and purity of

Orthodox Christianity, the Neopatristic theologians were also involved in many of the wider social and religious currents of their day such as ecumenism.[12]

In the view of these theologians, a wholly synthesized and harmonious storehouse of unaltered and unalterable teaching and practice has been safeguarded and conveyed (literally, as the very word "tradition" indicates, "handed down") through lines of bishops stretching from the earliest apostles (and Christ) to the present day. In effect, Tradition is, in the words of Fr. John Meyendorff, "the permanent presence of God in the community of the New Israel," as embodied in the continued work of the Holy Spirit in human life and history.[13] According to this view, individual Christians do not assume the roles of atomized interpreters of dogma and liturgy but are members of a corporate body, called upon to be as mindful of the experiences and teachings of the past as the present. In this way, Orthodox Christians today claim a far greater affinity with the ideas, images, and vocabularies of the earliest apostolic and church fathers than with contemporary Roman Catholics and Protestants.

As a point of contrast, modern Orthodox Christians frequently cite the Western churches' eventual inclusion of the *filioque* (Latin for "and the Son," denoting that the Holy Spirit proceeds from the Father and the Son rather than the Father alone) into the Nicene-Constantinopolitan Creed, the nineteenth-century doctrine of papal infallibility, and the multiplicity of churches and Christian teachings arising in the wake of the Protestant Reformation as evidence of the unsteady, fragmented nature of Christianity in the West. Indeed, many Orthodox Christian writers, including American converts, consider these issues symptomatic of *the* underlying distinction separating Eastern Orthodoxy from its Western counterparts—the supposed adherence and reverence of the former to the norms and forms of the past (to various notions of Tradition) and the supposed eagerness of the latter to embrace, meld, and merge with new cultural trends and developments through time. According to this view, these long-held tendencies to theological and liturgical changeability on the part of Protestant and Roman Catholic churches have only become more spectacularly pronounced over the course of the twentieth century. Orthodox converts, for example, often voiced their dismay over the widespread reforms introduced in the Catholic Church during the Second Vatican Council as well as Protestant propensities to adopt new forms of worship and change course on social issues such as divorce, abortion, the roles of women in the church, and homosexuality.

In addition to maintaining their Tradition as unchanging, Orthodox Christians employ a diversity of external forms—written, oral, visual, and kinesthetic—to express and convey it. While scripture, the creeds, and the writings of the church fathers represent the more textualized elements of Tradition, the rich liturgies and iconography of the church are no less important in embodying and making visual the basic stories and teachings of the Christian faith. In the Orthodox Church, worship is neither an addendum nor an afterthought to theological speculation; it is the very sensory and bodily enactment of theology itself. Even in contemporary America, Orthodox temples feature a ritual sensory elaborateness that has few parallels in either the Protestant or post–Vatican II Roman Catholic worlds. Incense, continual priestly and choral chanting, brocaded vestments and banners, and anciently inspired icons all come together (ideally) to transport worshipers beyond the mundane and provide a sense of being physically present in "an earthly heaven."[14]

Within the complex round of feast days, saints' days, fasting periods, and sacramental actions punctuating the Orthodox liturgical year and the lives of church members, the Divine Liturgy—the Eucharistic celebration performed each Sunday—serves as the meeting point of the individual and the communal and stands as the most obvious and pronounced expression of the fullness and catholicity of the Orthodox faith. The Divine Liturgy is marked by processions, epistle and gospel readings, as well as prayers and petitions for divine mercy and intercession, all of which lead to the distribution of the Eucharistic gifts. Consisting of leavened bread tinctured with wine and fed to the faithful on a spoon, the Eucharist is endowed with great mystical importance as the food of immortality, the actual Body and Blood of Christ that, when consumed, mystically knits Orthodox believers with one another. The fact that only baptized and chrismated Orthodox Christians may partake of "the heavenly gifts" further heightens the mysterious, exclusive, and communally binding nature of the ritual.

While the doctrinal and moral teaching of the Orthodox Church is maintained as essentially immutable, there is a recognition among Orthodox Christians that elements of its ritual practices (examples of which John Meyendorff identifies as "the order of services, hymns, liturgical vestments") are culturally determined and can change over time. These variations according to local custom and norm are frequently referred to in English as "little traditions" to distinguish them from the historically unchanged "Tradition" of the Orthodox faith.

Fr. John Meyendorff, in particular, stressed the need for modern Orthodox Christians to differentiate between "Holy Tradition" and "human traditions," given what he considered the Orthodox penchant to "preserve *everything*."[15]

As I will examine more closely in chapter four, these various strands of Orthodoxy's historical, theological, and liturgical experience act as powerful enticements for many Americans once they discover this "best kept" of marketplace secrets. In addition to its strong adherence to the fundamentals of Christian doctrine, the Orthodox Church presents would-be converts an opportunity to situate themselves within a wide narrative frame stretching back through history to the first apostles via the splendors of imperial Byzantium and reaching towards heaven in the sensory gravitas of its liturgical performances. In a contemporary American context so often thrust forward by the sheer adrenaline of novelty, Eastern Orthodoxy can appear as something of a haven, a last bastion of conservative Christianity, shielding its adherents from the ennui and angst of late modern life. Certainly, many American converts express this view, as we shall see.

Despite these illustrious historical and spiritual claims, Orthodox Christianity is not a religion of the abstract. The "one, holy, catholic, and apostolic church" is tangible, existing in mundane time and space and lived in actual brick-and-mortar parishes. Thus, to explore more deeply the issues of religious conversion and change as they occur within the "lived" and "everyday" experience of lay persons and clerics, I conducted participant observation and formal semi-structured interviewing in Orthodox churches in two regions of the United States—Pittsburgh, Pennsylvania, and Jackson, Mississippi. It is towards an elucidation of the social and demographic contours of these churches where I met and conversed with the converts who were so taken with and compelled by the Orthodox faith that I will now turn my attention.

Field Sites

Although Orthodoxy was first brought to North America at the end of the eighteenth century in the midst of Russian attempts to missionize the native peoples of Alaska, significant numbers of Orthodox Christians from various parts of eastern/southeastern Europe and the Middle East only began arriving in the United States towards the end of the nineteenth and beginning of the twentieth centuries. Rather than hand-selected monks and missionaries set upon the spreading of the Orthodox faith, these later immigrants were working men and women, lay persons attracted to the industrial centers of Pittsburgh, Detroit, Chicago, and Cleveland in search of factory jobs and economic betterment. Referred to as "New Immigrants," an appellation distinguishing them from the predominantly Protestant, northern European immigrants of a generation earlier, the newcomers were often the objects of intense discrimination on the part of Protestant Americans. This situation, coupled with the fact that immigrant groups were often suspicious of one another, encouraged their organization into distinct ethnic communities. Thus, instead of establishing pan-Orthodox parishes attracting the faithful from across ethnic lines, the newly arrived immigrants founded churches that largely preserved and bolstered their own languages and folk customs as distinct from those of other national and ethnic groups.[16]

Despite the relative aloofness of these ethnic Orthodox churches, John H. Erickson has cogently noted that conversions are by no means new to American Orthodoxy but part and parcel of its varied historical and contemporary experience within the United States. The Orthodox Church has always accepted converts and, indeed, received a good number into its fold over the course of the twentieth century, especially through intermarriage.[17] Additionally, two significant waves of conversions, in which parishes of Greek Catholics of Carpatho-Rusyn heritage entered the Orthodox Church en masse, occurred at the turn of the last century, first under the leadership of Fr. Alexis Toth, who has since been glorified as a saint in the Orthodox Church, and then again at the end of the 1930s. Most of the converts from the first wave were incorporated into the OCA while those from the 1930s were organized into their own Carpatho-Rusyn Archdiocese under the leadership of the Ecumenical Patriarchate in Constantinople. In fact, often unbeknownst to current parishioners, many Orthodox churches in Pittsburgh were originally Greek Catholic in orientation.[18]

Known among Orthodox Christians as the "Holy Land" of North American Orthodoxy, Pittsburgh, in particular, affords an important context for exploring the interplay of Orthodox Christianity with the supposed mainstreams of American religious life. In addition to serving as one of the historical centers of the "New Immigration," Allegheny County, where Pittsburgh is located, continues to be the municipal home of a number of Orthodox churches, 37 in all in the year 2000, representing a wide swath of different ethnic groups and jurisdictions. These included the Orthodox Church in America (OCA), the Russian Orthodox Church Outside Russia (ROCOR), and the Serbian, Carpatho-Rusyn, Ukrainian, Greek, and Antiochian (Syrian) archdioceses.[19] From this ecclesial plethora, I selected two churches—St. Michael's OCA parish and Ascension Greek Orthodox Church—based on the diversity of jurisdictional and ethnic affiliation, municipal location, size, demographic composition, and length of current pastoral leadership each represented. Let us examine these field sites in turn.

Founded in 1914 by an original "50 families" of Carpatho-Rusyn descent and continuously occupying the same building and neighborhood since 1917, St. Michael's parish had approximately 120 members in 2005–2006, of whom 20 percent were converts (individuals brought to Orthodoxy both through intermarriage and in the course of self-propelled religious seeking). While many of the cradle Orthodox parishioners of St. Michael's too claimed a Carpatho-Rusyn background, the church was Orthodox from its founding. The parish's Slavic past and Americanized present were, at once, reflected in its architecture and furnishings. Like many Orthodox churches, St. Michael's distinctive yellow-painted cupolas of the "Russian style," five in all and each topped with the triple-barred crosses common to Slavic Orthodoxy, immediately set the building apart from its surroundings. Meanwhile, a large, prominently displayed red, white, and blue sign stood in the church lawn announcing service times, "St. Michael's Orthodox Church. Saturday Vespers 6 p.m.; Sunday Divine Liturgy 10 a.m. All are Welcome." Welcomed visitors would then enter a warm, wood-paneled interior elaborately adorned with icons painted by early parishioners as well as a New York artist in the 1940s, a crystal chandelier, and stained-glass windows depicting an assortment of Orthodox saints. As usually found in Orthodox churches, an altar screen known as an iconostasis separates the sanctuary from the nave. St. Michael's also boasts rows of well-worn pews, a feature common to Pittsburgh-area and many other American Orthodox churches but a relative rarity in other parts of the Orthodox world where standing remains the primary bodily posture to be assumed by Orthodox worshipers at corporate prayer.

Despite the proud, if slightly pealing, cupolas and sign of welcome on the front lawn, the priest and parishioners of St. Michael's, at times, gave off an air of feeling besieged by the sharp, unmistakable signs of neighborhood decline that surrounded them. A once prosperous section of Pittsburgh during the city's manufacturing heyday, the neighborhood fell on hard times in the 1980s with the closing of nearby steel mills. While older church members recalled living close to the church as children and walking to Liturgy on Sunday mornings with their families, most parishioners by 2005 were scattered throughout Pittsburgh, with a few living in the city's outer suburbs as far as forty-five minutes to an hour away from the church. During the period of my fieldwork in 2005–2006, the neighborhood surrounding St. Michael's had a reputation for being a dangerous, high-crime area, an image reinforced by the dingy beer joints that dotted the block around the church and the fact that the police dismantled a methamphetamine lab in a house across the street shortly after I arrived to begin my fieldwork. Not surprisingly, a number of parishioners expressed worries about visiting the church after dark or allowing their children to play in its iron-gated yard during coffee hour.

Like many Orthodox churches in Pittsburgh, St. Michael's too had experienced a demographic decline paralleling that of the broader community. As manufacturing jobs dwindled, younger populations left Pittsburgh in search of other career and educational opportunities. Those who remained in Pittsburgh often left Orthodoxy as they married outside the faith or found the church services, which until quite recently were performed largely in Slavonic, arcane or incomprehensible. Indeed, "dying" was the most common adjective heard among parishioners when reflecting on the condition of their parish before their current priest, Fr. Mark, took over the pastorate in 2000 from his father who had also served as an Orthodox priest. An energetic man in his forties with a wife and three small daughters, Fr. Mark had worked as a music teacher for a number of years before taking seriously and acting upon the promptings of his family to become a priest. From that point, he said he had never looked back and was constantly surprised by the great joys as well as the momentary frustrations of the priesthood. Since Fr. Mark's appointment, parishioners maintained that an overall change in the social dimensions of the church had occurred—from an increase in educational and social activities to the increased use of English in the services to greater numbers of non-Orthodox inquirers walking through church doors to investigate Orthodoxy. Beyond Fr. Mark's direct influence, St. Michael's had experienced a sizable influx of Russian and Ukrainian immigrant visitors and members since the early 1990s with the fall of the Soviet Union. Thus, it was not uncommon to hear Russian spoken at church social functions.

Whereas intermarriage served as the primary means for bringing newcomers to St. Michael's over the course of its history, more recent converts, many of them young, twenty- and thirty-somethings like Karen, have evinced a more pointed interest in the theological/ritual offerings of the Orthodox faith. As I shall explore more fully in chapter two, these individuals typically discovered Orthodoxy after months, years, or decades of intense religious seeking. Parishioners, lifelong and convert alike, credited this spurt in conversions to Fr. Mark's interest in actively evangelizing the non-Orthodox of Pittsburgh and beyond. Quite simply, he made this "best-kept secret" of a church easier to find. A technology aficionado, Fr. Mark designed an attractive website for St. Michael's, which provided basic information about church belief and practice, a photo gallery of parish events, and an audio archive of his Sunday sermons among other features. Fr. Mark has also coordinated online "Ortho-convert" chat-rooms and discussion threads and established initial contact with at least two recent converts in his parish through these electronic channels. On official diocesan and national levels, he has been involved with the OCA's Department of Evangelization and has delivered talks on parish growth in a variety of Orthodox venues. Indeed, convert informants responded positively towards these welcoming attitudes and multiple avenues for learning about and accessing the Orthodox faith and commonly referred to the overall atmosphere of St. Michael's as "seeker friendly."

Another factor making St. Michael's an attractive parochial option for convert and lifelong church members alike (with so many Orthodox churches in the Pittsburgh area, even cradle Orthodox Christians shop within their tradition for a parish that meets their needs) was the rich round of liturgical, social, and educational activities the church offered. Attending as many of these events as possible, it was not uncommon for me to be at the church several times a week. As the Divine Liturgy is the focal point of Orthodox worship more broadly, so too this service remained at the center of St. Michael's parish life. Regularly performed on Sundays between 10–11:30 a.m., the Divine Liturgy drew the highest and most diverse cross-section of the church's parishioners, with approximately 60–80 in attendance each week. While English had become the primary language used in worship at St. Michael's, Fr. Mark occasionally chanted some of the liturgical petitions and prayers in Slavonic as a nod to his church's immigrant past and present.

In contrast to the Liturgy's rubrics, which changed little from week to week, the weekly sermon was more spontaneous and less bound by liturgical norms. Usually drawing upon the gospel or epistle readings of the day as illustrative of some wider theme of spiritual growth, Fr. Mark sprinkled his sermons with anecdotes drawn from current events and popular culture and, on more than one occasion, referred to convert struggles and reflections on Orthodoxy. Nearly always, Fr. Mark portrayed converts, especially seeker converts like Karen, in the most positive of lights in underscoring the value and richness of their contributions to the faith and faithfulness of the parish. In this way, converts were often presented as models for cradle Orthodox emulation. In addition to Sunday services, St. Michael's also held Saturday Vespers each week, a biweekly Wednesday Vespers service, as well as liturgies for all the major feast days of the Orthodox church calendar.[20] Fr. Mark asserted that a vigorous liturgical schedule with services beyond those of Sunday morning was important to the life of his parish, even if attendance numbers could at times be discouraging, "The worship of the Church is for God, it's not for us. Believe me, nobody will come if you don't have the service. If you don't have it, no one will come for sure, but if you have it maybe someone will come. But if they don't come, you have it again and then you try again and again and again. You have to offer the classes and you have to offer the services and different services like akathists and molebens.[21] The Canon to the Mother of God, we started doing that and people love it. They sing it and they like it and I want to have more and more services."

As significant as participant observation of the parish's worship services was for my research, it was the more informal encounters with priests and parishioners that really allowed me to document the social groupings and exchanges between them at my field sites. Chief among these opportunities was coffee hour, a weekly informal gathering after worship during which parishioners shared light snacks and fellowship with one another, which took place at St. Michael's in a below-ground community room attached to the church and fitted with two rows of long tables and a kitchen. Although self-selected, the coffee-hour attendees represented a reasonable cross-section of the church's population. Over the course of my fieldwork at St. Michael's, Ascension, St. Seraphim's, and elsewhere, coffee hour proved vital for meeting informants and charting the character and social makeup of the respective parishes.

Observations made during coffee hour and other functions allowed me to distinguish differences in the ways intermarriage and seeker converts organized themselves in parish life. For example, with the majority of its recent converts coming into the church after engaging in self-described searches and journeys, St. Michael's had an easily identifiable cohort of converts who sat together and socialized with one another at parish functions, such as coffee hours, for which they had their own designated table. Meanwhile, intermarriage converts of the parish generally sat and conversed with their spouses and children rather than with other converts on such occasions. St. Michael's more recent seeker converts also had extensive social ties with one another outside the church setting. They often met one another for dinner or moviegoing and played important participatory roles in one another's major life events, such as weddings and baptisms. These converts also established kinship ties through opportunities to "sponsor" new converts and stand as godparents to each other's children. Given this context, I had little difficulty initially identifying and meeting the majority of St. Michael's regularly attending recent converts, but found intermarriage converts much more difficult to locate, scattered as they were among the parish's many biologically entwined families.

Ascension Greek Orthodox Church, the second primary field site selected for my research, differed from St. Michael's in many crucial respects. Founded in 1954 when a group of parishioners broke from the municipal Pittsburgh Greek cathedral to establish a neighborhood parish closer to their homes, Ascension first occupied a former Lutheran church before moving to its present hilltop location in 1969 overlooking a wealthy suburban community filled with upscale shopping boutiques, restaurants, and coffeehouses. Although it is not uncommon to hear Greek spoken among the parishioners, Fr. Joseph (in his sixties), who had grown up in and served the church as its priest for over a quarter century, maintained that there had been no significant influx of immigrants from Greece to Ascension since the 1950s. While the church clearly identified itself as "Greek" in its ethnic orientation, one lifelong parishioner declared, "Our ethnicity is much more subliminal than on the marquee. Ascension has never really been a particularly ethnic parish, at least not in the overt kinds of ways people usually think. I am sensitive to people in the community who are uncomfortable with the ethnicity and there are also a lot of converts who have just embraced it and are probably more Greek than I am." Although some convert informants at Ascension did express a certain discomfort with the Greek-ness of the parish, most either defended ethnicity as compatible with Orthodox values (say, in strengthening family ties) or "made peace" with it in finding other features of church life (for example, the care of the priest or the bonds they had formed with parishioners) compelling enough to join and remain within the community.

In contrast to St. Michael's, a good many of Ascension's parishioners lived within a radius of five to ten miles from the church, and many of my interviews in informant homes occurred within close proximity to the parish. In 2005–2006, the church had approximately five hundred members, about 20 to 25 percent of whom were converts. The population has remained relatively stable over the past couple of decades, and thus Ascension has not experienced a population decline similar to St. Michael's. Ascension's parishioners tend to be highly educated, involved in professional careers, and economically well off. All members of the clerical staff (Fr. Joseph is the main priest, assisted in his endeavors by Fr. Andrew, a cleric who served the parish on a part-time basis, and a deacon, Morris, all of whom were interviewed for this project) observed that materialism and conspicuous consumption were among the deepest "spiritual" problems facing church members, and a number of Sunday homilies were preached on this theme during my time there.

Like many Greek churches in the United States, Ascension's architectural style evokes less the Old World than the modern with its large white temple compacted into a tight square, slit along each of its four sides with thin ribbons of vertical stained-glass windows and crowned with a single gold dome. A well-tended manicured garden, planted in honor of a deceased church member, greets visitors at the entrance. Also furnished with the ubiquitous pews, Ascension's interior liturgical space is a large white-marbled hall, which one convert parishioner described to me as "cold." Yet, it does feature a typical Byzantine Greek iconographic schema, in this case largely of gold mosaics, with Christ *Pantocrator* (Greek for "All-Mighty Ruler") peering down upon worshipers from the overhead dome and the Mother of God (common phrase used in reference to the Virgin Mary, in Greek—*Theotokos*) doing the same from the apse. Ascension also had an organ (another feature not generally found in Old World Orthodox churches), which was used to accompany the choir during its divine services.

Whereas St. Michael's often seemed insular in the midst of its high-crime neighborhood tightly enclosed as it was behind its black iron gate, Ascension possessed an air of openness and expansiveness to its surroundings. In addition to the church building's high visibility to passersby from its perch on the hill, the parish also sported a community center immediately adjacent to the temple, complete with an auditorium, full-service kitchen, gymnasium, offices (open to the public Monday through Friday), a library, bookstore, several classrooms, and a special "bridal room" where brides and their parties dressed for the many weddings that occurred at Ascension each year. During the time of my fieldwork, the community center also housed a pan-Orthodox day school, supported by the parish and other Pittsburgh Orthodox churches and founded by a convert parishioner of Ascension who remains active in both the parish and the school.

With its wide spectrum of highly specialized organizations, Ascension made ample use of these facilities. Fr. Joseph, as his OCA counterpart, maintained an active liturgical schedule of Sunday Divine Liturgy (about half of which was conducted in Greek), Saturday Vespers, and a weekly Monday-night Bible study preceded by a *Paraclesis* prayer service.[22] He also commemorated the regular round of Orthodox feast days with early morning liturgies. In addition to the strictly liturgical, Ascension housed chapters of GOYA (Greek Orthodox Youth of America, for teenage youth), JOY (Junior Orthodox Youth, for preteen youth), and Philoptochos, a national philanthropy for Greek Orthodox women that engaged in community-service work. The parish also provided new mothers support and fellowship through a group known as First Steps, and the Circle of Angels was another organization, dedicated to visiting the parish sick and shut-ins. Keen on integrating converts into Ascension's social fabric, Fr. Joseph often actively enlisted the help of converts for these organizations and invited them to assume key roles within the community such as sitting on the parish board.

Ascension's large membership rolls and high rate of intermarriage, which Fr. Joseph affirmed to be historically and during the time of my fieldwork the single most important motivation for conversions in his church, created a social and demographic climate that differed markedly from that of St. Michael's. Whereas St. Michael's converts, many of whom were single and brought into Orthodoxy without other family members, formed a cohesive, close-knit group, Ascension's (largely intermarriage) converts were scattered among the parish's many families and participated more widely and diffusely in its many ministries and social events. Thus, during coffee hour and at other social gatherings, converts were less socially segregated at Ascension, which did not have an unofficially designated "convert table" where converts tended to congregate together as was the case at St. Michael's. While coffee hour proved a key time for meeting potential informants and establishing rapport with parishioners, I generally had more difficulty identifying converts as such at Ascension than at St. Michael's.

However, as Fr. Joseph maintained, an increasing number of individuals in recent years had begun contacting him out of sheer interest in Orthodox Christianity. "We have others who literally walk in off the street that have read something about the Orthodox Church, Timothy Ware or some other source, the Internet, and they just develop and they start coming to the services, to Bible studies and we start talking." While less overtly evangelistic than Fr. Mark, Fr. Joseph was clearly encouraged by this development and provided the time and support converts needed to learn about and decide whether to join the Orthodox faith. For their part, converts, regardless of motivational stripe, generally held Fr. Joseph and his kindly pastoral tutelage in high regard and reported feeling welcomed to and comfortable at Ascension.

While nearly all my participant observation occurred at St. Michael's and Ascension, I expanded my interviewing beyond these two churches to include priests and lay parishioners of five additional communities. Three of these parishes—a Ukrainian Orthodox, a Carpatho-Rusyn, and an Antiochian church—were located in the Pittsburgh area, while the remaining informants were from a Ukrainian Orthodox and an OCA parish near Cleveland. These churches reflected diversity in jurisdiction, church size, and numbers of converts. The priests of both Ukrainian Orthodox churches reported that less than 10 percent of their respective populations were convert, while the priest of the Antiochian parish reported over 40 percent of his congregants to be converts to Orthodoxy. I only interviewed lay parishioners at the Carpatho-Rusyn and Cleveland area OCA churches, while my informants from the other churches were exclusively clerical. In addition to these informants, I also interviewed a Pittsburgh-area bishop.

While the experiences of the Pittsburgh converts sit at the heart of this book, I reentered the field in 2009 to conduct a second, much shorter round of ethnographic research at St. Seraphim's, an OCA parish in Jackson, Mississippi, a city and state little associated in the popular imagination with Orthodox Christianity either historically or today. However, despite the dominance of evangelical Protestantism in the history and cultural life of Mississippi and portions of the Deep South more generally, Orthodox Christians have had a long-standing presence in the state with the founding of an early parish by Syrian/Lebanese immigrants in Vicksburg in 1906 and another by Greeks in the state capital, Jackson, in 1951. Furthermore, in recent years, the Orthodox Church in America and the Antiochian Archdiocese, in particular, have marshaled significant resources and human-power to build mission parishes throughout the length of the American "Bible Belt" stretching from North/South Carolina to Texas.

While the earliest Orthodox churches in Mississippi, as in Pittsburgh, were closely associated with immigrant communities, St. Seraphim's was established in 1977 specifically as a convert-oriented, pan-Orthodox parish geared towards welcoming inquirers and Orthodox Christians of diverse ethnic backgrounds into its ranks. Located in a Jackson suburb, the parish has occupied its present building, a former Presbyterian church, since 2006. Prior to that, parishioners worshiped in a nearby house that had been transformed into an Orthodox chapel. Despite the fact that the building had previously been in Protestant hands, the rectangular brick structure possessed the regular trappings of an Orthodox temple, including a cupola, Russian bells, and an icon-laden interior with a large, pewless center space for worshipers to stand and bow during the liturgies. St. Seraphim's layout and liturgical performances held a perfect balance of attempting to make the church discursively inviting and intelligible to non-Orthodox visitors and accentuating the supposed "otherness" of Eastern Orthodoxy. Like many of the other churches in the area including a Baptist church down the road, St. Seraphim's sports a prominent message board in its front parking lot, from which drivers-by can read messages such as "The Saints Are the Evidence of the Holy Spirit."

A native Mississippian from the Delta who has served at St. Seraphim's continuously from its very beginning, Fr. Timothy converted to Orthodoxy in 1977 from the Episcopal Church, the denominational home of his family for over five generations. Although he had served as an Episcopal priest for many years before becoming Orthodox, this pastoral experience did little to prepare him for the heady task of organizing different ethnic (for example, Syrian and Ukrainian) and convert constituencies, each of which often held competing expectations of what the small parish should look and sound like. He recalled the early years of establishing St. Seraphim's as the most challenging of his pastorate since, in his words, "It was a very difficult time for us not because of being Orthodox but just because of the circumstances of starting a brand new mission with a very diverse group of people and with me having so little training. I had plenty of book learning, but I had really no practical experience of what an Orthodox parish is like." Despite the many conflicts that ensued in the early days of its founding and the fact that, in Fr. Timothy's words, "they [the parishioners] almost ran me out of here," his bishop provided unswerving support for the parish and for Fr. Timothy, who never left the church.

At St. Seraphim's, conversion was not the select experience of a minority within the parish but the common denominator experience for most church members. Therefore, parishioners attempted to smooth out the rough edges of unfamiliarity for visitors and inquirers. Fr. Timothy, for example, took time to explain basic components of Orthodox services, especially ritual gestures such as prostrating during Lent, that may make visitors uncomfortable. Converts themselves often reported being taken in hand and guided through the intricacies of Orthodox worship by parishioners from their very first step into the church. Fr. Timothy held a regular "Inquirer's Class" at the church each Wednesday evening throughout the year and the church had a well-stocked bookstore that provided church members and would-be converts reading materials to learn more about the faith. One woman, in her mid-60s, recalled her first visit to St. Seraphim's: "So, I showed up one morning and I was scared to death because I didn't know what to do or anything like that. So, I went in and kind of stood in the back and one of the people, well, of course, everybody was so friendly. They had me all under their wing immediately. And I thought, 'Oh, I just love this. This place is just gonna be the right place for me.'" Strikingly, despite the fact that two other Orthodox churches are in the Jackson area (the aforementioned Greek parish and a convert-dominated Antiochian church) and many informants have opportunities to travel around the state and elsewhere, most parishioners whom I met admitted to never having visited another Orthodox church besides St. Seraphim's.

Fieldwork

To make sense of communal and individual meanings of conversion within Eastern Orthodox churches in Pittsburgh and Jackson, I employed the classic ethnographic field methods of participant observation and formal, semi-structured interviewing to collect data for this project. From February 2005 to May 2006, I conducted seven months of participant observation each at St. Michael's and Ascension in order to observe the social placement and relationships of converts in everyday parish life. While participant observation was a significant component of my research, the focal point of this project remained 48 formal, semi-structured interviews conducted with the clerics, converts, and lifelong church members of St. Michael's, Ascension, St. Seraphim's, and the aforementioned Pittsburgh and Cleveland-area communities. Since it was difficult to establish the exact size and composition of convert and lifelong lay populations at these field sites, given the frequent population shifts that occurred in these communities and the fact that the priests of St. Michael's and Ascension, in particular, did not have complete records of converts, I relied on snowball sampling to identify interview subjects (see Appendix B for interview guides). The interviews were conducted with both women and men between the ages of 19 and 75 years who had been Eastern Orthodox, in the case of converts, anywhere from 2 to 32 years at the time the interview took place. Eight of these interviews were conducted among informants from St. Seraphim's (see Appendix A for a demographic overview of the informant populations).

While data collected over the course of this fieldwork remained central to my analysis, I also examined documentary evidence and published Orthodox conversion narratives, as well as depictions of converts and conversion found in Orthodox Christian print and electronic sources. Although secondary, these materials allowed me to gauge resonances between the conversion experiences and perceptions of study informants and those found within American Orthodoxy more broadly. I used NVIVO, a computerized qualitative data analysis program, to code my interview transcripts, field notes, and imputed documentary evidence and took a "grounded theory" approach to my examination of these data, whereby themes were allowed to emerge and guide interpretation. Through this data analysis, I detected patterns and variations in language and thematic content that were not generally available to individual informants themselves.[23]

In this way, I also subscribe to Victor Turner's multilevel approach to symbolic meaning, here applied to perceptions and experiences of religious conversion. In his essay "Symbolism, Morality, Social Structure," Turner argues that anthropologists must be aware of three "fields of meaning," which include indigenous, operational, and positional interpretations.[24] While anthropologists must certainly rely initially on indigenous interpretations, they also can draw conclusions that are unfamiliar and contrary to those of indigenous informants based on their wider vantage in conversing and observing a variety of social actors in multiple venues over a period of time. Not only did I collect multiple informant perspectives, but I also observed how notions of conversion were wielded in different parochial and interview contexts as well as their positioning vis-à-vis other categories, such as that of the lifelong church members.

It is based on these observations from multiple perspectives that I justify interpreting Orthodox conversions and their meanings in ways with which informants themselves may feel uncomfortable and may take issue. For example, informants, whether clerical, convert, or life-long church members, often expressed disdain over potential "secular" interpretations of phenomena. One of the parish priests with whom I worked once declared to me that, "In the end, this [ethnographic] research will tell us nothing about the Orthodox Church," given its *sui generis* nature in his eyes. Therefore, the overall validity of my analysis is not dependent upon an informant's recognition of herself in this book, but in the careful charting of phenomena as used and conceptualized repeatedly over time at these field sites and across informants.

However, it is important to stress that this book in no way presents a complete, comprehensive, or generally representative portrait of "the conversion experience" of American-born converts to Orthodox Christianity. Still, even localized case studies such as this provide a valuable glimpse into how the participants of Orthodox communities often characterized as ethnic can imbibe and utilize marketplace metaphors and mechanisms as well as those of Orthodox belief and practice. These processes may manifest themselves in other ways in other Orthodox churches or parts of the country, but my analysis of the above documentary evidence, potent in its shaping of Orthodox attitudes, allows for the tentative conclusion that the points of view and experiences of the Pittsburgh and Jackson informants are not unique but reflective of those found within American Orthodoxy at large.

One of the most consistent themes that emerged in my analysis was the language and methodology of the spiritual marketplace that so concertedly framed the conversion experiences of informants. It is towards a fuller charting of these experiences as informants began their pre-conversion investigations as well as the overarching issues of conversion they illumine that we will now turn our attention.

CHAPTER Two

Eastern Orthodox Conversions
in a Pluralistic Context

In discussing their pre-conversion religious experiences, Orthodox converts regularly drew upon vocabularies and images that resonated deeply with the prevailing marketplace of American religious life. Few informants, for example, referenced classic Christian models of conversion in their narratives, especially those derived from sacred scripture often historically evoked in other Christian contexts, to describe the phenomenon. In contrast to the early Puritans' penchant for publicly charting how divine providence transformed their inevitably wretched and sin-ridden lives, as Patricia Caldwell observes in her study of their narratives, contemporary American converts rarely liken their experiences of seeking and finding the Orthodox Church to famous New Testament stories such as the Prodigal Son or Paul's Damascus-road conversion. Even the more general contours of Christian conversion as a movement from sin through repentance to salvation were largely absent from the narratives. While references were certainly made to the divine as well as more occasionally to repentance and salvation, they were scattered piecemeal within the narratives rather than giving them shape as a whole.[1]

In this regard, the language and themes of "searching" and "journeying" appeared in informants' narratives in theologically vague or secularized ways that highlighted conversion as a personally orchestrated choice rather than a response to divine intervention. As Karen had undertaken a "personal journey" in the course of discovering and entering the Orthodox Church, so too other converts had engaged in self-described religious seeking and church shopping in attempting to find the right venues for enacting their religious lives.[2] To this effect, one convert from Ascension Greek church likened his Protestant-driven, pre-conversion investigations for a church to a shopping excursion:

> And I knew countless times that my friends church shopped. Even my friends who I was very close to, like this couple I met. They went church shopping with me and we'd try a different one [church] each Sunday. You know, if you didn't like what the pastor said, you just left. Then you went down the street and found somebody else who said something you liked.

The coupling of shopping, with its highly charged connotations of commercial exchange, materialism, and programmed novelty or obsolescence, and church, a supposed venue of permanence and solidity at least as it is often popularly imagined, rested uneasily in the mouths of many informants, for as one convert maintained: "People church shop because they're not happy somewhere anymore or the pastor doesn't speak to me anymore. I mean, I've heard that a hundred times from people, 'Oh we have to go find another church.' And we knew church shouldn't be that way."

While shopping, in contrast to the more romantically tinged metaphors of search and journey, at times possessed this hint of a moral taint, all of the above tropes suggested conversion to be a *process* of self-propelled movement through landscapes dotted with a diversity of worldview options rather than a sudden, all-in-a-moment *event*. According to Wade Clark Roof, these all-pervasive metaphors, saturating as they do media airways and commonplace backyard discussions of religion and spirituality, reflect the process-dominated "reflexive spirituality" that has become normative to post–World War II American culture.[3] These representations of conversion to Orthodoxy as searches or journeys are by no means anomalous but are deeply engrained visions of what it means to be religious today and point to a general homogenization in the language used across American religious groups.

Books such as M. Scott Peck's *The Road Less Traveled* as well as the easily media-packaged teachings of figures like Deepak Chopra and Joseph Campbell, the latter with his pithy exhortation to television viewers "to follow your bliss," have popularized the notion of spiritual questing and reassured their audiences that ambiguity in life's meaning and direction may, in the end, just be part of one's overall "spiritual journey." As tropes common to what Anthony Giddens and Ulrich Beck refer to as "reflexive biographies," "searching" and "journeying" underscore a situation in which the circumstances of one's life are increasingly divorced from traditionally fixed natal determinants such as familial and ethnic heritages, which also have been pried from their moorings and await individual scripting and interpretation in their own right.[4]

The processual qualities of conversion to Orthodoxy as a choice-making endeavor are explored in this chapter. In this respect, Orthodox conversions reflect what scholars of other religious contexts have identified as the gradual, deliberate nature of modern religious transformation and boundary-crossing as individuals confront and compare worldview options. After providing a brief overview of how scholars more recently have conceptualized the roles of choice in modern conversions, I will explore how three different social actors in Orthodox parish life in turn consider the spiritual marketplace and its methodologies. First, we will focus on the narratives of seeker converts such as Karen, who frequently engaged in intense, religiously driven investigations spanning years or decades. We will examine how the spiritual marketplace affects their pre-conversion biographies along with the sources of information that informants consult as they discover and learn about the Orthodox Church. Second, we will turn to a category of convert all but ignored in contemporary discussions of Orthodox conversions, intermarriage converts, whose experiences converge with and diverge from those of their seeker counterparts in important ways. Finally, we will conclude with a brief overview of clerical experience with and attitudes towards the spiritual marketplace.

Conversion and Its Literatures

In his famous psychological account of the phenomenon in *The Varieties of Religious Experience*, William James outlines two models of conversion, the "volitional type" and "the type by self-surrender." While "volitional" conversions involve change that "is usually gradual, and consists in the building up, piece by piece, of a new set of moral and spiritual habits," the "self-surrender type" involves "a complete division" that "is established in the twinkling of an eye between the old life and the new" and produces "subconscious effects that are more abundant and often startling." Despite the fact that James brackets superhuman agency in his analyses, the psychological forces he highlights in this ideal-type conversion effectively act upon persons in rapidly changing their understanding of self and world. Thus, in focusing on the "self-surrender" variety, James consistently portrays conversion as a passive endeavor, in which the self is alternately "to be converted, to be regenerated, to receive grace, to experience religion, to gain assurance," in other words, to be the vessel of massive psychological shifts.[5]

After giving a brief nod to the "volitional type" as, at least, an alternate model for conversion, James summarily deems it to be "as a rule less interesting than those of the self-surrender type," given the latter's often highly dramatic and emotional character. As Paula Fredriksen notes, James's emphasis on "self-surrender" as paradigmatic of religious conversion is heavily influenced by Christian theological models of instantaneous change such as those epitomized in the stories of the Apostle Paul and Augustine of Hippo. The drama of these stories, encapsulated in a precise moment of divinely induced transformation, eclipses the choice-making potential of religious conversion and reduces what may be quite extensive processes (as Augustine himself painstakingly recounts in his *Confessions*) to a single moment. These classic, theologically imbued models, as Talal Asad aptly observes, suggest a phenomenon so fraught with the "mysterious" and the "inexplicable" that it seemingly borders on the irrational. As a conceptual and practical category, conversion often appears, in Rudolf Otto's sense, to be something "wholly other," a kind of mystical occurrence divorced from the processes and ambiguities of everyday life.[6]

These early, theologically informed views of instantaneous conversion, however, came to be largely supplanted in the 1960s and 1970s by new theoretical models of and methodologies for the study of conversion. Rather than considering conversion as an interiorized, socially decontextualized event involving a lone person and her psyche or, from a theological perspective, her god, sociologists and social psychologists wielded the field methods of interviewing and participant observation to understand the meaning-making and group-individual dynamics of conversion within specific religious communities. A number of significant studies emerged illuminating these processes within New Religious Movements (NRMs) in particular, such as the Divine Light Mission

(James V. Downton, Jr., 1979), the American Hare Krishna movement (Francine J. Daner, 1976), and Scientology (Harriet Whitehead, 1987). As Lorne L. Dawson discusses in his overview of this scholarship, the relative freedom and choice-making capacities of the neophyte members of NRMs remained key themes of these and subsequent studies, given the periodic, popular depiction of these movements as "cults" bent on "brainwashing" the gullible.[7]

Certainly, the most consistent and innovative theorizing in regard to conversion as a platform for strategizing and choice-making over the past 30 years has come from scholars evaluating conversion and missionization in colonialist contexts such as the historical research of Jean and John Comaroff, Gauri Viswanathan, and Christopher Queen.[8] The work of these scholars is significant, again, in demonstrating the vital multidimensionality of conversion processes as standing beyond monolithic determinants however socially, economically, politically, or ideologically defined. Missionaries do not simply force religious ideologies on the missionized or colonized, but the "converted" are themselves active participants in conversion processes as they *strategize* (that is, make choices) and effect religious change in their lives and societies. As Gauri Viswanathan points out in her cogent work on conversion and modernity, convert emphasis on personal religious choice and choice-making fundamentally alters the contours of modern conversion and its narratives. Viswanathan writes in this regard:

> Recent scholars have drawn attention to the crucial role of choice in distinguishing conditions of modernity from those of premodernity. . . . If modernity comprises a complex range of ideas, philosophies, and systems, the ability to process them calls not only for reason to make the requisite discriminations between them but also the skill to evaluate the quality of their respective demand on one's attention. Such evaluation is itself a form of choice, but the important point is that choice is possible only when the heterogeneity of belief-systems is made visible. Such acts of conscious selection account for new types of conversion narratives, which reflect the individual subject's greater access to a range of traditions, ideas, and doctrines.[9]

From this "evaluation" and "access to a range of traditions, ideas, and doctrines," Viswanathan concludes that modern conversion is fundamentally a "knowledge-producing" activity. Thus, it appears as "an interpretive act, an index of material and social conflicts" since "spiritual autobiography shades into critiques" of both the rejected and adopted religious contexts as well as society at large. It is precisely the making and articulating of religious choices that makes the convert, both historically and today, such a powerful and often suspect figure of social life. The act of consciously evaluating and crossing religious and cultural boundaries not only blurs the supposedly distinct margins of communities and institutions but also provides the convert a wide vista of experience from which to compare, analyze, and critique alternatives and milieus. Choice-making, therefore, is nearly always, at least to some extent, an analytical process of categorization, comparison, and deliberation.[10]

As vital components of the spiritual marketplace and its choice-making imperative, active knowledge acquisition and self-reflexivity lend shape to the Orthodox conversions under consideration here. At each point in their conversions, from initial religious seeking to settling into life as Orthodox Christians, Orthodox converts in Pittsburgh and Jackson consistently relate a kind of ongoing negotiation between self and other, as they research religious differences and experiment with practices and beliefs. Such processes virtually ensure that converts arrive at the doors of the Orthodox Church with these marketplace skills and attitudes fully intact and ever more deeply engrained and habitualized in their lives. For seeker converts, these skills and attitudes are often found in the earliest of their pre-conversion religious experiences and environments.

Seeker Converts

In casting their pre-conversion lives as journeys and searches, informants were simply following well-worn patterns dominating their childhood homes rather than setting off as pioneers of religious experimentation and conversion. Given the fact that the vast majority of study informants were either baby boomers or their progeny, demographic groups long noted for their religious or spiritual restlessness, few converts with whom I spoke stepped directly from mono-religious birth families into an adolescence or adulthood of sudden multireligious possibility.[11] They often grew up in households where religious investigations were part and parcel of their everyday lives. The varied narrative strands bringing the context of religious diversity and choice-making for these American Orthodox conversions into sharp relief typically began to unfold in answer to the open-ended question invariably starting off my 48 interviews, "Can you tell me a little bit about your religious life growing up?" (See Appendix B for interview guides.) The responses from converts along with those of clerical and lifelong Orthodox Church members made abundantly clear that personal religious conversion and change were well-established features of informants' lives.

Such was the case with Alex, a nuclear engineer and current parishioner of St. Michael's church, in his early 20s, who converted to Orthodoxy while in college. The young man recalled a childhood largely shaped by the religious experimentation, albeit of a wholly Christian sort, of his baby boomer parents. When asked about his religious life as a child, Alex responded that it was "pretty complex" beginning with his parents' interfaith Roman Catholic and Presbyterian marriage for which Lutheranism appeared as "something in the middle," a "compromise" denomination as the couple began their life together. The Lutheran Church did not remain the family's primary church of attendance for long but simply served as a prelude to 15 years of ardent church "hopping" as the family moved to various parts of the United States. Alex provided an overview of his religiously eclectic childhood:

> During the time between when I was first born until I was about 15 years of age we went to a lot of different churches. We lived here in Pittsburgh a little bit after I was born [he was born in a town near Pittsburgh] and then we moved to New Orleans, Louisiana, where we went to some sort of Protestant church and then we moved to Lawrence, Kansas, and there we probably attended some form of Protestant church and then from there we moved to Tulsa, Oklahoma. And I guess the reason I'm bringing these up is because this is sort of the influence my parents had. They had all these different locations that they lived and when they lived in the Midwest they experienced more of an evangelical and charismatic faith.

It was precisely in this fashion that Alex, in his words, came to be exposed to "the full spectrum of all of Western Christianity." Such was the case with another woman in her late 30s who responded to my opening query by characterizing her birth family as a kind of casual, if rather haphazard, religious pastiche, "Okay, I was baptized Methodist but everybody in my family was baptized a different Christian religion. . . . My father's a lapsed Catholic who loathes the Catholic Church. My mother is United Church of Christ. My sister was baptized Episcopalian and married a Baptist so they go to a small evangelical church outside of Alexandria, Virginia. So we never had formal religious training at all. I would occasionally go to different churches."

Even if exposed to the concept and actuality of religious seeking in childhood, informants did not typically embark upon their own searches until mid- to late adolescence or early adulthood, with college and other postsecondary educational settings being commonly cited venues for their inauguration. In what some commentators, such as Catherine Bell and Bradd Shore, have argued is the general dearth of contemporary American rituals marking the transition from childhood or adolescence to adulthood, "going away" to college has become a veritable *rite de passage* for many Americans.[12] Invested with a subliminal, ritual-like cachet as well as, in many cases, actual movement from the parental home to new physical surroundings, social situations, and academic expectations, college looms large in a number of narratives as a period of intense questioning and experimentation. Much of this questioning revolves around issues of moral and religious decision-making. Not only are informants confronted with a vast array of religious and moral options, but away from the familial eye often for the first time, they have an opportunity to explore and appropriate them. Through classroom studies and social contacts with persons of different faiths and cultures, the university affords individuals, in a relatively short span of time and space, access to what appears to be "everything" in religious and world cultures, for as one woman remarked of her own experience: "And then you get to college and there's so much there. There's everything from Hinduism to everything there and I searched around a lot, but nothing really clicked."

Alex, for example, situated his eventual conversion to Orthodoxy within a wider imperative of deciding upon a "more moral lifestyle" his freshman year of college. Even before encountering Orthodoxy, the young man became intensely aware of the necessity to make fundamental lifestyle choices. "I have decisions to make. Once you're going into a culture where decisions are necessary and you could lead this form of life or this form of life—life A or life B or life C or life D, how do you make a decision? Which one is it going to be?" Alex's questioning extended to Christianity itself: "I knew I was brought up Christian and I think I just wanted to know, wanted to verify, is this the right religion? I was brought up with this religion and I tend to believe in God . . . but how do I really know that God is the Christian God and, is not, the Muslim God or that Hinduism isn't the right religion?"[13]

In the midst of trying to establish moral or religious certitude, Alex discovered an "objective" means by which to test and verify his childhood faith—an introductory world religions course offered at his university. Alex said of his newly found "objective" measure: "And so that class really helped to clarify things for me and there was no bias to the teaching of it. It was a very well-instructed course taught specifically about different religions and I really saw a drastic difference between Christianity and the other religions at that time and that drastic difference I concluded to be love." While, in Alex's view, religions such as Buddhism and Confucianism provided "this mental form of how you create society or how you come up with laws or teachings," Christianity offered a vision of "sacrificial love," something he felt to be lacking in the other religions he studied.

In the realization of this "sacrificial love," at a single stroke, Alex's moral and religious dilemmas seemed to be settled. He continued, "From that point, I was very motivated, very interested in anything Christian—reading scriptures, really dedicated to a lifestyle that was in line with Christ's lifestyle." In the midst of gaining this increased surety, however, that Christianity was the "right religion," Alex encountered only new choices to be made, now in the guise of which church to attend, again a choice for which no clear objective standards of decision-making seemed readily available. "Let's say there's twenty churches in the area, well why do I choose one over the other? Why would I choose the Presbyterian Church as opposed to the Lutheran? They all had their own problems, their own misunderstandings." Furthermore, the few criteria he could identify as critical to the congregational selections of other Christians were suspect in his eyes: "Some people made a decision because, 'Oh, I like the pastor or I like the way this pastor does his sermons.' I didn't really feel that was a valid reason to choose, just because you like something or you don't like something and so then I said, 'Is there a good reason that I should choose one church over the others?' And so I was kind of just not real sure what I was going to find, but I was going around and seeing if I did find anything." Eventually, Alex came to learn about Orthodox Christianity through the efforts of a controversial Pentecostal cum Orthodox Christian street preacher, who has spent more than 20 years evangelizing a large state university in Pennsylvania and initially engaged Alex in debate. The preacher introduced the young man to the writings of the church fathers, which he began reading in earnest. Over time, Alex came to visit a local Orthodox parish, where he converted two years later.

As Robert Wuthnow points out, other major life transitions including marriage, divorce, the birth of children, and travel or geographical relocation can also serve as significant prompts for religious seeking since they often bring into relief questions of meaning and belief.[14] Such was the case with Pam, one of the very few informants interviewed who had never attended college and who in her early 60s was a vivacious, stylish woman who worked the perfume counter of a local department store. A Pittsburgh native raised in a Roman Catholic home with paternal ties to Russian Orthodoxy, Pam married a Methodist man immediately upon graduating from high school, and, in her words, "We both sort of started searching then. We thought maybe we should try other churches and we moved away from Pittsburgh too, after we were married, to California. So we just sort of went to every church in Bakersville that we thought we might like to attend. And we found one. It was Southern Baptist." These ecclesial venues eventually extended from this initial Southern Baptist church to include the Assemblies of God as well as other Pentecostal and non-denominational charismatic churches. Pam encountered and considered Orthodox Christianity as a personal religious option only years later when she returned to Pittsburgh to care for her elderly and ailing parents (her mother had in the meantime left Catholicism to become Orthodox along with her father) in the early 1990s.

At the same time, another man was prompted to search for "a more spiritual influence" in the midst of a painful divorce, for as he explained, "As we are all like that, you know, when times are tough what do we do? We always glorify God and ask God for help when we have problems. But then, when everything's nice and happy we just forget. Right? That's how life works. So, that was a very trying period in my life going through this divorce and I was searching for something but I didn't know what. I wasn't sure."

Informants consistently took for granted the idea that religious or church affiliation was a private, individual decision often made in the hope of attaining personal satisfaction and peace. From her post-conversion vantage as an active Orthodox church member, Pam continued to hold the diversity of Christian churches in high esteem and saw church affiliation more as a matter of personal taste than an imperative to find the doctrinally true. She explained: "It doesn't matter how you believe. It's everybody's general preference. I mean, I can tell people to come to my church [St. Michael's] but everybody's going to find their niche somewhere." Another convert echoed Pam's sentiments in quoting William Shakespeare's "To thine own self be true" as her guiding principle for maneuvering through the terrain of religious options and offered this as advice to would-be converts. Even in narratives where "truth," of the decidedly unique and absolute variety, was cited as the hoped-for end of religious searching and believed to be found in Orthodoxy, this subjective view of religion as a kind of handmaiden to the needs of the self was not easily shaken. Karen, too, at times favored subjective measures over the "truth" as the ultimate criterion for selecting a church, for she advised: "Find a very good teacher. Find someone you can ask questions and keep trying until you're satisfied. Keep searching until you find yourself satisfied and, in fact, that's what I did."

Sources of Convert Information-Gathering

As intimated, the American religious marketplace influences not only how converts talk about their conversion experiences but also the ways in which these come to be enacted as a constructive meaning-making, "knowledge-producing" endeavor. Although the making of personal choices is a complicated amalgam of rationality, emotionality, happenstance, habit, and external persuasion, among other features, the activity itself can be defined in rather broad strokes. Arising from and reflecting conditions of marked contradiction and mutual exclusivity, choice-making involves the nullification rather than the expanse of possibility as options are evaluated and discarded, even if only temporarily. While individuals may welcome the potentialities a world of competing alternatives can offer, the actual selection of *one* alternative to the exclusion of others can create situations of acute anguish and doubt. Given the heavy responsibility accorded to modern persons, fatefully determined to make choices at every turn in their lives down to the finest of the fine print, the making of choices is *work*, at least if the individual is at all concerned with the possibility of choosing the wrong option among the many rival alternatives, whether material or ideational, to be examined and decided upon.[15]

Given its continued obscurity on the American religious landscape, converts' discoveries of Eastern Orthodoxy, indeed, often required considerable effort and persistence. While, as discussed in chapter one, American religious seekers may have some knowledge, however cursory, of Western Christian and non-Christian religious options including Hinduism, Buddhism, and Islam, they often have little early experience with the Orthodox Church. Therefore, in contrast to other religions with which converts may experiment, Orthodox Christianity was rarely encountered in the course of natural "shopping" excursions in visiting different churches from week to week. Therefore, print and electronic media as well as social contacts and encounters became the primary sources of information available to would-be converts. They have also become increasingly important within American Orthodoxy as a whole.

Certainly, over the past 30 years, Orthodox Christians, for their part, have endeavored to make their religion better-known through the expansion of English-language print and electronic media and active evangelistic efforts including the establishment of new parishes and, more rarely, face-to-face proselytism. While not all informants necessarily engaged in extensive reading, nearly all the converts who did were individuals who came to the church primarily for theological or liturgical reasons rather than through intermarriage. Reading and studying, either independently or in formal postsecondary settings, proved to be the most common ways that converts learned and accessed information about the Orthodox Church. In their studies on Orthodox converts, Paisios Bukowy Whitesides and Richard Cimino too have noted the book-driven, rather intellectual nature of these conversions.[16] Informants reported hearing about Orthodoxy in history or literature classes and often set out upon years of intense personal research into topics of Christian theology and history in an attempt to understand the differences between Christian churches or to find the "early church." Translations of the church fathers, from Ignatius of Antioch (second century) to Gregory Palamas (fourteenth century), as well as the writings of more recent interpreters of Orthodoxy to English-language audiences such as Bishop Kallistos Ware (b. 1934), Fr. Alexander Schmemann (1921–1983), Fr. John Meyendorff (1926–1992), and Vladimir Lossky (1903–1958) were among the most frequently consulted works.

Significantly, the influence of converts as a collective force (and voice) within the church becomes apparent with even the most cursory glance over the array of Orthodox print materials published in the United States in recent years. Publishing houses such as Conciliar and Regina Orthodox presses, each established by a different cadre of former evangelical Protestant converts to Eastern Orthodoxy, have been especially active in disseminating materials with an eye towards educating the would-be or initiated newcomer to the faith. Pamphlets ranging from the not so subtly titled "What on Earth Is the Orthodox Church?" to "First Visit to an Orthodox Church—Twelve Things I Wish I'd Known" introduce the Orthodox Church and the intricacies of its worship and doctrines (as much as can be relayed in a small, folding pamphlet) to persons largely unfamiliar with the faith. Once an individual's interest in Orthodoxy has been piqued by a pamphlet, a host of handbooks, primers, and periodicals of various sorts are widely available for more sustained study into aspects of Orthodox history, beliefs, and rituals.

Conciliar published *Again* magazine and *The Handmaiden* (the latter was a periodical for women), which provided readers ongoing perspectives on contemporary Orthodox life and experiences in the United States before both publications were discontinued in 2009. Not only did these magazines furnish advice and information of special use to converts (for example, *The Handmaiden* dedicated an issue to dealing with non-Orthodox friends and relatives), but they, importantly, also published their stories of conversion, of finding and embracing the Orthodox Church. In fact an entire subgenre of published (and unpublished on the Internet) Orthodox conversion narratives have sprung into being, both as anthologies and in book-length formats with well-known American Orthodox convert commentators such as Frederica Mathewes-Green and Frank Schaeffer offering their personal accounts of becoming Orthodox.[17]

Like Karen and many other convert informants, Fred too became Orthodox at Ascension along with his wife, Mary, in the early 1990s after years of self-directed reading and studying. A self-confessed "banker by day and theologian by night," Fred described the intensity with which he approached his religious search: "It was a ten- to twelve-year process where I would stay up to two or three in the morning studying everything I could, the best scholarly materials I had access to, which weren't always the best, but the best that I had access to on the New Testament, the early church, theological critiques of the church, processes of transformation. I kept thinking to myself, 'Somebody out there has to know a way. It was simply beyond my ability to believe that the power that transformed the early saints couldn't still transform us.'" Alex remarked upon the comparative nature of his personal pre-conversion readings: "If anybody is in touch with the correct teachings [of Christianity] it would be the disciples of those who wrote the scriptures. So I went off and I read those and I also read Augustine. I had heard the Protestants and Roman Catholics use him for a lot of their theology and when I read Augustine, it tended to support what was in the Protestant faith. But when I read the other church fathers, I tended to see how they spoke differently and they seemed more Orthodox. That reading made a big difference."

The Internet too proved to be a significant means of convert infor-mation-gathering. Not only do all the canonical Orthodox jurisdictions in the United States have official websites, often complete with book recommendations, pastoral contacts, parish directories, and basic question-answer pages devoted to explaining the church to inquirers, but many parishes, including Ascension, St. Michael's, and St. Sera-phim's, do as well. Indeed, increasingly, would-be converts can preview an Orthodox Divine Liturgy or investigate the layout and architecture of any number of churches from the comfort of their own homes as some parishes regularly broadcast their Sunday services on the Internet and offer pictorial web tours of their temples. Furthermore, a host of more informal Orthodox blogs (many authored by converts, both lay and clerical), chat rooms, and inquirer forums in which priests and other Orthodox Christian insiders answer questions on church doctrine and etiquette exist for individual perusal. As Barbara Adam and Timothy W. Luke have maintained, religious traditions in no way stand outside of or in necessary opposition to these modern technologies but have quickly and effectively marshaled them for the dissemination of their teachings.[18]

While most converts described their Internet activity as supplemen-tary to other means of religious inquiry (reading books, conversing with religious practitioners, and so forth), Carl relied primarily on the Internet in his active, highly self-conscious search for a church. With a Presbyterian mother and avidly non-religious father, Carl, a middle-school educational assistant and music teacher in his early 30s, claimed little interest in church or religious matters in general throughout his adolescent and college years. Still, he reported learning about Orthodox Christianity in the culture portion of a Russian language course he took in high school. Given his deep love for music, Carl mentioned being particularly struck by the Russian liturgical chant his teacher played for the class and which he heard again in a college music history class. Carl speculated, "At that point it was like I guess the seed was planted in the back of the brain."

Disgusted with the informal worship services of the Presbyterian Church, Carl turned to the Internet as a research tool for finding a new church, an endeavor that unexpectedly germinated the "seed" still lying dormant from his high school and college days. He explained, "So I started in the course of '97–'98. You know, the dawn of the Internet comes and I go well, 'Okay, let's see what's out there.' I go, 'Well, this isn't for me. This isn't for me.' And somehow I come in contact with this Orthodox website and music comes playing and I went [he gasps], 'Oh, yeah. What's this all about?'" In this passage, the twin constituents of the contemporary American religious scene, religious diversity and subjectivity, are underscored. At the click of a mouse, Carl could instantaneously investigate a wide swath of competing alternatives from the privacy of his home. Rather than looking to history or theology as a means of narrowing choices, Carl relied on personal intuition and taste underscored by the curt litany that one or another option "isn't for" him. Only the beauty of the liturgical chant wafting through his speakers flagged Orthodox Christianity as somehow distinct, an incident that further highlights the power of electronic media to appeal directly to the senses of sight and hearing.

Carl's search was also a highly private affair, occurring within the confines of his own home and revolving solely around his own decision-making. Initially, he consulted no religious practitioners and visited no worship sites; no physical "church shopping" occurred at any point in this search. After making his Internet discovery, he quietly returned to this and other Orthodox websites. He explained, "So, I started looking into it [Orthodox Christianity] and I started seriously just thinking about it and just keeping it to myself because I didn't want to make a decision that was gonna be in haste or anything, one that I would regret later on. If I'm gonna do it, I'm gonna do it and that's the end of it." From the official OCA website, Carl quickly found the link to St. Michael's parish and Fr. Mark's e-mail through which he first made contact with the cleric. Carl became Orthodox in 2002.

Nearly all the clergy interviewed attested to the rising significance of these electronic media for bringing seekers to their doorsteps. Interviewed in the spring of 2006, one Antiochian priest in Pittsburgh, for example, observed that the Internet had risen in prominence as a recruitment tool in the last two to three years at his parish. Meanwhile, Fr. Mark said in this regard: "I just knew that God would bring people into the [Orthodox] Church. I just knew that if we did certain things. I knew that if we put a face on the Internet. I knew that if we put the sermons out there, you know. I knew that we have something good here and something holy." In addition to maintaining a strong Internet presence for his parish, Fr. Timothy expressed a desire to televise Sunday church services even if he had not taken steps to do so: "If I had the money, I'd be on television. I would televise the Liturgy. I think there are people who have never been literally exposed to anything like that and have no idea that it exists and would find it beautiful and would want to come here."

Even in the midst of this proliferation of media resources, face-to-face encounters between seekers and religious insiders or participants as well as others investigating religious options (religious seekers often meet up, compare experiences, and make recommendations to one another) continue to be significant ways of learning about religions and should in no way be discounted. Certainly, American converts to Orthodoxy are not unique in this regard. As Rodney Stark and William Sims Bainbridge have long pointed out in their studies of conversions to New Religious Movements, the formation of social ties with religious insiders is a critical component of modern recruitment and conversion. Despite the fact that individuals may favor certain beliefs and practices over others, they are often introduced and encouraged to explore religious options more concertedly through preexisting and newly developed social networks. Furthermore, stronger and better-developed bonds between potential recruits and religious insiders also increase the likelihood for conversion, even if resistance to fundamental tenets of the newly adopted group remains. Ethnographic studies, such as those conducted among converts in Orthodox Jewish and Taiwanese American contexts, confirm that strong relationships often long precede acceptance of official religious ideologies in the course of conversion processes.[19]

While this relational element is obvious in cases of conversion through intermarriage, it is also present for seeker converts as well. No amount of reading makes one an Orthodox Christian, for at some point would-be converts must establish contact with Orthodox clerics and other church members and undertake a process of socialization and integration into the local community. Relationships developed with clerics and other religious insiders also become increasingly important in providing knowledge and comfort as individuals come ever closer to crossing institutional boundaries, as we shall see in the processes of formal catechesis discussed in chapter three.

Intermarriage Converts

Not all converts encounter Orthodox Christianity in the course of active religious seeking, however. Indeed, one of the fundamental distinctions made in Orthodox parishes was between intermarriage and seeker converts. Although the latter variety of convert has received more scholarly and popular attention in highlighting the viability of Orthodox Christianity as a marketplace player attractive to certain

constituencies of Americans, there was always a steady stream of persons entering the faith in the course of marrying an Orthodox spouse,
for as one lifelong Orthodox woman in Pittsburgh in her midfifties
recalled of earlier decades: "There were no converts outside of marriage.
I can't think of one. I mean, nobody came into the church because they
had an epiphany or discovered the church and I'm here because, you
know, for whatever reason. Everyone who came in came because of the
spouse." The priests of St. Michael's and Ascension attested to this shift
of conversion motives in their parishes. Fr. Mark observed, "There has
been an increase in conversions and converts not just from marriage,
but conversions of people who are just looking for Orthodoxy. I think
all of the Orthodox churches have [experienced] that to one extent
or another." St. Seraphim's was distinct from the Pittsburgh churches
in having a majority convert population who had become Orthodox
through religious seeking. Fr. Timothy, therefore, maintained that the
impact of intermarriage conversions on his parish was negligible.

In a manner similar to religious seeking and conversion itself, interfaith marriages too reflect a religiously and ethnically diverse landscape favoring individual wants and needs over societal and familial
constraint. Sociologist Robert Wuthnow, for example, observes that
there has been a significant increase in Americans marrying outside
their own religions since the 1950s, with very few Christian churches
today escaping the readiness of their adherents to cross institutional
lines in search of husbands and wives. Furthermore, the acceptance
and undertaking of religious intermarriage by ever larger segments of
the American populace do not appear likely to abate in the near future
if the attitudes of contemporary college-educated young adults are
any indication. According to Barbara Dafoe Whitehead's study of this
cohort, "fewer than half (42%) of single young adults believe that it is
important to find a spouse who shares their own religion," and when
religion is cited as an important quality, they "seem to want their ideal
mate's religious faith to be as syncretic and blandly 'spiritual' as possible."[20] As in the case of other Christian and religious contexts, internal
social barriers such as intra-parish strictures or stigmas discouraging
marriages outside one's ethnic or religious group have relaxed considerably, and increasingly bi-religious families, in which no postmarital
spousal conversions have occurred, have come to quietly populate
many Pittsburgh Orthodox churches.

While intermarriage conversion is naturally correlated with marriage itself, the Orthodox Church, as it understands marriage in

practice today, permits a certain amount of choice-making leeway in regard to the church affiliation of non-Orthodox individuals who marry Orthodox Christians, a flexibility that is fully embraced and exercised in the parishes under consideration here. For example, church-sanctioned marriages, sealed with the official rituals of the sacrament, are permitted between Orthodox Christians and baptized persons of other Christian denominations, although intermarriage between Orthodox Christians and non-Christians is strictly prohibited.[21] The official Orthodox position on interfaith marriage, therefore, presents an on-the-ground decoupling of conversion from nuptial rituals and the commencement of the marital estate. Thus, informants often began their married lives as part of an interreligious couple. For the purposes of this research, intermarriage converts are persons who learn about and embrace Orthodoxy over the course of meeting, marrying, and living with an Orthodox spouse, not necessarily out of an ecclesial or familial imperative to become Orthodox. In this definitional regard, scholars of conversion have observed that marriage often acts as a vehicle for introducing a faith that is only embraced many years after the marriage has taken place in Jewish and Muslim contexts as well.[22]

In popular parochial parlance, however, as relayed by priests and laity, the individual choice-making potential of intermarriage conversions is typically lost in the institutional glare cast by its entrenched association with the duty-bound estates of marriage and family, of hearth and home. In this way, intermarriage conversions were frequently perceived by others in parish life, by Orthodox clerics, lifelong church members, and other converts, as motivationally far removed from the apparently unalloyed and preferable desire of uniting one's self to the faith solely out of personal affinity with its doctrinal and ritual aspects and regardless of external social or familial circumstances. Informants typically exhibited an unabashed admiration for the effort self-proclaimed seekers and journeyers expended in learning about and entering the Orthodox Church. Fr. Joseph, for instance, said in this regard: "I think in some instances because they [intermarriage converts] are coming in to unify themselves with the Orthodox family member, there is a certain motive, while not bad in itself, that is not speaking to a deeper conviction [of conversion and the religious life]. So, we have those converts and they're not gonna be as much on fire, so to speak, as are the ones who are more deeply drawn into the faith through study, through prayer." Still, Fr. Joseph found much to be pastorally hopeful about in these conversions, as he continued, "That convert may be lacking in that type of conviction. But, again, with something to build on we try to bring them in. I mean, it's a good start. They've taken this step."

While many Orthodox priests and parishioners characterized inter-marriage conversions in simple and dismissive terms as the everyday concomitants of marrying an Orthodox spouse, a strong strand of American individualism certainly coursed through the narratives of intermarriage converts as they emphasized their own religious choice-making. Keenly aware of the overarching contexts framing their conversions, intermarriage converts often delayed their entries to the Orthodox Church for years or decades as they developed what they considered to be appropriately deep and enduring spiritual ties to the Church. Concerns over establishing mono-religious households for the maintenance and transmission of religious practices and beliefs were of lesser importance than that the converting spouse felt and expressed personal affinity for the Orthodox faith.

A part-time physical therapist and mother of four in her midforties, Olivia embraced Orthodox Christianity a number of years into her marriage with a man who had himself converted to the faith in his late teens. A former Roman Catholic who described herself as "the good little kid" who "didn't ask questions, just learned all the stuff" taught her by the clergy and nuns, Olivia only learned of the existence of the Orthodox Church upon meeting her future husband while in college. Although her initial encounters with Orthodoxy were pleasant as her future husband, James, took her to Orthodox churches over the course of their dating, Olivia recalled the lack of enthusiasm with which she greeted the idea of changing religious affiliation at the time: "I was not looking for anything when I met him or even after I met him. I was not necessarily going to convert or anything like that." Olivia did receive some pastoral instruction on church doctrine and practice prior to her Orthodox wedding but said of her early relationship with the Church, "It wasn't like I found 'home.' It took me a little bit longer to decide this is where I always wanted to be."

Although her husband certainly introduced her to Orthodoxy, Olivia maintained that he played little to no role in affecting her ulti-mate decision to become Orthodox, which occurred shortly after the birth of the couple's first child. According to her, from the very be-ginning of their marriage James seemed to recognize and respect her choice-making autonomy in regard to ecclesial affiliation:

He didn't really say anything. He can be very outspoken, very exuberant about his faith and for the longest time I really didn't want to hear it. And he was smart enough to know, okay, step back, just let it go, which tends to work better for me. So, he pretty much stayed out of the whole thing. But, of course, he was very happy when I converted, but he did not encourage, discourage, nothing. He really didn't do much at all. And I think if he would have pushed, I would have pushed harder and that just would not have worked. I wouldn't have even converted at all.

If her husband, in this assessment, "didn't do much at all" in bringing about her conversion, Olivia's birth family played an even more diminished role in her eventual acceptance of the Orthodox faith. She concluded, "I never had anybody saying, 'Oh, that's not a good decision.' Or 'Are you really sure about this?' They were supportive in not being unsupportive. You know what I mean?"

As in Olivia's case, intermarriage converts generally reported minimal spousal involvement in their decisions to become Orthodox while at the same time recognizing that the conversion itself probably would not have occurred apart from the initial circumstances of marriage. Occasionally, Orthodox spouses expressed surprise and skepticism at their husbands' and wives' interest in joining the church. Such was the case with Ken, an accountant in his early 40s who married a lifelong member of Ascension parish. He described his wife's reaction when he converted 11 years later: "I think she [his wife] was really surprised. She was like, 'Are you sure?' And I said, 'Oh, I'm sure.' You know, it was really my decision and it was something I thought about. I mean, this is where I need to be and there's no reason that I need to straddle this fence. So, it was my decision and she was kind of like, 'Make sure. There will be repercussions.'"

Despite this emphasis on personal choice-making, the narrative contours of intermarriage conversions, in particular the constituents of their pre-conversion phases, can differ markedly from those of seeker converts. Whereas individuals who discovered and were drawn to the church apart from circumstances of marriage often presented their pre-conversion lives as comprised of a series of movements across religious boundaries, this ardent movement and its concomitant descriptors of "search" and "journey" were frequently absent from the narratives of intermarriage converts. Significantly, most intermarriage converts claimed that even the very notion of leaving their home faiths had *never* occurred to them before their premarital and postmarital encounters with Orthodoxy. These informants, however, were by no means unaware of the religious diversity surrounding them or of the fact that individuals can and do change religious affiliation at will, but simply refrained from placing themselves into its midst as seekers.

Based on my fieldwork observations of these events, I conclude that in addition to these differences in language usage, intermarriage converts much less frequently consulted print and electronic media in gathering information on Orthodox Christianity either before or after their conversions and were less likely to participate in the educational offerings of the parish, such as Bible studies, special lectures, and so forth than those attracted to the church primarily for theological or liturgical reasons. In learning about Orthodoxy, intermarriage converts relied on firsthand encounters with church life as well as conversations with family, clerics, and other members of parish communities. A more in-depth discussion of the contours and ramifications of the socialization of intermarriage converts will be offered in the next chapter.

Clerical Perspectives

In their ready engagement with new technologies and other avenues for making Orthodoxy better-known, clerics certainly demonstrated a keen awareness of the spiritual marketplace, which appeared as an integral, experiential component of clerical and lifelong Orthodox Christian biographies as well. Certainly, none of the priests could in any way be considered unversed in the thematic and terminological intricacies of American and world cultures. All clerical informants, for example, were American or British-born, possessed college degrees, and had traveled at least once outside the United States. Four of the priests interviewed were themselves converts to Orthodoxy, in turn, from Methodism, Byzantine Catholicism, Roman Catholicism, and Anglicanism/Episcopalianism.

Meanwhile, Orthodox clerics often mentioned the changes in religious affiliation that had occurred among their family and friends. Fr. Joseph, for example, candidly discussed the pain and disappointment wrought upon his family by a brother's abandonment of Orthodoxy for Zen Buddhism. Having moved from Pittsburgh years earlier the brother, whom Fr. Joseph pointedly described as a "seeker," today regularly practices meditation at a Zen Buddhist temple in California. Fr. Joseph attributed his own sensitivity to the "religious struggles" and conflicts of converts to the necessity of confronting questions of religious change in his own family. Meanwhile, another priest from a Pittsburgh-area Antiochian church mentioned that his mother and father each hailed from different Christian denominations, in this case Roman Catholicism and Presbyterianism, and consciously decided upon Orthodoxy as something of a compromise faith for their married life together, since each had ancestral ties to the Orthodox Church through immigrant grandparents.

Priests also drew upon the cultural repertoire of the spiritual marketplace in describing conversions to Orthodoxy as the natural outcomes of church shopping and religious seeking, though often imbuing them with a certain connotative distinctiveness. While converts, for example, often directly castigated "shopping" as an unsavory practice, clerics tended to view it as morally neutral or, more positively, as the very vehicle bringing inquirers to their churches. Fr. Mark, for instance, used this language in assessing the reasons for the recent spike in the number of conversions in his parish: "I think that the interest in Orthodoxy has increased due to the liberalism in other faiths. There are certain issues that are going on in the Roman Catholic Church or the Episcopal Church. People start shopping. They start reading and discover Orthodoxy and they never knew what it was." The Orthodox bishop attributed what he considers to be the mental astuteness of converts to the self-reflexivity and knowledge-gathering inherent in religious shopping in the first place. "In some cases, some of the people that convert to Orthodoxy, as far as their mental knowledge of the church, it often supersedes the people that were born in the church, 'cause these people have made a conscious effort to shop, to shop for a faith and deciding to come to Orthodoxy. They've gained knowledge and they've been able to achieve a certain mental maturity that you deal with them on a different level."

In evoking the language of "searching" and "shopping," clerics repeatedly stressed the significance of the knowledge and experience gained in the course of these processes. Converts in no way could be considered wholly reborn persons for whom entry into the church represented a radical departure from all previously learned ways. Echoing the sentiments of the Orthodox bishop, another cleric commented favorably upon the "very sophisticated backgrounds" of many converts, "Many of the people come from very sophisticated backgrounds and they don't come because of the [church] building or for the ambience. They come for the fact that they've studied and they've searched and God has led them to the Orthodox Church as a place for them to express their desire for tradition and traditional worship. Give thanks to God." Although not directly involved in counseling converts or bringing them into the church, since this remained the responsibility of Fr. Joseph, the deacon from Ascension discussed his "fascination" with converts since they were "serious" about Orthodoxy and took "their faith to heart," characteristics directly resulting from the earnestness of their religious searches. As he explained: "By and large, people who convert to another faith do so because they're making a very serious investment of themselves in the pursuit of truth and if they didn't think that this was going to be the way they could advance that, they wouldn't make that investment."

Conclusion

Not surprisingly, the spiritual marketplace and its attributes of religious diversity and individual choice-making are at their most pronounced and explicit in the pre-conversion phase of these reconstructed biographies. Whether in their overarching and largely theologically indistinct utilization of the language of seeking or journeying or in the concrete particularities of early familial lives and methods of learning about different religions, converts repeatedly expressed appreciation for and confidence in their ability to make religious choices for themselves. Informants thus stressed the self-propelled nature of their encounters with and investigations of a wide swath of competing religious options. Even intermarriage converts never questioned their ability to make religious choices for themselves apart from spousal expectation or influence.

Although clerics too often positively wielded marketplace terminology in their discussions of conversion, they reported a wariness of allowing newcomers into their respective folds without appropriate counseling and discernment. The same forces bringing converts to their church doors may also steal them away since weakened commitment and fickleness are potently present in a context where one can quickly and easily exchange religious venues and allegiances at will. It is towards a fuller understanding of how these perspectives affect Orthodox catechesis more generally that we will now turn our attention.

CHAPTER Three

Processes of Catechesis and
Socialization for Orthodox Converts

A vivacious woman in her early 60s with silver-spiked hair and wrists full of dangling bracelets, Lorraine lived in the heartland of the Mississippi Delta where she served as a music manager for a number of top blues musicians. Disturbed by the fact that "there wasn't any Mississippi representation" at an international blues competition she attended years ago, Lorraine dedicated herself to promoting her home state and its music since, in her words, "Mississippi is the birthplace of the blues, which ultimately birthed rock-'n'-roll and everything else. It's the authentic American music. It's influenced the whole world and everybody had forgotten about it." Energetic and persistent in her work, Lorraine credited her eventual conversion to Orthodox Christianity precisely to the blues, since a young Orthodox musician from the former Soviet republic of Georgia whom she met in the course of her work introduced her to the faith. Fascinated by the many religious conversations she began to have with the devout young man, Lorraine consulted the Internet, "looking for anything I could find about Orthodox Christianity," an endeavor that allowed her to make a critical decision. "All this time I was checking out all this information. And so, I said, 'Andrei [her Georgian friend], I'm gonna become Orthodox. I've made my decision.' Well, he looked at me and said, 'I think you better go to church with me.' You know, I'd never been to an Orthodox service at all."

Arriving at St. Seraphim's with the expectation that she could join the Orthodox Church with the same ease with which she had become a member of her former Baptist and Presbyterian churches, Lorraine quickly learned that desiring to become Orthodox was not the same as doing so. As she recalls: "I didn't know you had to be a catechumen or anything like that. I thought I could say, 'Hey, I want to be Orthodox. Okay.'" Discovering that being a catechumen often involved quite lengthy intellectual and spiritual preparation for conversion, she continued, "When I first got into the Orthodox Church I felt like I wanted them, I'm not sure they want me. You don't just come in and decide that you want to be Orthodox and you're in. I mean, it takes a little while and it should, because it's not something you should be changing your mind about, obviously after you're in. It's a serious thing."

Fr. Timothy directed Lorraine to his Wednesday evening inquirer's classes especially geared for introducing Orthodox belief and practice to persons interested in learning more about the church. She faithfully attended the classes and weekly Sunday services for nearly seven months before officially becoming Orthodox, a time frame Fr. Timothy shortened from the usually expected year or more of study and reflection. Another informant, at St. Michael's, recalled the mild frustration she and her son too experienced in having to wait and receive formal instruction from the priest. Such instruction followed nearly a year of private reading and studying on their part. "I think we kind of pushed him a little bit [to convert]. I know he [Fr. Mark] made a comment or something like, 'Bob [her son] wants to be Orthodox today, but that's not possible.' Then I guess I was sort of like once you know it, why do we need to wait? We know. Why can't we just do it right now?" When asked why she thought Fr. Mark had insisted on delaying their reception into the church, the woman answered, "Well, I think he wanted us to wait to be sure that we weren't gonna change our minds."

Informants in Jackson and Pittsburgh are in no sense the only Orthodox converts bewildered by clerics' requirements for lengthy periods of instruction and counseling prior to being officially received into the Orthodox Church. This is a common theme found in American Orthodox convert literatures as well. One perplexed inquirer into the faith wrote to *Again* magazine, which was especially geared to featuring the stories and concerns of converts: "I decided to convert to Orthodoxy. I have been seeing a priest in a monastery. I am now a catechumen. The father said it could take six to twelve months. I have seen him three times now and there seems to be no formal approach, he asks me if I have questions and things go from there. . . . What troubles me is the length of time till I am baptized. . . . Why does this take so long?"[1]

Given the hierarchical and sacramental nature of the Orthodox Church and the fact that the initiatory rituals of baptism, chrismation, and confession are not available for self-administration, Orthodox clerics assumed a pronounced "gatekeeping" function in protecting the theological and social boundaries of Orthodox Christianity by ensuring that would-be converts were adequately prepared for and knowledge-able about a church whose doctrinal and ritual purity was touted as a key constituent of its present and past identities.[2] In assuming this role, Orthodox clerics attempted to control the "traffic flow" of converts across ecclesial borders (although their influence was largely one-way since they could do precious little to prevent people from leaving the church) while at the same time sharing the language and conceptual framework of seeking and shopping with the converts (discussed in chapter two) as a matter of course. On the one hand, this seeking and its resulting conversions provided a sense of excitement and pride in highlighting Orthodoxy's potential arrival on the American scene, as a viable option among the many to be perused and appropriated in the spiritual marketplace. In a sense, converts and conversions raised Orthodoxy's "spiritual capital," a phrase Wade Clark Roof and others scholars wield in conscious reference to the work of Pierre Bourdieu to indicate the relative value different marketplace goods acquire in the course of social interaction.[3]

On the other hand, a desire emerged on the part of the clergy to maintain ecclesial distinctness and to fortify the church's boundaries against the fickle, conversional faint of heart, the perpetual seeker. In this way, clerics endeavored to set Orthodox Christianity apart from the crowded field of religious options to ensure that it was not cheap-ened and rendered just another church in the raising of its visibility and attractiveness to religious seekers. These clerical assessments of conver-sion and its seeker culture undergirded pastoral responses to and in-teractions with converts, especially during the critical pre-conversion stage when priest and convert have frequent conversational contact with one another in the course of catechetical instruction.

Although the processes of Orthodox catechesis are varied in their form and content (or, in the words of the aforementioned letter writer, lacking a "formal approach"), catechesis serves two purposes in con-temporary American Orthodox churches. First, as in the case of the early church, it involves a period of instruction into the formal tenets and practices of the religious community. In this instance, the parish priest ensures a would-be convert gains knowledge of selected aspects of the Orthodox faith such as the creeds, sacraments, and basic church history. While lay persons may certainly be involved in the catechesis of converts, primary responsibility for instruction invariably fell to the priest himself at all the studied field sites.

Second, Orthodox catechesis becomes a field for determining the spiritual state and preparedness of the catechumens, to gauge their overall commitment level to the Orthodox Church. Nearly all the interviewed clerics reported holding regularly scheduled one-on-one conversations with potential converts to discuss inquirers' past religious lives and experiences, their motivations for possible conversion to Orthodoxy, family obstacles or objections for such a course of action, and even personal problems and past traumas, religiously incurred or not. Through these conversations and observations of the catechumen in parish life (for example, how often and consistently catechumens attend divine services, how well they develop social ties with others in the community, and so forth), clerics attempted to discern the seriousness and depth of the individuals' personal commitment to conversion as well as their overall spiritual development.

While clerically supervised catechesis was the most common venue for socializing and determining the commitment levels of seeker converts, another pattern emerged among informants initially introduced to Orthodoxy through intermarriage. For these individuals, official catechesis was much less important than the naturally developing relationships forged in the course of marrying and adopting the social and familial connections of an Orthodox spouse. These individuals usually possessed deep social ties with Orthodox church members apart from the priest and often did not receive the same level of instruction and scrutiny afforded those drawn to Orthodoxy through other circumstances. Thus, the contours and criteria for conversion differed between the two conversion types. While commitment came to take on a singular, overriding importance in determining whether seeker converts should enter the church, priests were more interested in maintaining marital and familial religious unity, even if individuals themselves were not initially concerned with this issue (as discussed in chapter two).

The ways that converts are catechized and integrated into parish life are, therefore, explored in this chapter. We will first turn our attention to the significance formal church catechesis holds for fomenting and discerning religious commitment among seeker converts before examining the alternate channels for its establishment for those introduced to Orthodoxy through marriage. Our exploration will then conclude with a look at the ways that convert-clerical relationships, forged through the processes of catechesis, impact local Orthodox communities. Converts are perceived as being receptive to pastoral influence in a way that many lifelong members are not, and converts can come to be readily seen and to act as allies to the priest within the parish setting. The personal intensity of these pre-conversion clerical-catechumen relationships frequently continue as part of converts' post-conversion experiences within the church as well.

Formal Catechesis of Seeker Converts

Despite its varying degrees of formality, the processes of catechesis remained the appropriate venue for clerical interaction with and oversight of converts, especially those of the seeker variety. As in centuries past, the term "catechesis," originally derived from the Greek and meaning "to teach by word of mouth," today refers to the process of educating would-be converts and preparing them for the official rituals of reception into the Christian community. While adult baptisms preceded by years of formal instruction predominated in the early church from the first to the fourth centuries, the rise of infant baptism over time eventually led to the decline of the catechumenate as an engrained aspect of liturgical life.[4] Interestingly, however, adult catechesis as a topic of more ardent concern for Roman Catholic and Eastern Orthodox Churches has made something of a comeback in the twentieth century, with the unfixing of individual ecclesial affiliations and the onslaught of seeking that bring adult inquirers to church doors.[5]

Within contemporary American Orthodox churches, especially in the OCA and Antiochian archdioceses, which have received the greater numbers of recent seeker converts, something of a revival of the catechumenate as a term and concept within parish life has occurred as well. Persons demonstrating serious interest in studying and learning about Orthodoxy may have special prayers said by the priest on their behalf, effectively marking them as "catechumens," a practice especially common at St. Michael's and St. Seraphim's given the larger numbers of seekers eager to join these parishes. Fr. Timothy even insisted that persons preparing for conversion come to the front of the church during Sunday Liturgy as he read the "Litany of the Catechumens," which concludes the first half of the service. Would-be converts themselves often looked upon this first step towards membership with great seriousness and readily wielded "catechumen" as a label of self-description in their social dealings with other parishioners.[6] When two young catechumens from a Kentucky parish visited St. Michael's in the summer of 2005, thorough coffee-hour conversations ensued between the couple and other convert parishioners over the length and character of their respective pre-conversion statuses within the church.

Strikingly, despite this revival, the Orthodox Church in the United States today, in contrast to many mainline Protestant and Roman Catholic churches, has no uniform, cross-jurisdictional program for instructing and bringing new adult members into its fold. Given its largely decentralized nature as well as the emphasis placed on determining more interiorized religious states, catechetical preparation was consistently cast by clerics as a highly individualized endeavor, with length of time, format, and contents dependent upon the experiences, knowledge, study, and desire of each person standing at the gate of entry to the Orthodox Church. Rather than marshalling converts through well-established institutional patterns of instruction, of conforming converts to the processes of catechesis, the Orthodox priests featured here usually tailored preparations for conversion to the needs and interests of each person. Thus, the one-on-one catechetical interplay between priest and catechumen in the course of their developing relationship bore no resemblance to the tightly scripted, thematically arranged dialogues so common to other Christian settings.[7]

The instructional methods employed varied from person to person but usually consisted of reading, studying, discussions, and on-the-ground living and worshiping in the local community—in effect, the same vehicles of information-gathering consulted by seekers alone. Fr. Joseph mentioned drawing upon a variety of these approaches in introducing Orthodox Christianity to would-be converts in his parish: "We give them a period of time and then I give them a book to read and then they meet with me on a one-to-one basis over a period of months and then I see how things are going. I try to get them to meet other people in the parish who can more or less mentor them in some respects." A Pittsburgh bishop with ample experience in catechizing converts in over 20 years as a parish priest employed a similar multisourced approach:

> It was very individualized, but in most cases, however, there was a period of time that they [the converts] would study and attend services of the church, get involved with the church in its completion, its totality, the total life of the

church. I had one man who came to the church for 20 years and we didn't bring him into the church for 20 years. And there's people for a shorter period of time. Every case is separate, separate unto itself, depending on the needs of the person and the needs of the parish, but as I said, it does require that the person is able to do some reading, some studying, some counseling with the priest.

Fr. Mark similarly underscored the uniqueness of each convert and case of conversion. As he explained: "In my experience, conversion is different for different people. . . . I think everyone is on a different road in terms of conversion, they see different things and they experience different things. It's kind of like a diamond, a jewel, where people look at it and certain people see different colors, you know. They'll see certain blues or certain reds and I think the faith is like that." Fr. Mark kept this conversional variation in mind, while drawing upon the same grab bag of catechetical tools outlined by his clerical colleagues. "It's different for every person. Ideally, I would like to catechize someone for six months and that may not be a formal catechesis, but something more informal that would include discussions. I'm meeting them on a regular basis talking to them even if they're not a catechumen the whole time and I'd like to see that they're coming to church regularly."

Although Fr. Timothy held an ongoing "Inquirer's Class" every Wednesday evening, he flatly declared that he cared far less about what catechumens learned than that they were developing the necessary spiritual disciplines to stay the course within the Orthodox faith. "I'm not too concerned about what they learn, but that they are around long enough to make sure this is what they want to do. I try to get them to read some things but basically more of it is just meeting with them and talking to them from time to time. See how they're doing, if they've got a life of prayer and so forth." Charlie, a convert at St. Seraphim's who had been under Fr. Timothy's Wednesday evening tutelage, concurred that individual monitoring and interest seemed to take precedence even in a group setting: "I saw it [catechesis] as a lot more personal, one-on-one study even though it was in a large class setting. But that's just the way Fr. Timothy does things. He speaks to people. He speaks to individuals even when he's speaking to a group. But, the same with his catechism class. And, they were pretty informal little gatherings and we all had a tendency to just kind of wing it."

Clerics also varied in their expectations as to the appropriate length of time required for preparing a person for conversion, with the norm being several months to at least a year. The Orthodox bishop, however, was critical of all preconceived time frames for conversion, especially any born of catechumen eagerness to embrace the faith: "I think it [conversion] is a gradual thing if you find sometimes people converting and their conversion is something that they want to do in three days, three months, even three years, they've got a time frame on it, you become suspicious of that because as a matter of fact they do it in God's time, not in their time. So, I think impatience is a definite concern and lack of preparation is a concern."

While converts appreciated receiving the sustained time and attention of the parish priest and the amplification of their personal queries and interests in regard to Orthodox Christianity or their lives more generally, this case-by-case, nearly episodic, approach to catechizing inquirers practically ensured that the base knowledge converts possessed of Orthodoxy was uneven and wildly divergent from one person to the next. Furthermore, priests relied heavily on catechumens' own motivations and abilities to read and study the faith and, in many cases, expected that converts discovering Orthodoxy over the course of their searches had engaged in some amount of prior reading. As one priest asserted: "You know, most often folks start having read two or three introductory books before I've ever even met them." Not only did clerics assume catechumens to be at least minimally self-directed in their explorations of Orthodox Christianity, they also in some cases took into positive account the religious educations that catechumens had received in other Christian settings. In fact, a few converts commented that clerics and other lifelong Orthodox parishioners recognized them as experts in religious matters, based on their prior studies (especially former Protestants in familiarity with the Bible), and they were occasionally drafted to teach Sunday school or serve other educational functions within the parish *before* officially converting to the church.

For most clerics, however, the type and amount of discursive knowledge conveyed during official catechesis was less important than that converts, in the words of one priest, simply be "willing to do it" and demonstrate a genuine commitment to the Orthodox Church. In emphasizing convert commitment, informants reflected a fundamental paradox of the contemporary "culture of choice," to which scholars have long pointed. In her study of modern American conceptions of love and marriage, Ann Swidler, for example, notes that two apparently contrasting vocabularies, of choice and commitment, dominate the discussion. In a context where familial, ethnic, class, and economic constraints concerning whom one may marry have weakened com- mitment, the conscious and willful determination to remain involved regardless of external circumstances arises as the single, all-important thread holding marriages and love relationships together. In a sense, these conversion ideals are analogous to Anthony Giddens's "pure relationship," which he argues has become the model for interpersonal relationships under conditions of late modernity. Writing extensively on the topic, Giddens defines a "pure relationship" as one "in which ex- ternal criteria have become dissolved: the relationship exists solely for whatever rewards that relationship as such can deliver." Such relation- ships are based on "trust" and "intimacy" and come to be decoupled from the "criteria of kinship, social duty or traditional obligation," the supposed moorings of relationships in past eras.[8]

In the general absence of external determinants for religious affili- ation, priests were encumbered all the more to stress commitment to the Orthodox faith from potential converts. As the bishop observed: "It's difficult for people that live in a society where everything is in- stant. They have instant eggs. They have instant soup. They have instant this and instant that. They want their religion that way too." Fr. Joseph echoed these concerns: "I think that's one thing we have to be aware of with any kind of conversion. They come in through the front door, but the question is how many of them are leaving through the back door? We have to make sure when they come that we can really engage them and let them get to know people in the parish."

While church shopping remains an everyday American practice of importance to the conversion narratives featured here, informants, convert and clerical alike, were at the same time adamant that religious expression should not at all resemble a visit to a mall. In contrast to many Americans for whom religious seeking appears to be an end unto itself, study informants naturally held to a kind of mono-religious ideal whereby fidelity to a single religion was considered the appropriate means of enacting and living one's religious life. Fred from Ascension, for example, likened his Anglican father's Eucharistic participation at his mother's Roman Catholic church to premarital cohabitation. "Well, I told him, 'Dad, it's like living together before marriage. You're living together. You're not married.' He said, 'Oh, I didn't think of it that way.' He didn't care for it, but he got the point." Similarly, clerics often likened conversion itself to marriage and eyed even the anger and disappoint- ment individuals may feel towards former confessions with suspicion. The bishop maintained in this regard:

> If you're getting married, you don't marry somebody because you got dumped by somebody else, right? That's not a reason to get married. You get married with a person because you love them and you care for them. . . .You want to be married to Holy Orthodoxy, it's because you love Holy Orthodoxy, not because you're mad at the Episcopalian Church or the Roman Catholic Church. It's because you love Holy Orthodoxy and you want it to be part of your life eternally. You want it to be your focus eternally. So, we have to be sure of that and we do everything we can to ensure that.

This analogy necessarily established a high bar for determining religious commitment. While perhaps acceptable for inaugurating respective searches, discontent with other religious venues was not, in and of itself, considered by clergy an appropriate reason for converting to Orthodoxy. Rather, a kind of romantic ideal of "love," "commitment," and "eternal fidelity" should propel converts into the church. In fact, commitment to Orthodoxy was even more highly valued than conversion itself, with the former's lack signaling that the latter should not be enacted. While they cheerfully and matter-of-factly embraced commitment as a positive grounding for these current conversions, clerics really had no choice but to do so, for commitment became the only anchor by which to tie religious seekers to specific contexts in the midst of a milieu characterized by wanderlust.

In emphasizing commitment, priests were left with the thorny dilemma of ensuring that autonomous, self-taught seekers who had picked and chosen their way to Orthodox Christianity remained compliant church members and held their substantial, often valorized, choice-making skills in firm check. People endowed with the all-encompassing task of choosing a religious worldview in the first place may feel entitled to choose specific tenets and practices by which to abide. Furthermore, if or when the ever-vague experience of post-conversion fulfillment waned, as it sometimes did even among the most initially well-intentioned, shopping for either new parishes or new religions may become enticing once again.

Clerics' concerns in this regard are echoed in other contexts, for as Gauri Viswanathan points out, unbridled, autonomous choice-making, especially that exercised by "strangers," always stands as a potential threat to established religious powers since it embodies latent tendencies for deviance from authorized forms of teaching and governance. At its most extreme, personal choice-making poses threats of straying into "heresy" or, at the very least, precociousness as individuals crossing into new religious contexts marshal their knowledge and experience to the rearrangement of interior decors. In his characterization of the stranger, Zygmunt Bauman notes the deep unease newcomers arouse in communities since their ultimate allegiances can forever remain in question: "The episode of entry brands the 'former stranger' forever—as a *changeling*, a person who can pick and choose . . . whose status can never have the same degree of solidity, finality and irreversibility as that of the natives." In a similar fashion, Patrick Allitt notes the deep hierarchical suspicion awaiting Anglo-American converts to Roman Catholicism throughout the late nineteenth and early twentieth centuries. John Henry Newman, himself a convert from Anglicanism to Roman Catholicism, once announced that "all converts are dangerous" since, as Allitt continues in his characterization, "converts, intellectually adventurous and unused to clerical censorship, were likely to take speculative excursions that challenged orthodoxy rather than fortifying it."[9]

In the American Orthodox context, regular church attendance and the formation of social ties within the parish remained critical ways for effecting and determining potential convert commitment. Although emphasizing that "the model is going to be different for every single person," Fr. Mark said he looked upon church attendance as a favorable indicator of the seriousness of an inquirer's intentions: "I have a girl right now that's been coming for six months and I've been talking to her on and off. She's been coming every week, *every week*. She's not going anywhere else and this has been happening for six, eight months. We just made her a catechumen last week and she'll be chrismated on Holy Saturday. That's about a month away." Meanwhile, Fr. Joseph affirmed repeatedly in his interview the necessity of would-be converts' "putting down roots" in his parish through the establishment of close friendships with other church members who could offer mentoring and encouragement to the inquirer.

Not only did these conversions to Orthodoxy take place after active commitment had been demonstrated on the part of the catechumen but the measured, deliberative quality of these preparations had the added psychological effect, in some cases, of enhancing Orthodoxy's overall desirability in the first place. In a cultural context in which Christian denominational boundaries appear rather fluid and individuals can with little preparation or serious intent easily attach themselves to a telephone book's listing of different, competing Christian churches at will, this emphasis on spiritual and intellectual readiness coupled with the fact that conversion is not granted on demand heightens the "spiritual capital" of the Orthodox Church. With an already well-developed ecclesial self-perception of theological and historical singularity conveyed to the convert through books and conversations, the Orthodox Church appears much more serious and distinct among the array of religious options clamoring for attention. Furthermore, a glimmer always remained, however faint, that despite the catechumen's best efforts the conversion may in the end be denied at pastoral discretion. Orthodoxy is presented in these accounts as something rare and hard-won, a treasure to be cherished and savored once one has been officially admitted into its membership ranks.

Inquirers could not just want to be Orthodox, they had to *really want it* as demonstrated in their active engagement with the faith. When asked how he recognized this moment of readiness concluding the process of catechesis, Fr. Joseph, again, framed it within the context of wider social integration into the parish:

> I can just see that they're eager. It's just sort of a sense that they really want it now and they've been thirsting for it—the integration into the community. They're seeing people and meeting people. They are coming to the [Bible] studies. They're getting caught up in the enthusiasm of being part of the faith. And I think at a certain point you kind of have a sense that he or she is really ready now to make the big step.

Fr. Mark made a similar assessment of the moment of decision-making for both priest and catechumen: "I think [the converts] have to be at the point where they have no other choice. This is what they want and they just see no other alternative. They have to *really* want it. So really it's not so much how I know, it's hearing what they're saying. Are they saying this is absolutely it? I'm not turning my back and this is what I want and you've seen their commitment coming to church. You've heard it in their answers and their discussions." Meanwhile, the Orthodox bishop evoked his marriage analogy in addressing this issue of convert readiness:

> I wouldn't be able to put that into words. It would be like asking you if you told me you were going to get married, for me to be able to say to you, how do you know that you're ready to get married? I wouldn't know unless I saw you with the person for a long period of time. That's why we make people go to counseling 'cause we don't marry people just because they ask us to.

> . . . I think that you can see that a person has really made the [Orthodox] Church their life, has made Christ their main focus and if you see that in their lives, then you think it's probably a good indication that they should become Orthodox. . . . If a person doesn't have a commitment to being immersed in it then you don't bring them in.

Although a joint decision is made in which both priest and catechumen assent to the next step of formal reception into the church, a significant thread coursing through these characterizations was precisely that of conversion as a choice, a decision to be made in the first place. Furthermore, the imperative of this choice, made visible through words and actions, did not remain an interiorized event in the life of an isolated individual but, rather, a communal experience for all parties (if mainly priest and catechumen), to see, study, and understand. In a sense, the catechetical process was one of setting convert decision-making on display, of making it available for pastoral and communal inspection and comment. Interestingly, even the bishop's analogy equating marriage and conversion, in which mysterious qualities seemingly beyond articulation dictate their respective courses, only underscored their ultimate ability to be inspected and discursively understood. Observed over a "long period of time," both the suitability of marriage partners and catechumens and their church can be pastorally determined and granted official seals of approval.

Intermarriage Converts

The notion that wider cultural views of religious seeking play a direct role in shaping the contours of catechesis and its resulting spiritual discernment is highlighted all the more by my observation that intermarriage converts as well as others accompanying a seeker convert into the church (a spouse or other family members, for example) were generally subject to less rigorous standards for conversion than seekers themselves. A curious pattern emerged. The more purely theological or liturgical an interest an individual demonstrated in joining the church, the more rigorous became the requirements for entry, further reinforced by the largely informal, individualized nature of the catechetical proceedings in the first place. While clerics frequently insisted that seekers coming to their doors wait for months or even years before converting, as they attended the yearly round of services, read theological and historical works, and engaged in lengthy conversations about their religious lives, converts through marriage were often admitted into the church solely on the basis of a stated desire to join. Extensive, line-by-line explications of the Nicene Creed or expositions of the intricacies of early church history were jettisoned in these cases for much more abbreviated discussions of conversion intentions and family life. If, indeed, conversion occurs at the time of the marriage ceremony itself, catechesis, in the form of brief overviews of ecclesial belief, may be conflated with general preparations, emphasizing the meanings and responsibilities attendant with marriage itself.

Rarely, however, is conversion delayed or cancelled due to the supposed casualness of the candidate's attitudes. Indeed, Fr. Nicetas, a British-born Orthodox convert and priest from a Cleveland-area Ukrainian church, cited intermarriage conversion as a prime example of a situation in which his criteria of regular church attendance and intellectual effort to learn and study the faith came to take on a lesser significance for the sake of expediting marriage proceedings: "Exceptions are in cases of a marriage where somebody who had not been baptized at all needs to be hastily baptized in order to get married. In those circumstances, in marrying into Orthodoxy as it were, hopefully the person's married someone who's strong enough [in her faith] that he will pick it up afterwards."

In addition to generally receiving different levels of catechetical instruction, seeker and intermarriage converts also represented alternative patterns of socialization into parish life. While most clerics drew distinctions in conversion type (between seeker and intermarriage converts) along the lines of convert effort expended and enthusiasm demonstrated in becoming Orthodox, Fr. Andrew, who himself converted from Byzantine Catholicism to Orthodoxy in the early 1970s, considered the differences to lie primarily with the patterns of convert social integration into Orthodox parish life. Quite simply, intermarriage converts had ready-made familial networks and supports that seeker converts largely lacked. He discussed the differences he had observed in his 25 years of serving as a priest, 18 of which were spent at Ascension:

> If a non-Orthodox marries an Orthodox person, particularly in this parish, you are automatically brought into a familial situation, so therefore, by extension you are a part of that family once removed so to speak. If a person is not coming to the church through that means, but through being received into the church because they are seeking Orthodoxy or Christianity in its

fullness, in Orthodoxy, it's different. Just obviously there's going to be made a distinction between person one and person two.

Again, Fr. Andrew offered a more detailed assessment of the social situation of seeker converts who are not "automatically going to be brought into a familial situation" but need, in his estimation, "to really be a family unto themselves in a greater sense." He further explained: "I think any Orthodox convert in a parish as such needs to be brought in and I think there really needs to be more of a connection between converts to one another so that they can themselves develop into a family relying on one another because their own families are predominantly non-Orthodox and they don't have those family ties." While intermarriage converts can rely on marital and biological bonds once children are born as bases for social interaction within Orthodox communities, seeker converts must "have their family linkage among that small group of individuals (other converts). So, that becomes their family, in a sense, not their biological family, but their family unto themselves within the faith."

In this regard, intermarriage converts themselves frequently saw their acceptance into Orthodox communities as closely tied to their spouses' established social standing within it. Rather than fretting over the potentiality of sitting alone at church picnics or coffee hours, these converts often underscored that they were accepted as "part of the parish family" as a matter of course. Olivia, for example, attributed the warm, immediate reception she received in Orthodox churches to the fact that she came to be coupled with her future husband in parishioners' minds. She asserted, "The people were very welcoming, but the simple fact is that most people know who James is [in Pittsburgh-area Orthodox churches]. So, the fact that I was there with *him* automatically put me into the group. So, that was very nice, and people took me under their wing and made me feel very much part of what was happening in the group, you know, the whole church and the whole nine yards." Olivia even recalled singing with the church choir along with her future husband on her very first visit to an Orthodox service, which happened to be a Carpatho-Rusyn parish accustomed to singing their hymns in Slavonic. She continued, "He had me up in the choir loft which probably helped because at least I was singing—didn't know what I was singing, but at least I was singing."

From this initial sense of feeling "very much part of what was happening" in the parish, Olivia became more involved in the activities of the church in the early years of her marriage even though she did not, as mentioned, initially convert, and she continued to attend a Roman Catholic Church by herself on Saturday evenings. During these early pre-conversion years, Olivia taught Sunday school at her husband's Orthodox parish and eventually became its director, a position she continues to hold in her parish. When Olivia decided to become Orthodox shortly after the birth of her first child, her chrismation simply strengthened ties already well established with other parishioners and represented a simple continuity with her pre-conversion life within the Orthodox Church. Olivia said of her conversion itself: "We went through the whole service and, of course, people said, 'Well, it's about time.' They had already accepted me, you know. . . . I was already part of the church when I joined the church. So, it wasn't a major thing."

The experiences of intermarriage converts, however, do vary, and despite the ready-made entrée spousal relations to a parish may present for the non-Orthodox partner, social discomfort and even a sense of wholesale rejection may still be part of one's parochial experience. Despite the fact that her husband was an active lifelong member and church councilman of Ascension, Christine, a woman in her late 30s with no prior religious affiliation before her marriage, maintained that she never felt "wholeheartedly" accepted by the church, a factor contributing to the family's eventual move to St. Michael's, where she felt a much greater degree of social acceptance: "I don't feel like a visitor here like I did at Ascension. And Fr. Mark has always stressed to all of us, that no one's a visitor here, you know what I mean? It's like you're here, you're here. You're a member of our church, which is really cool." Still, she considered herself "philosophically an outsider." As she explained: "I don't feel I've embraced the church wholeheartedly in all aspects and I don't know if I ever will. I told Fr. Mark that it would be artificial of me to embrace the church wholeheartedly when I've never been a Christian. I wasn't baptized as a baby. You know, it's not in my bones."

Convert-Cleric Relations in Parish Communities

These many months or years of priest-catechumen interaction within the wider context of establishing and detecting commitment have implications for the quality and depth of these relationships in parish life, since priests rarely instruct or engage in spiritual counseling of their lifelong parishioners in quite the same manner or degree. Brought into the church as infants and typically catechized, if at all, as children in some cases many years or decades before current pastors assumed their pastorates, many lifelong parishioners only contact their priests for in-depth discussion of their personal lives in times of crisis and tragedy and in many cases never at all. Even for lifelong Orthodox parishioners participating in Bible studies or catechetically designed inquirers' classes, the same level of intense one-on-one discussion and scrutiny of individual spiritual life and motivation typically does not occur. Nearly all the priests interviewed remarked that the pastoral needs of converts (both before and after conversion) differed markedly from those of their lifelong church members. Priests often maintained that the intensity of convert interest in Orthodoxy and their own spiritual development made greater demands on their time and attention. Fr. Joseph offered his perspective on the matter:

> Because [converts] have a better spiritual focus in many instances they expect more. They have to be fed and you have to give them the real thing. You can't just tell them, "You're a good kid." There has to be programs. They come to confession a lot so I have to be available when they come, which I'm happy to do. But you're engaging them on a different level, whereas the parishioners who are cradle Orthodox, some of them are just sort of laid back about it all, and they don't expect much, as much, unless there's a crisis—a death in the family, marital problem, a sickness, something like that in their lives, then they begin to open up a little more.

In relating to persons whom they considered in possession of a "better spiritual focus," priests often felt that they could hold higher-level theological discussions with well-read converts and more directly influence their spiritual and religious lives than might be the case with either lifelong Orthodox or intermarriage convert parishioners. One priest, for instance, was enthusiastic that converts, as a rule, "elevate" the entire tenor of a parish with their religious knowledge and zeal. At the same time, Fr. Mark mentioned to me in casual conversation one coffee hour that he had long given up trying to influence most of the older, lifelong members of his church, to change their long-engrained, often erroneous practices and notions of the church taught to them by "bubbis" (a colloquial term of endearment for "grandmother" related to the Russian word *babushka*) rather than priests. Rather than harboring hopes of substantially increasing the knowledge and interest levels of many of the elder members of his flock in the tenets of the Orthodox faith, Fr. Mark decided to concentrate his pedagogical and pastoral efforts almost exclusively on "the children and the converts" of his church, groups that he considered more malleable and receptive to his influence.

For their part, converts often emphasized the personal qualities and likability of the priest as essential to their conversions and eventual choice of parish affiliation. Certainly, American converts to Orthodoxy are not unique in this regard but reflect wider changes in how lay persons across the span of religious contexts have come to consider and interact with clergy in late twentieth-century America and elsewhere. Rather than standing as the mere public face of ecclesial authority, clerics are increasingly viewed as discrete persons, offering individualized perspectives on and approaches to religious faith and making attempts to connect on a personal level with their congregants. Indeed, more than one commentator of contemporary American religions has noted how electronic media (for example, radio, television, and the Internet) have transformed religion itself into a realm of "personality" and "celebrity" where the individual quirks, foibles, and temperaments of religious leaders commonly take center stage over issues of doctrine and church practice in the lives of the laity. Sociologists Grace Davie and Enzo Pace among others have noted that established clergy and religious leaders are increasingly expected to fill the role of the "prophet," in the classic Weberian sense of embodying charismatic energy and appealing to certain emotional states in their followers. Pace, for instance, has noted that much of the intense popularity of the late Pope John Paul II stems from his manner of communication (his charismatic delivery and the overall warmth and approachability of his personality) rather than the doctrinal contents of his message itself.[10]

On more local levels, as religious affiliation itself is now largely a matter of personal preference, so too clerical personalities are subject to scrutiny, with the overall compatibility between pastor and congregant a key factor in determining whether or when persons may engage in active religious seeking. For example, despite the fact that a few, especially former Protestant, informants were highly critical of the American penchant to premise church membership upon pastoral likability, many others seemed to equate finding the "right church" with locating a pastor who was personable and demonstrated great concern over their needs and problems. While the motives for converting to Orthodoxy are numerous and complex, the charisma and care of the local priest, in the varied styles that clerics exhibited, was vital to encouraging conversions and ensuring that converts stayed in their parishes.

These more generalized understandings of the roles of modern religious leaders and leadership were heavily supplemented, in many informants' narratives, with strong doses of the significance of personal spiritual elders and teachers as culled from Orthodox literatures. Certainly, notions of spiritual fatherhood and mother-hood—in which more religiously advanced and enlightened elders, known as the *geron* in Greek or *starets* in Russian, take responsibility for and offer direction to novices in the religious life, especially in determining levels of interior consciousness and parceling out prayer rules—remain deeply engrained components of Eastern Christian piety. Arising in the desert monastic communities and hermitages of Egypt and Palestine in the second through fourth centuries, the tales of which are immortalized in the *Apophthegmata Patrum*, "spiritual direction" found its most concerted home in monastic milieus for which innumerable rules and directives for "spiritual fathers" were penned and deep traditions of obedience culled.[11]

Even the most basic modern literary references to Orthodoxy, long familiar to and beloved by many converts, frequently highlight spiritual elderhood as a vital component of religious life. Heavily influenced by the elders of the famed Optina Monastery (an important focal point of pilgrimage in late Imperial Russia), Fyodor Dostoevsky's Elder Zosima from *The Brothers Karamazov* stands as a fictionalized exemplar of Orthodox spiritual guidance. At the same time, the monastic republic of Mt. Athos produced a string of powerful teachers throughout the twentieth century. Silouan the Athonite, a barely literate ascetic recognized in death as a saint, has become familiar to English-language audiences through the popular writings of his spiritual son Archimandrite Sophrony. The ever popular book *The Way of a Pilgrim*, deeply influential on how people, Orthodox and non-Orthodox alike, have come to regard Ortho-dox spiritual practices such as the Jesus Prayer, features the agony of an anonymous narrator, who is neither a monk nor a priest, over locating a spiritual father who can teach him to "pray ceaselessly." Even in death, the once-located elder continues to offer the narrator-pilgrim assistance from beyond the grave through dreams and other rather ambiguous supernatural directives. While clerics were careful to differentiate these extraordinary examples of largely monastic spiritual eldership from the more circumscribed relationships forged between priests and laity in par-ish life, converts often carried into Orthodoxy these lofty ideals.[12]

Just as the plethora of ecclesial options appeal to varied consumer tastes, so too clerical personalities and approaches resonated with different constituencies of the laity. For example, each of the presiding clerics of my primary field sites, Frs. Joseph, Mark, and Timothy, exhibited quite different sets of qualities attractive to convert informants. Often standing outside the fray of daily parish activities, Fr. Joseph was described by a number of parishioners, both convert and lifelong Orthodox alike, as a "holy man" for his dedication to Orthodox prayer practices and his quiet, calm manner with others. A number of converts discussed the deep, penetrating insight he seemed to have into their psychological states and problems, an insight that seemed mildly tinged with near superhuman powers. Describing the agonizing situation of delivering a stillborn child, Mary, who converted to Orthodoxy with her husband, Fred, mentioned Fr. Joseph's quick arrival at the hospital to be so "weird" and uncanny, she said, "He must have been carried there by the angels." Meanwhile, another woman said of her first meeting with the man, "He was so generous, just so generous and I knew the minute I walked in and sat with him the first time and I told him a little bit about myself. . . . And I looked at those slacked eyes looking at me so intently and thought, 'I've really come. I've been in touch with the source here and I'm gonna continue.'" Another parishioner simply declared of Fr. Joseph that "he has no guile, absolutely no guile," and she was astonished at his kind and trusting nature, especially in agreeing to take her and her husband on a pivotal mission trip to the Holy Land slightly after their introduction to him and before the couple had converted to Orthodoxy.

The convert informants of St. Michael's, on the other hand, were impressed by Fr. Mark's down-to-earth quality, the fact that he lived in the midst of life's everyday frays, not above them, and regularly spoke to his parishioners' practical concerns. One woman who converted at St. Michael's, for instance, was impressed that Fr. Mark assumed the role of a "peer" more readily than that of an authority figure: "I think having Fr. Mark there [at St. Michael's] really spoke to me on a lot of levels. So, here's this guy who has three kids, a wife, had worked day jobs and so, I mean, even confession, I go in and I talk to Fr. Mark about marital problems or life problems or whatever, and you understand he knows what you're talking about. He's a peer, you know."

The formerly unchurched Christine was relieved that she had finally met a clergyman who was a "real person," who never gave off priestly airs and who seemed interested in making Christian teaching practical and relevant. As she enthused about his sermons: "And the first Sunday, we were there [at St. Michael's], we were just blown away by Fr. Mark.

I mean, I just had never heard a priest's sermons like that before. I had only heard something very dry, you know. Whereas he weaves passages from the Bible into real life and he makes me understand the Bible better by doing that—making analogies of our real lives and the Bible." In addition to his accessible teachings, Fr. Mark informally socialized with his young, mainly convert, parishioners by organizing young adult outings that involved visits to ice cream parlors and movie nights showcasing popular flicks such as *Batman Returns*. He also tended to meet parishioners at coffee shops and restaurants (in addition to the church itself) rather than in his formal office.

At the same time, Fr. Timothy, with his shock of thick white hair and soft southern drawl, seemed to epitomize a courtly gentlemanliness that at once exuded kindliness and firmness of purpose. Known for his erudition, given his deep love of literature (especially Flannery O'Connor, whom he referenced on more than one occasion during my interview and other communications with him) and ability to quote poetry from memory, Fr. Timothy was respected for a straightforward, no-nonsense honesty that seemed to cut through pretension and premature spiritual enthusiasms. One parishioner of St. Seraphim's, for example, recounted with deep gratitude the honesty and care that accompanied Fr. Timothy's wise spiritual counsel: "It's so great to have somebody that you can talk to who will be honest with you. And not sugarcoat anything. Not be scared to tell you, 'Hey, look in the mirror every once in a while,' and be supportive of you and love you no matter what you say. No matter what you share. He's gonna guide you, pray with you, forgive you as a human being himself. It's just been a fantastic experience for me."

Given the importance of the priest-convert relationship, formed and strengthened over the course of the catechetical process and well beyond, converts were often seen in the parish, through the prism of intra-parish power relations and struggles, as natural allies of the priest, although priests themselves rarely spoke of this dimension directly. While lifelong members with whom I spoke at both St. Michael's and Ascension were generally excited about and encouraging of converts coming to their church, this enthusiasm was by no means a universal sentiment, either at the field sites at hand or in other parishes. The starkest example of this came from the experience of Fr. Andrew of Ascension church who, although now a full-time social worker, had begun his clerical career as a young man successively in charge of what he referred to as two largely "geriatric parishes," both of which "would have accepted converts only because of the fact of what it meant to them financially." When asked why the parishioners of these communities were not generally open to new, previously non-Orthodox, church members, Fr. Andrew forthrightly speculated: "I think they really felt threatened by it [conversion]. I think it threatened the power base to have new people come in who were in some sense loyal to the priest instead of the power base [of some lifelong parishioners]—itself being typically antagonistic to the priest. The converts would be seen as loyal to the priest rather than loyal to *them*, you know, the power base."

However, as is the case with all categories of human endeavor, relationships between priests and converts themselves were not always idyllic. While more than happy in most cases to offer counsel and assistance to their convert parishioners, priests often commented on the dangerous tendency exhibited in a few, rare converts to idolize the priest and look upon him as something of a "guru," to be deferred to on all the major decisions of their lives. Again, these notions were often drawn from the aforementioned Orthodox literatures. Fr. Mark emphasized the dangers of converts' interpreting his spiritual fatherhood in this way: "But where I am concerned sometimes is the tendency of some converts to place either in me or some other spiritual father a sort of guru-ship that is extremely dangerous and extremely harmful and extremely un-Orthodox. And it is dangerous in ways that they will never understand." He further coupled these warnings with concrete examples from his own pastoral experience:

> If [converts] come to me and say, "You know, I'm thinking of buying a car or something and I don't know if I should really spend all this money" it becomes—I mean, if it's a truly spiritual issue, I think that's all well and good and should be encouraged. But when it starts to seep over into their private life, into their social life, I want to step away from that as quickly as possible and sometimes they want to encourage that. Sometimes they want to have that type of a relationship on that level, which is certainly the level that an abbot would have with their spiritual children in the monastery, the monks in the monastery. But this is *not* appropriate at all for lay people to have this type of a relationship with their spiritual father. It's simply not appropriate.

As a monk himself, Fr. Nicetas framed the issue of teacher-disciple relationships within the wider tableau of Orthodox religious life and counted their idealization a common problem found among converts to the faith. "A tendency to be unrealistic in expectations is probably the main problem I see. Certainly, I think I've seen this more in the Orthodox Church than anywhere else, but a tendency to idolize people. So, I think this is a pitfall for converts in *any* church and I think particularly among the Orthodox there's this real expectation of the sanctity of certain people and they can feel awfully let down when their idols have feet of clay and most of us have, I'm afraid, in one way or another."

Conclusion

While observers of American Orthodoxy generally place it on the margins of the American spiritual marketplace, the metaphors and actions of seeking and choice-making inform nearly every aspect of catechesis as implemented in the Pittsburgh and Jackson Orthodox churches. Demonstrations of convert commitment to Orthodoxy are of far greater importance in these proceedings than the conveyance of doctrinal and ritual information from priest to catechumen. Deftly wielding the language of seeking and choice-making in their interviews, clerics at once valorize converts for consciously choosing Orthodoxy from the midst of competing options available, a sign of Orthodoxy's rising marketplace value, and wrest sole choice-making control from them through the pastoral "gatekeeping" function of ensuring the purity and earnestness of conversion motivations. At the same time, the potentiality of pastoral delay or denial of a catechumen's desire to become Orthodox can serve as a potent means of distinguishing Orthodoxy from ecclesial competitors eager for new members.

The duration and personal intensity of these pre-conversion clerical-catechumen relationships frequently continue as part of converts' post-conversion experiences within the church and have important ramifications for the parish as a whole. Converts, like "children," are perceived as receptive to pastoral influence in a way that many lifelong members are not, and converts can come to be readily seen and act as allies to the priest within the parish setting. More will be discussed on the intra-parish parsing of lifelong and convert church members in everyday parish life in chapter six. For now, there will be a discussion about the issue of conversion motives themselves, an issue of central concern to Orthodox parish insiders and observers alike.

CHAPTER *Four*

Meanings of and Motivations for
Conversions to Orthodox Christianity

At the precise moment of the recording of informants' interviews a clear destination, the Orthodox Church, had been reached and transformed from an unknown ecclesial terrain into a place and space of long-term dwelling. Over the course of my interviews, informants recounted a multiplicity of features they found attractive about the Orthodox faith. So too have scholars who have examined the phenomenon of American conversions to Orthodoxy. Phillip Charles Lucas, for example, maintains that such "conversions include both individuals and communities drawn to the rich liturgies, firm moral theology, mystical spirituality, and claims of apostolic continuity offered by Orthodoxy." Meanwhile, Richard P. Cimino has noted the "different visions of the church" conveyed by young Orthodox converts. "Just when I thought I could pinpoint a common tendency of thought among most of the young adults, there were usually several exceptions that would break the rules." Cimino attributes this finding to the natural variability found within Orthodox Christianity as a religious system, in its expanse of ritual and conceptual offerings.[1]

Despite the variation that exists in the views converts hold on the motives and meanings of conversion, their stated reasons for embracing Orthodox Christianity generally fell into two categories, each of which provided distinct, if entwined and mutually informed, perspectives on Eastern Orthodoxy. These two categories represented fundamental aspects of Eastern Orthodoxy's "cultural repertoire" that are set in potent interplay with, rather than remaining set apart from, the concepts and language of the American marketplace. First, in direct, explicit reaction against this marketplace culture, informants such as Karen (in the introduction) were often profoundly interested in Eastern Orthodoxy as a staid, doctrinally and historically conservative form of Christianity offering its members a profound sense of stability and continuity with various real and imagined pasts. Many informants affirmed a strong attraction to the external, institutional qualities of the Orthodox Church as a preserver of doctrinal formulae, hierarchical structures, and absolute, exclusivist notions of truth and tradition. In this regard, Orthodoxy was frequently valorized as offering the strong doses of moral certainty and community needed to assuage the social isolation and existential uncertainty of contemporary existence.

Yet, these same informants commonly described Orthodox Christianity as liberating in providing new arenas for individual self-expression, growth, and transformation, all of which were usually gauged in terms of positive personality change or a heightened awareness of divine workings in their lives. The Orthodox Church, especially in offering its adherents a rich assortment of strategies to adopt and implement, was depicted as a powerful platform and context for individual self-discovery. Even informants with an avowed interest in Orthodoxy's supposed unchanged and unchanging "truth" did not want to remain unchanged themselves in their encounters with and lives within the church but freely wielded the theologically indistinct language of growth and fulfillment in describing their desires for an ecclesial context to call their own. Convert use of this vague, largely therapeutic and psychologized language resonates deeply with that of the surrounding American culture, where theologically specific tropes and vocabularies have been supplanted by a generalized focus on the development and satisfaction of one's "self." However one may wish to interpret moralist Philip Rieff's assertions regarding the modern "triumph of the therapeutic," convert informants regularly took for granted the notion that religion, and the Orthodox Church in particular, should provide psychological benefits such as comfort, happiness, and satisfaction.[2]

At the same time, converts fully expected to exercise their choice-making skills within the church setting and to formulate self-expressive and individualized post-conversion identities within Orthodoxy. Sociologists H.B. Cavalcanti and H. Paul Chalfant similarly observed of Orthodox converts in Boston that such individuals were "not simply robotic followers of a rigid faith." Rather, as persons bouncing "their individual, implicit feelings off the traditions of the Orthodox faith," they often held different interpretations regarding the nature and meaning of their newfound church.[3]

The different motivations that informants cite for becoming Orthodox Christians are explored in this chapter. These motivations are intimately tied to the competing visions of Orthodox Christianity that informants wield in their narratives. First, Orthodoxy as a vessel of absolute, immutable, if individually discernable "truth" will receive our focus. In this regard, the Orthodox Church is presented as standing in sharp contrast to the surrounding American culture, in providing what converts consider to be surefooted moral stability against modern relativism and pluralism. Second, the ways in which Orthodoxy provides a strong sense of community and belonging to its new adherents, especially intermarriage converts, will be featured. Third, Eastern Orthodoxy as a venue for personal spiritual growth and fulfillment will be discussed. Here, special attention will be paid to the specific ways in which the external, institutional features of Orthodoxy, as embodying and conveying truth and tradition, are featured as promoting growth and fulfillment. This last discussion will allow us to chart the improvisational interplay of the two visions of Orthodoxy that emerge in the narratives. A more pointed treatment of the ritual and aesthetic attractions of the Orthodox Church, so often cited as a significant motive for Americans' embrace of Eastern Christianity, will be treated more fully in chapter five.

Orthodoxy as Truth

Informants commonly responded to the question as to why they had converted to the Orthodox Church with the rather simple answer that it was true. Orthodoxy was frequently described in informant narratives as the "true church" or the "true faith," not in the sense of a church or faith adequately suited to personal liking, as if it was true for the informant alone, but as an objective, universalized reality, a fact of the world, against which other worldview options could be measured and deemed inadequate or false. This image of the Orthodox Church as the "true church" was also forged in narrative opposition to a variety of cultural "isms," the very engines of the spiritual marketplace itself, pluralism, multiculturalism, relativism, individualism, consumerism. These many, often quite interchangeable, concepts were generally considered by informants as detrimental to the integrity and viability of Christianity and the moral fiber of American society in general. These many cultural phenomena were believed not only to limit Christianity's influence over American culture and society as a whole but also, perhaps more insidiously, to weaken Christianity from within by creating a climate in which ecclesial fragmentation, religious and spiritual individualism, and doctrinal and liturgical innovation, rather than unshaken and unshakeable authority and belief, had become normative to contemporary Protestantism and Roman Catholicism.

Certainly, American converts to Orthodox Christianity are not alone in holding suspicions of these trends and tendencies believed in many quarters to contribute to modern existential uncertainty and insecurity. Across the span of world religions, fundamentalisms of various sorts have arisen, in negative reaction to these late modern tendencies, and throughout the twentieth century, individuals have actively sought adherence to various conservative movements and churches as a way of escaping the vicissitudes of late modern life. As Patrick Allitt and Adam Schwartz observe in their respective studies of nineteenth- and twentieth-century British and American converts to Roman Catholicism (especially writers and other members of the intellectual elite), many individuals converted to the Roman church for precisely the same reason claimed by Orthodox converts today; they found the "true church," in this case the Roman Catholic Church. In characterizing the conversion motives and later apologetics of a number of British converts of this period such as G.K. Chesterton, Ronald Knox, and the like, Allitt wrote: "Why should anyone want to become a Catholic? Because it is the one true religion. . . . All [the converts] shared the view that human beings without a dogmatic teaching church and a definite principle of religious authority were too vulnerable to their passions, prone to idolatry. . . . A dogmatic church would protect them—first, spiritually and, by extension, politically—from the chaotic forces loose in the twentieth-century world."[4]

Convert informants, both former Protestants and Roman Catholics, made regular reference to the "chaotic forces" that they felt endangered contemporary moral life and Christian teaching. Karen, as we recall, repeatedly referenced her disdain for cultural and religious pluralism and considered most of contemporary Christianity (apart from the Orthodox Church, of course) as rife with dangerous relativistic tendencies. While Karen referred to the "liberalism" of most Protestant churches today, in attempting to accommodate personal tastes and temperaments, Fred offered more extensive and detailed critiques of what he perceived to be America's social and religious ills. Fred and his wife, Mary, certainly had wide-ranging experience upon which to draw since they had spent nearly 12 years studying and investigating a wide range of religious options that took them far from their respective Roman Catholic childhoods. Having made their way through a vast array of non-denominational Protestant churches, the couple arrived at Orthodoxy's doorstep after learning of its existence from a friend who himself had converted to the faith. Of all the study informants, Fred offered the most pointed analysis of the relationships between American consumerist popular culture, of which he was highly critical, and the "egoism" he felt infected most American Protestant churches:

> We're a consumer society. America is structured that way. It's wonderfully productive on an economic level but the danger is that you can take that category and it can become formative. Let's face it, six days out of the week that's how you live. I'm a consumer. I want what I want as I want it. I have a hard time accepting if I can't get what I want at the price I want. Most people seem to. I mean, what are these shows on T.V., *Extreme Makeovers*? Why can't I be like *this*? I expect to be like this and I expect it to be within a reasonable price. . . . But then go to church, which does not live that way. As I've said before, if you're a Protestant you go, what's in it for *me*? I mean, church should bless you, but really it's not about you it's about God.

For Fred, the entwinements between (especially evangelical) Protestantism and American market mind-sets and strategies weakened Christian teachings and made them increasingly susceptible to individual whim and desires for economic gain. Fred explained of his experience: "Every year, somebody would come down the pike with this new thing that will open up your eyes and change your life and we're only going to charge you 'X' dollars. And I'd think, 'How dare you? If this is actually the gospel of Christ you have an obligation to give it away freely. You have no right to turn it into a product and franchise it.' What I saw in most of these was just marketing. Just another selling scheme." Even beyond the realm of motivational seminars and Christian book tours, Fred concluded that most Protestant clergy were "natural sales-men or women" hawking an ecclesial good that "in retrospect turns out to be a billboard. Look, here's the message but there's nothing behind it." For Fred, the easy coupling of Christianity and consumerism made apparent the malleability of modern Christian culture.

In addition to pluralism and consumerism, other informants found the general relativism of knowledge worrisome, especially as fomented in academia. When asked what was meant by the term "modernism," the constantly evoked bane of another conversion narrative, Sam, a young iconographer from a Cleveland-area OCA church, replied, "It's this questioning that's going on in academia of anything that even strikes of being ancient or standard. Like nowadays they're questioning whether or not Christ actually lived. Of course, he lived. It's like why are you guys always trying to reinvent the wheel?" On the verge of complet-ing a master's degree, one Pittsburgh convert noted his general disdain for the "intellect worship" of university life, premised as it was on the accumulation of degrees and the constant questioning of once certain truths. "Well, you're questioning everything all the time and you've got to be bringing in every single perspective possible to a subject. I don't like the way that a lot of people around here at the university will think that a person's entire value can be measured by their ability to think and their ability to accumulate degrees and—and it's intellect worship and I just don't like the idea that the university embodies civilization and that it is all good. I just don't really see that."

While these cultural tendencies, especially in their impacts upon Protestantism, were key emergent themes in the collected narratives, former Roman Catholics often lamented the doctrinal and liturgical changes wrought upon the Catholic Church by the Second Vatican Council. Catholicism came to be regarded, in many informants' eyes, less as the venerable preserver and conveyer of objective truth than an institution losing its bearings in attempting to appear modern and rel-evant. Although many former Protestants had simply come to expect ecclesial fragmentation and doctrinal debate as part and parcel of their religious worlds, however distasteful it appeared to them, informants who grew up under pre–Vatican II Catholicism recalled the Council as a jolt, precisely because they considered the church beyond the reach of widespread cultural change. As their Protestant counterparts, former Roman Catholics reiterated similar questions of the reconcilability of historical change and truth and more often than not concluded them to be mutually exclusive.

Growing up in a family that was firmly "entrenched in the Catholic faith," Kay, who eventually became Orthodox nearly 20 years into her marriage to a lifelong parishioner of Ascension church, found the changes effected in local parish life by Vatican II confusing and disconcerting. She explained how the ritual and doctrinal ground seemed to shift beneath her feet on a near weekly basis: "I just couldn't imagine every Sunday you went to church and something new was happening. One Sunday, they turned the altar around and the next Sunday they got out the guitars and they had a folk mass and there were just so many changes. . . . I was *very* disillusioned. . . . I went to a Catholic college and we had nuns and they had the habits what-have-you, then all of a sudden [the habits] were all gone." In the end, Kay only found her deep childhood love and respect for the Catholic Church decidedly eroded, for, as she explained, "I wanted something steadfast and pure and real and I didn't feel that anymore in the Catholic Church. I felt that it had been adulterated." Another informant echoed these sentiments: "It seemed like it was the style to have mass *anywhere* but church, whether it was out in the woods, the top of a tower, just anything new and exciting and I just never understood. We have these beautiful chapels and churches. Why don't we have mass where we always did? It was just common practices that were always changing and being relatively conservative, it was just hard for me to accept."

Against this backdrop of constant flux, Orthodox Christianity appeared attractive in offering potential stability, in remaining (in converts' eyes, at least), historically and doctrinally unchanged and unchanging. Orthodoxy was true because it possessed a Tradition, one that could be empirically verified rather than just accepted "on faith" in an almost scientific manner through informant reading and studying of Christian history and theology. The writings of Neopatristic theologians, in particular, influenced converts' readiness to equate Orthodoxy with Tradition. Fred, for example, described what he meant by Tradition, a word he frequently evoked in his narrative: "Tradition is, well, literally is the Latin 'what's been handed over.' God doesn't just sort of drop truth in on you from outside." Rather, it finds expression in "the votes, as G.K. Chesterton said, 'Tradition is the vote of the dead.'" Fred further appealed to the depths of an unchanging historical past in tracing the church's teachings from Christ through chains of apostolic tradition, to the modern Neopatristic theologians (Lossky and Meyendorff) he found so compelling. "If it's been handed by Christ it's not gonna change. Look, I can read St. Ignatius, I can read St. Maximus (the

Confessor), I can read St. Symeon the New Theologian. I can read St. Tikhon or St. Theophan and I can read John Meyendorff and they're all speaking the same language. Here you see a family resemblance. And, of course, if you're at Ignatius, you're right next to the apostles anyway and that's as good as you get." Fred's characterization is echoed in John Meyendorff's assertion that "Tradition is the sacramental continuity in history of the communion of saints; in a way, it is the Church itself."[5]

Coupled with this Neopatristic interpretation of the Orthodox Church as Tradition was the long-held reverence many informants held for Christian origins, to find the early church or the church as described in the New Testament, a perennial theme of Christian self-reflections as Fred's remarks intimate. Lucas too has reflected upon Orthodox converts' fascination with early Christianity, a mainstay theme of American Orthodox convert literatures.[6] To this effect, one Mississippi convert declared her early, pre-conversion desire "to go back to mama," to what she considered the historical roots of Christianity. Within a contemporary context marked by pluralism and relativism, the notion of a church impervious to historical change was attractive to many informants, especially given the supposed "empirical" nature of this interpretation available through a comparison of present-day Orthodoxy with the early church as described in the consulted literatures. Informants rapidly catalogued the similarities: the early church had bishops and priests, so does the Orthodox Church; the early church had a liturgy, as does Orthodoxy; veneration of Mary, saints, and images was documented in the early literatures and has remained significant in the present-day Orthodox Church. No other Christian confessions, informants maintained, fit this mold between past and present so neatly, for various Protestant churches have discarded these structures and practices and Roman Catholicism have "adulterated" them by introducing innovations.

Significantly, in all of the above cases, the discernment of religious "truth" did not belong to the category of divine revelation but to that of human effort and reason. Paul, a convert from St. Michael's in his early 20s, asserted that he had concluded Orthodoxy to be the "true faith" based on the "very concrete research" he had conducted. "It was about reading scriptures and reading the church fathers too. I was getting answers from an Orthodox perspective of the very concrete research I did that this is what the church fathers believed." Characterizing himself as a "very black and white person" in regard to beliefs and issues of morality, Paul maintained that "research" was fundamental to his approach to the religious life. "So, I tend to think that I try to research what I believe and research what I think and research what I do in order to make sure that I am doing the right thing and not to just go through with it with a carefree attitude about things that I do." Recalling the "point in time" when he decided to become Orthodox, young Alex from chapter two asserted: "There came a point in time when I said, 'I've searched for almost two years now the Orthodox Christian faith and I haven't found anything that seems not to be the message of the scriptures,' that I can point at and say, 'the Orthodox Church is wrong here.' I found nothing in Orthodox doctrine that was inconsistent with the early Christian church. I also didn't learn anything in that time period that was counter to my own reasoning, what I thought made sense."

Orthodox Christianity as Community

In addition to the temporal dimension of community encapsulated and conveyed in the narratives through notions of truth and tradition, many informants discussed the deep yearnings for a like-minded network of believers with whom they could find concrete social acceptance and belonging. Here, the spatial dimension of establishing one's current place in relationship to others took precedence.[7] Again, Orthodoxy as community was presented as a point of contrast to what some informants identified as a trenchant American individualism that left persons with few resources beyond the singular self. Other converts, however, simply saw community within the framework of their own lives as providing a love and support woefully missing in their encounters with other churches or within their families.

An informant for whom community was a constantly evoked motivation for becoming Orthodox was John, a young graduate student at St. Michael's, who became interested in finding a church after attending his great-uncle's funeral and realizing that his relative was divinely "taken care of" and "that everything you wanted to do you couldn't just straighten your own back and say, 'Well, I'll do it. I'll be strong. I'll believe in myself.' You needed to have God's help." From this early realization, John moved from his largely unchurched childhood to explore a number of religious options, including Unitarianism as well as the Methodist and Lutheran churches, before encountering Orthodoxy through a friend.

Along the way, themes of being "taken care of," of finding divine and communal support for problems, coursed through John's narrative and contributed to the rather dim view he held of individualism in American life. Here, he sharply contrasted this mind-set from that found, in his view, within Orthodox Christianity: "Yep, self-reliance, we [the Orthodox] just don't do that. That seems to be the common belief that out of any strand that [American] people believe in is that you just put your mind to it. You just be independent. You just get up and do it. It's the stuff they're teaching in the public schools these days, 'Believe in yourself and you can do the math assignment. Have self-confidence. Build up your self-esteem,' which isn't always a bad thing. . . . But when you just leave it there at self-esteem you're going to end up at the end of the day pretty sad, I think."

At another point in his interview, John qualified these remarks slightly, while at the same time underscoring the difficulties this "self-reliance" can engender for the religious life: "I guess I should also add I mean not *all* Americans believe in this extreme self-reliance thing. But if you're a believer in this kind of self-reliance, 'I'll figure it out all myself. I'll believe in myself.' That's an obstacle to conversion. You have to get over that." For John, this "self-reliance" also had profound social and moral consequences for modern America: "It's hard to live according to Christ's commandments in this society. I mean, just as regards to a number of things that society views as basically acceptable. 'You know, well, you're not hurting anybody. It's your right.' Despite the fact that they're wrong, society says, 'Oh, it's okay, just as long as you take care to keep the HIV rate from going up or whatever whether it's sex or intravenous drug use or whatever.' They'll say, 'What's wrong with that as long as you're not hurting anybody?' And you just have to stop the conversation right there."

Despite John's deep longings for community he did not, from his brief encounters with Orthodoxy, immediately see the Orthodox Church as the direct fulfillment of these desires. Indeed, as he repeatedly remarked, he found the church's ritual practices "just too strange," even after multiple visits, to grant it serious consideration although he did find the church's theology rich and agreeable. However, his attitude and course of religious direction "changed very abruptly" as he delivered a paper to a professor one spring afternoon his senior year of college. John described the events that unfolded precipitating his immediate desire to join the Orthodox Church:

> I'm just walking across campus and about 75 feet behind me was this music professor. He was walking in the same direction I was. I had no idea he was there, 75 feet behind me. Seventy-five feet in front of me was this crazy guy

with a gun and I didn't see him either. But I walked into the building to take the article to the professor. And this angry guy walked up to the music professor, took the gun, and shot him four times and then he shot himself and I came out of the building and there were these two guys lying there and the music professor died on the scene. Um, crazy guy died later that night at the hospital. So, I was just standing there watching the nursing students try to save the professor and I just thought to myself, "So, I'm going to be one of those eternal guests [to the various churches he was visiting at the time]?" And I said, "The hell I will." I decided right then and there I was going to be Orthodox and I said the "Our Father" over and over again. I couldn't really believe I was saying that I was going to be Orthodox. But I just wanted it so bad at that moment.

Against the backdrop of these harrowing circumstances, Orthodoxy immediately sprang to John's mind as an ecclesial dwelling, a place of safety and stability for him to inhabit and "be taken care of" in the midst of an unpredictable and dangerous world. Faced by an event that, in John's words, "didn't make any sense at all," the young man did not cling to false fortitude but at once looked for "God's help" in repeating the Lord's Prayer and in making the surprise decision (to himself anyway) of converting to Orthodoxy, which he carried out in fairly quick order. As John related: "From there I went to church throughout the course of the summer and in the fall I was baptized." When asked what his conversion personally meant to him, John declared without hesitation, "It [Orthodox Christianity] represented community. That was the most important part. . . . I wanted to have a community of believers, together repenting, helping each other, supporting each other in a common tradition. . . . And I was brought into that community. That is what I was really looking for."

Other informants too affirmed the strong sense of connectedness they experienced in becoming Orthodox and in entering into relationship with their fellow parishioners. This relationship was made manifest and strengthened through the shared tenets and sacraments knitting the community together. Lorraine of St. Seraphim's described the profound feeling "of being home, at the right place," after becoming an Orthodox Christian in 2007. "It's the relationship with other people within the church and I think that has something to do with us all being Orthodox. It's a communion of people. There's a love here I think that's just a little different than what I've experienced in other places. You don't come to church and share Communion with people that truly know what all of this is about and not seem to develop a sense of unity with them in general."

Intermarriage converts often also counted the close ties they had formed with fellow Orthodox parishioners as fundamental to their eventual conversions. Although disillusioned by Vatican II liturgical changes, Kay all the more attributed her eventual conversion to her husband's Orthodox faith and to the positive bonds of love and friendship formed at Ascension church: "It's just very pleasant. You're greeted. People reach out to you. The Liturgy's always the same, the message of love." Again, she said, "I've met such wonderful people here. It's a very loving atmosphere and forgiving and it's unchanging. It's so nice." In a similar vein, another former Catholic and intermarriage convert remarked of her former confession, "There were a lot of things about the Catholic faith I didn't agree with. I didn't feel like it was a loving church, an open church."

If marital and familial relationships lend shape to intermarriage conversions especially in providing social placement of (initially) non-Orthodox spouses within communities and eliciting decisions in the handling of religious matters in the home, they also serve as powerful factors in bringing about conversions themselves. While these informants cast their decisions to become Orthodox as autonomously made, especially apart from spousal influence, feelings for hearth and home appear as significant subtexts both coloring these "freely undertaken" actions and easily merging with other needs and desires. While forthrightly eschewing the view that marriage and family as *social institutions* had any part to play in their conversions, informants did consider them potent arenas for the meeting of emotional and psychological needs and desires. To a certain extent, marriage and family (much as religion itself under conditions of late modernity) have been pried from their institutional moorings of societal expectation and obligation to become sources of self-fulfillment and happiness.

Rather than necessarily envisioning marriage and family as means of ensuring economic stability or enhancing social standing, contemporary scholars argue, Americans fundamentally consider these estates as venues for personal love, intimacy, and commitment (for example, Giddens's "pure relationship"). The late historian and moralist Christopher Lasch, for instance, attributed the much-discussed rise in American divorce rates over the latter portion of the twentieth century to higher than fulfilled expectations for the meeting of emotional needs at marriage outsets. Meanwhile, a number of empirical studies highlight the importance Americans place on such matters as marrying one's "soul mate" and having opportunities to share feelings with partners and other family members, even if as Ann Swidler observes, practical concerns often naturally overwhelm the first flush of early relationship romance. Child-bearing and rearing too have become less obligation than choice, with parenting for its own sake, as a source of personal satisfaction and fulfillment, trumping the more utilitarian, economically driven motives of past eras (for example, extra pairs of hands for household chores or economic security for one's old age) as stated reasons for having children.[8]

In some contexts, family runs parallel to religion as a "secularized" rival in providing meaning and support to its members; in others contexts, they appear wholly entwined and barely distinguishable one from another. Indeed, as Robert Wuthnow points out, the religious groups in the United States most vehement in their institutional support of the family, such as conservative Protestants, are also the ones "emphasizing expressivity and emotional bonding" within the familial unit.[9] Certainly family in its daily rounds and earmark events comes closely coupled, in the minds of many, to the enactment of one's life in the church and feelings of religiousness, however that may be defined. For example, when one intermarriage convert described her attraction to the Orthodox Church it was precisely formulated in terms of the strong attraction its familial rites of passage, "its baptisms and weddings" in all their sacramental splendor, hold for her.

In this vein, even if spouses remain in the background of these conversions, the eventual birth of children to informants often figures prominently into decisions to officially step across the ecclesial threshold and become Orthodox. Interestingly, however, these births seem to awaken subjective feelings of religious longing in the non-Orthodox parent, rather than simply bringing into focus any external imperative that parents should be of the same faith as their children. Intermarriage converts repeatedly attested to being emotionally overwhelmed by the beauty of the Orthodox baptismal service and coming to a realization, in the midst of witnessing this event, that they too wanted to be connected to the church through official membership. Her daughter's baptism, for example, only confirmed for Olivia the all but finally made decision that she herself needed to join the Orthodox Church, for, as she said, she was "already accepted" by the church's parishioners, which offered her a spiritual "completeness" she had not even realized was lacking in her early years as a Catholic. Despite her avowal that her conversion "wasn't a major thing," given the long-standing relationship she had with the parishioners of her church, Olivia still considered it a major event in her life. For example, she teared up when describing her decision to become Orthodox: "When we had our first child, we baptized her and by that time, I had pretty much figured out [Olivia starts to cry; pause of about 20 seconds] that this is what I wanted to do, that this was the faith that I wanted to belong to. So, after she [her daughter] was baptized, . . . I went and saw the priest and I said that I wanted to join. And he was like, 'Well, that's good.'"

Despite his growing attraction to Orthodoxy, Ken attributed his decision to finally convert, like Olivia, to the birth of his first child. "When my son was born, I saw how important it was that you be part of the sacraments and that you physically take part in the Liturgy. We went to the baptism and it was such an overwhelming experience that I was like, 'This isn't right. I need to be part of this community to actually share and benefit.'" When asked what he found so "overwhelming," Ken discussed the "interactive" and "participatory" nature of Orthodox liturgical life, which became so forcefully apparent in the midst of his son's baptism and clearly appealed to him on a personal level: "So, I felt that in looking at the baptism and seeing that you are physically receiving communion very early [as a child]. You physically experience a baptism with all the screaming and the crying and I just felt a physical connection that I felt was lost with the Catholic faith. It wasn't participatory anymore."

Occasionally, conversion followed upon personal tragedy. Renee converted to Orthodoxy at her husband's Pittsburgh-area Carpatho-Rusyn parish shortly after suffering a miscarriage in the early years of her marriage. Renee said that the church provided a supportive community and a conceptual frame of reference for enduring and making sense of her loss. "I would say there was just a sense of peace knowing that there's somebody kinda watching over you and there's a bigger reason for why things happen and you might not know why or understand why or even like why, but there's a bigger purpose for everything that happens and things aren't always as it seems." In the aftermath of this crisis, Renee realized the largely reciprocal nature of her relationship to the Orthodox Church, for the deep comfort and sense of "belonging" the church furnished her demanded, in turn, a demonstration of long-term commitment on her part. Thus, her conversion appeared as an act of solidarity with a faith that, in her words, "had been there for me" in a time of personal need. "About the time that I'd converted, it was shortly after the miscarriage like within the first year and everything. So I felt at that point, okay I need something I feel that I'm belonging to. You've [the church] gotten me so far through this point and through this horrible mess and so at that point it was like now I needed to commit to you, being my faith, since it had been there for me."

Beyond the direct context of births and losses, a few informants cited more mundane events and concerns of hearth and home as drawing them closer to the Orthodox Church. Kay, for instance, cited the many years she worked as a nurse at her children's Orthodox summer camp as critical for the formation of lasting bonds with other Orthodox Christians and the "love" she felt so strongly within the Orthodox Church: "I found so much love there and I knew that I wanted to become Orthodox through that camp experience. And I just met such wonderful people there and my godmother was from Lancaster and we were always at camp together and we had kids the same age and there was just a lot of good things goin' on."

Orthodoxy as a Source of Intellectual Freedom

With increased contemporary focus on the "self," necessarily understood in highly psychologized ways, religion as *process*, as providing sets of strategies for the care, fostering, and growth of one's inner life (soul or self) has taken center stage. Even convert informants who spent years at intense intellectual labors in attempting to find the "true church" wielded theologically vague and fluid terms such as "growth," "transformation," "fulfillment," "betterment," "integration," and "illumination" in describing the goals of their religious lives. Fred, for instance, remarked that his years of searching for the "right church" were fueled by an ultimate desire to "be deeply transformed," a process he described: "There had to be some insight into how people were transformed. I couldn't find it. There had to be some way to implement the promises of Christ in such a way that your life can be deeply transformed—not just transformed through momentary emotional conversions that frankly do dissipate over time. But transformations that are borne out in some deep fundamental restructuring of the personality and its issues. . . . first and foremost, how is this transformation effected by Christ?" As an Orthodox Christian, Fred felt assured that he was now on the proper path to "transformation." In his view, this path to transformation remained firmly within the structures of Orthodoxy's "ancient Tradition" while at the same time retaining the dynamism necessary for bringing about a "changed heart." It was precisely this "changed heart" that Fred so long sought to assuage the disappointment he felt in his life. "Yeah, it's, you know, a changed heart and seeing the pain and suffering in my own life, how important that change was."

Significantly, this dynamic personal growth and change in no way stood in opposition to the supposed authoritative and doctrinal immutability of the Orthodox Church but remained vitally connected to these structures. A number of ethnographers have observed that individuals who assent to external religious doctrines or authorities (or to absolute "truths" and "traditions"), even in contexts that might be deemed "fundamentalist," frequently do not consider this in any way an act of limitation or restriction. In her study of Southside Gospel Church, for instance, Nancy Ammerman maintained as much and quoted Frederick Bird, who found the same phenomenon in his investigations of converts to New Religious Movements. As quoted by Ammerman, Bird wrote: "By acknowledging these [religious] authorities, [converts] gain thereby a kind of license, a derived sense of personal authority, which authorizes them to ignore or to count as of only relative importance the claims made by various other secular authorities." Similarly, the interpretive space and ambiguity necessary for the dynamic personal growth and transformation so often sought by Orthodox converts in no way stood in opposition to the view of Orthodox Christianity as an upholder of unchanged and unchanging truth and tradition, but rather, these two poles of Orthodoxy's "cultural repertoire" were mutually reinforced by convert informants. The remainder of this chapter is dedicated to an exploration of this interplay within the narratives.[10]

First, in the case of converts to Orthodox Christianity, a reliance on the doctrinal and authoritative verity of Orthodoxy allowed informants to shift their attention and energies away from general, "big canvas" questions such as the nature and location of "truth" and the "true church," ecclesial polity, the nature of the divine, and so forth, to focus more concertedly on personal development. No longer encumbered by parsing competing theologies and churches, converts were now free to devote themselves with greater verve to the spiritual life, by appropriating and experimenting with the ritual practices of the church (a point to which we will return in the next chapter), reading devotional literatures (such as books on prayer or saints' *Lives*), and developing relationships with religious teachers and other members of their local parish communities. Not only could informants dedicate themselves to such activities, but they could do so with the security and certainty that the Orthodox Church would never lead them astray by imparting inaccurate teachings. They could move about and explore their new ecclesial world uninhibited by concerns that they might be heading in the wrong direction in their search for God. In this way, converts could selectively filter out of the range of their immediate concern not only the many modern cultural ills (the aforementioned "isms") stirring beyond the ecclesial boundaries of the Orthodox Church but weighty theological concerns that appeared contested in other Christian confessions. With the belief that the matter had been settled at the Council of Chalcedon (the church council in 451 declaring Christ to be both fully human and fully divine), for instance, informants no longer had to devote their time to mulling over the nature of Christ.

Alex, for instance, described his post-conversion religious life as a highly personalized encounter of intimacy with the divine, an encounter he likened to the dynamic love that could develop between persons. He said, "In the relationships we have in life we're meant to get to know each other better and better, deeper and deeper, more intimately. . . . And so the better you know that person, the better you know how to care for that person. And this analogy I applied to my mind-set in the sense that you're always going to be learning about another person." From this, Alex continued with his analogy: "So, if it's possible to always live the rest of your life learning more about another person, then how much more is it that we can spend the rest of our lives learning more about God, learning about who God is, what he desires for us." This personal human-divine relationship for Alex, however, found its proper outlet within the Orthodox Church: "I've learned so much from the Orthodox Church about God, so much from the writings of the church fathers, the traditions of the faith and that they all make sense to me and they've all moved me closer to God." Alex reiterated his appreciation for the church: "And I've just grown so greatly and I know that if I continue in the Orthodox faith, becoming deeper and deeper in my relationship with God if I so choose, that I could spend the rest of my life learning about God and how I should live my life through the Orthodox faith."

Orthodox Christianity, as Tradition, lent this growth a firm foundation in providing concrete frameworks for understanding and relating to the divine, but in ways that allowed for a fair degree of freedom. In this way, Alex's analogy is certainly apt, for the same is found in human relationships, which allow for multiple, at times quite idiosyncratic, strategies within wider social and cultural norms. Within Orthodoxy,

Alex could both explore the divine and do so with the certainty (a rare commodity of the spiritual marketplace) that, provided he remained within the church's theological frames, he would never learn or encounter incorrect teachings that might cause him to misunderstand or misapprehend the divine he sought to know. The young man concluded as much in his narrative: "I had complete confidence that I would never learn anything that would be incorrect in the Orthodox faith. I had complete confidence in that. That's how I knew that it [conversion] was the right decision to make."

Former Protestant converts to Orthodox Christianity, in particular, counted the church's authoritative structures a far more reliable and preferable alternative to the pastoral opinion often masquerading as the "voice of God" espoused in many of their previous denominations. To illustrate this point, Brad, who converted to Orthodoxy at Ascension in the late 1970s, recounted a traumatic visit to a Baptist church he made in his early 20s where the minister railed against alcohol consumption in such an adamant and hateful manner that the young man fled the church in tears (a particularly sensitive issue for this informant since his mother had died of alcoholism when he was a boy). Brad explained his intense reaction: "I mean, that's so presumptuous. This man was presuming to speak for God in this authoritative fashion and it was really his own opinion." He contrasted what he considered to be a Protestant propensity to cast opinion as teaching with the traditional safeguards of Orthodox Christianity: "You don't find that in Orthodoxy. I mean, you'll find strong personalities and firebrands, but they're always held in check by something else—by some hierarchical authority, by some ecclesiology or something traditional that's gonna keep them in check."

In addition to envisioning ecclesial authority itself as a form of liberation in keeping inaccurate doctrines or the tyrannies of personal opinions at bay, informants also introduced another category, "legalism," into their narratives against which Orthodox Christianity was routinely and positively compared. Informants asserted that Orthodox Christianity had firm moral and doctrinal frameworks, to be sure, but that it was *not* legalistic, especially as compared with other Christian confessions like Roman Catholicism or the Wisconsin Synod Lutheran church of one woman's childhood. These latter churches were characterized as possessing inflexible rules that made little sense and offered little to no real life applicability as well as punitive measures for their enforcement (usually in the form of accounting church members as "sinners" and readily assigning "guilt"). By contrast, Orthodox Christianity was variously described as "natural," "organic," "healthy," and "understanding" of human foibles, in recognizing the individual need to experiment, question, and doubt as well as in providing ample conceptual terrain, in the form of mysteries and miracles, for their exercise.[11] Years after entering the Orthodox Church, Fred found the relaxed attitudes of his Orthodox Christian friends a welcome change from, in his words, the morally "neurotic," fundamentalist Protestants with whom he had associated before. "These were people we could just be people with and never worry we were violating our faith. It was wonderful. We could just sit down and chat and laugh and have a great time and talk about family and friends and seeing movies and stuff like that. You know, the worst of the Nazarenes and the Baptists are you don't drink, dance, or chew or go with girls that do. . . . Anyway, they're just real people and we [he and his wife] both looked at each other and thought, 'These people are *real* and Christian and dedicated. They're sort of normal healthy. And 'healthy' is the best word for it.'"

Sam, who alternately characterized himself before his conversion as a "pope-loving" and "hard-nosed traditionalist" Catholic, quickly became discouraged by the "legalism" he found guiding the one year of Roman Catholic seminary training he undertook. "Something started to happen when I was there. I started to become disgusted with legalism. You know, we could be discussing in class silly things, like at what point is a person married during the marriage ceremony? At what point are you really forgiven for your sins? Really stupid things. This can't be the way God is. He can't be this legalistic. He can't be sitting up there with a score card keeping score on me and every other billion persons alive."

From his current post-conversion vantage, Sam found the apophaticism of certain strands of Orthodox theology preferable to the "legalism" of Roman Catholicism, a difference he cut along geographical lines:

> The West is very legalistic or at least Rome is. They've very legalistic. I mean, if you read the *Catechism of the Catholic Church*, they explain everything. The East follows a line of thought called apophatic theology, which basically says God is a giant mystery. . . . And so they basically, the East will say, "We don't know what God is, but we can pretty much pin him down by what we know he's not and then the rest of that is mystery." And the East is rather content with letting God be a mystery. I mean, if you ask a [Orthodox]

priest, he will tell you, "I don't know how the Eucharist becomes the Eucharist, it just does." They don't pretend to understand things that the human mind can't understand. The human mind can't understand these things, so I'm a lot more comfortable with that. Because you'll get to heaven and then God will laugh at you and say, "You're wrong."[12]

In Sam's estimation, Orthodoxy presented a divinity that transcended rules and measurements and appeared as "much more loving, more understanding, a more personal type of being" on his religious horizon. Rather than experiencing God as an authoritative, rule-enforcing deity bent on judging the errant, Sam, now as an Orthodox Christian, saw sin and his entire relationship with God much differently, "The Orthodox understanding [of sin] is you get back up. You do whatever you can to repair and you go on with life. . . . And that idea's so different than [the one with which] I was raised. It's actually liberating, because it makes God much more personal. It makes it much more like this friend who had done everything for you and he's given me all of this and I failed a little bit."

In the eyes of many informants, the verity and universality of the Orthodox Church was demonstrated all the more through its ability to move beyond the staid "ideal" of the history books into the "real" of everyday life, to answer questions through alternative strategies instead of unyielding laws. One informant evoked the example of abortion to wax enthusiastic about Orthodoxy's real life applicability:

> Orthodoxy looks more at the human being as a human who has faults. And I love the fact as I studied it more and more that Orthodoxy believed in *gray*. You know, so let's deal with the issue of abortion. . . . Despite the fact that in Orthodoxy we have a fervent love affair with life, there is no taboo in Orthodoxy that under *no* circumstances abortion. It is, you consult the priest and the bishop to find out what to do if a woman's been raped or if there are risks to health in particular. Orthodoxy allows for the exception 'cause Orthodoxy isn't legalistic in the way the Roman church is. And I always found that so attractive, because it's like a religion made for real people, people who make mistakes.

As illustrated in this passage, the interpretative spaces to be culled within Orthodoxy in no way abrogate the authoritative structures of the church (that is, the priests and bishops are to be consulted in the above example) but serve as the very arena for their exercise.

Conclusion

In addition to the interplay of Eastern Orthodox and American marketplace cultural elements, Orthodoxy itself possesses a multitude of voices and dimensions, in providing its adherents theological justifications for considering it, at once, a vessel for "absolute truth" and organic, natural "shades of gray." Although informants often demonstrate a keen interest in historically immutable "truth" and "tradition," they also want a church with "real life" applicability that allows them to forge quite distinct, post-conversion identities within the church. In providing moral certitude, Orthodoxy allowed for many informants to focus more concertedly on their spiritual lives. Orthodox Christianity furnished its adherents a cultural repertoire of such richness and intricacy that it, at once within a single narrative, can appear the most stalwart and flexible of religious options. Among the most potent sets of strategies Orthodox Christianity affords its adherents are its ritual, liturgical, and ethnic elements. We will now turn our attention to the ways in which converts adopt and experiment with Orthodox ritual and liturgical life in the course of their conversions and post-conversion lives within the Orthodox Church.

CHAPTER Five

Convert Perspectives
on Eastern Orthodox Ritual

While desires for truth and community loom large as stated motivations for American conversions to Orthodoxy, the more historically celebrated reasons for embracing Eastern Christianity—namely, an aesthetically driven love for its liturgy and iconography (the proverbial "smells and bells" of the faith)—also figure prominently in converts' stories. The conversion of Prince Vladimir and Kievan Rus' to Byzantine Christianity in 988 as recounted in *The Russian Primary Chronicle* is often cited by theologians and commentators as illustrative of the sensual power and beauty Eastern Orthodox worship exercises in effecting religious conversion and transformation. Although historians generally deem the tale apocryphal, the Kievan envoys' assessment of the Liturgy in Hagia Sophia, "We knew not whether we were in heaven or on earth," does, on occasion, approximate the experiences contemporary American converts report of their initial encounters with Orthodox Christianity. In characterizing what they consider to be the historically consistent traits of the Orthodox Church, historians Valerie A. Kivelson and Robert H. Greene have argued that, at least in the Russian context, "Orthodoxy valued altars, relics, and icons over complex theological argument. The material realm quite literally embodied the incandescent presence of the divine. The sensory and experiential dominated over the textual."[1]

At the same time, as observers of the spiritual marketplace point out, ritual-starved Americans more generally have gravitated to practices emphasizing bodily expression, explicitly religious or otherwise. Interest in yoga, meditation, labyrinth-walking, and rites of passage (both traditional and newly devised), among a host of other practices, has been wide and expansive in recent years. Certainly, the sheer physicality of Orthodox worship served as a powerful enticement for many study informants, with nearly all converts, even those initially confused and dismayed with its services, developing powerful attachments to Orthodoxy's ritual components. Informants in Pittsburgh and Jackson appreciated the fact that Orthodox worship seemed, in Ken's characterization, "interactive" and "participatory" in appealing to their physical senses and in providing strategic options for the forging of their own quite individualized post-conversion identities within the church. Richard Cimino too has commented on the significance that ritual flexibility holds in the lives of those interested in the faith. Writing directly about the Orthodox Liturgy rather than other ritual practices per se, he notes, "The Orthodox liturgy, the central and sometimes only function of many parishes, also illustrates and may even help explain the 'loose-fitting,' flexible nature of the faith. . . . The sense of individual freedom allowed in the liturgy seems to be carried over by the subjects into other parts of their lives."[2]

As a rich repertoire of cultural materials for individual appropriation, the use and interpretation of Orthodox rituals were manifold, complex, and highly contested among church members, both convert and lifelong. Not only were converts eager to experiment with Orthodoxy's wide cachet of ritual practices, they also frequently distinguished themselves in assuming the role of ritual critic in their communities in eagerly pointing out what they considered to be deviations from traditional Orthodox church practice. Culling their visions of a universal, crystalline Orthodoxy from history and theology books, many converts, especially of the seeker variety, were disdainful of the on-the-ground Americanizations or modernizations they felt had entered into the worship and architecture of the church over the years. Converts of long-established ethnic parishes such as St. Michael's and Ascension frequently clashed with priests and lifelong parishioners over these matters. Finally, as an example of the considerable attitudinal variation converts held in regard to issues of ritual, a surprising number of convert and lifelong informants reported engaging in the worship and practices of other non-Orthodox and even non-Christian religions.

In what follows, there is an overview of some of the means and outcomes of convert ritual interpretation and appropriation, serving as they do as significant arenas for pre- and especially post-conversion choice-making within the Orthodox Church. First, brief mention will be made of pre-conversion interest in and investigation of Orthodox ritual practices among (would-be) converts to the church. Second, the discussion will shift to the ways in which converts assume the role of ritual critics in their newly adopted parishes as they stress what they deem to be "correct" ritual performance over those often found in long-established communities. There will follow an examination of Orthodox converts who continue to cross ecclesial boundaries in order to participate in the rituals of non-Orthodox religious groups, a common occurrence that to date has received little scholarly or popular attention but too dramatically highlights the malleability of ritual adherence in informants' lives.

Pre-Conversion Uses of Orthodox Ritual

Orthodox ritual figured into informants' pre-conversion experiences both as a spectacle to behold and as a set of actions available for individual appropriation as would-be converts explored and "tried on" Orthodox Christianity for spiritual size. Indeed, as scholars such as Lynn Davidman have observed in studying conversions in other contexts, experimenting with ritual behaviors is a common way that converts can explore target religious communities before committing to full and official membership. While the Orthodox Church still possesses a stronger emphasis on convert acceptance of fundamental belief structures than the Orthodox Judaism American women embrace in Lynn Davidman's study, ritual remains central to modern Orthodox identity, for as Fr. Georges Florovsky maintains, "Christianity is a liturgical religion. The Church is first of all a worshipping community. Worship comes first, doctrine and discipline second."[3]

Furthermore, given the overwhelming tendency of would-be converts to read, study, or converse with others about Orthodoxy before appearing at church services, they typically carried into their first Liturgy some mental picture of what to expect, with the reality of its performance exceeding or eschewing these initial expectations. The potency of these visions coupled with the sensory overload Orthodox worship can provide elicited an array of informant reactions falling along the spectrum of dismay and discomfort to exhilaration. While

Prince Vladimir's ancient emissaries may not have known "whether we were in heaven or on earth" in attending the Constantinopolitan Liturgy, many American converts promptly identified any number of earthbound annoyances as fundamentally constitutive of their first experiences with Orthodox worship.[4]

Alex, who had visited a wide swath of Christian denominations during his short collegiate search for a church home, admitted that Orthodox worship "was something I had never experienced before." In contrast to the many other churches of his experience, Alex recalled that when he arrived at the small, pewless church, "I was actually really afraid to go in," at which point he located and asked a parish greeter, "I've never been to an Orthodox Church before. What do I do?" This liturgical disorientation and discomfort, however, at the same time served an important educational function:

> I felt extremely uncomfortable and I thought it was the weirdest thing. I mean, to be honest, like it was weird. I don't mean in a negative way, but I don't mean in a positive way either. It was something I hadn't seen before. It was a different sort of world, people coming and kissing what I considered pictures [icons] at the time. It was just very odd to me and I started asking questions after the service, "Why are people doing this? Why are they doing this?" And it was interesting to find out all the answers to those questions.

All of the constituent elements of the Liturgy, the unfamiliar gestures enacted by its participants, the a cappella music, and constant chanting rather than straight reading of texts, came together to form the "different sort of world" Alex found so "weird." Even the most basic of Christian symbols, the cross, appeared completely different in its Orthodox setting. As Alex recalled: "I saw the cross. It was three-barred and I'm like, 'Why are there three bars on there? I've never seen that before.'"[5] Despite the "weirdness" he felt in the midst of this first liturgical encounter, Alex, with his natural curiosity, immediately set out to learn the origins, reasons for, and meanings of the church's practices from the parish priest and other church members.

Meanwhile, John described his initial reaction to Orthodox worship in less than positive terms: "I thought they [the Orthodox] were strange as regards how they stood up all the time and kissed the icons. Their services drug on forever. . . . It was just men dressed like the Byzantine emperor making smoke and kissing icons and never sitting down because there were no pews and singing everything. . . . I'd go out and, boy, these people sure are weird." He contrasted these impressions with those he had heard from other converts. As he continued, "And a lot of people will spend a long, long time searching for the right church and they come into their first Orthodox service and they're just blown away. It's something I hear over and over again from converts and it had just the opposite effect on me."

Many converts, indeed, were emotionally "blown away" by "their first Orthodox service" in developing an almost immediate appreciation for Orthodox worship. Joan, a convert at St. Seraphim's who had entered the church in the late 1980s, was immediately "taken" with the beauty and "holiness" of a baptism to which she had been invited by a coworker:

> I wasn't offended by the candles or the incense or the icons. I was so in awe of what I saw and felt. I mean it sounded like when you read in the Bible about worship reflecting heaven's worship. That was it. I remember Fr. Timothy when he baptized the baby. He dunked her once. He dunked her twice and then he held her up to God and the blinds were open and the sun was coming in and the water was dripping and it was like diamonds from heaven and the baby cried out and there was laughter. There were tears. There was joy. There were hugs. It was just so deeply spiritual and joyful.

Asserting that she "fell in love that minute with Orthodoxy," Joan never returned to the Baptist church of her youth as she joined Fr. Timothy's catechism class and entered the Orthodox Church a year later.

In their ardent attempts to transform Orthodox Christianity into a place of familiarity and social comfort, converts, at least for a time, possess what Ann Swidler refers to as "unsettled lives" as they come into contact with new cultural elements. Until unfamiliar norms are essentially practiced into familiarity, "unsettled" persons rely heavily on "ideologies" or "explicit, articulate, highly organized meaning systems" grounded in discursive understandings of doctrine and ritual. Not only are converts themselves choice-makers arriving on the parochial scene with a swirl of dynamic, process-driven experience, but they simply *must* exert more intellectual and practical effort than their lifelong Orthodox brethren in gaining competency in their new environment. Indeed, Zygmunt Bauman makes a similar claim in relating the role of the "stranger" in various contexts: "Being a stranger means, first and foremost, that nothing is *natural*; nothing is given of right, nothing comes free. . . . In all these respects the stranger's stance differs drastically from the native way of life, with far-reaching consequences."[6]

On the other hand, lifelong church members stand as exemplars of "settled lives," grounded in habit and taken-for-granted practices often diffuse, difficult to identify, and implicit in daily social interaction.[7] Participating in the liturgical life of the church since childhood, some cradle Orthodox Christians, in particular, found it difficult to answer converts' questions about ritual performance. Marguerite was a young woman born and raised in a Greek parish before becoming a member of St. Michael's, who counted many converts among her closest friends. She observed that converts, in their attempts to understand and master the liturgically unfamiliar, focused on details she accepted as a matter of course: "It always fascinated me that they [converts] were concerned with the order in which things were done. While it is important, it's these 'little traditions' [those the Orthodox deem culturally and historically determined] they would focus on. In a Greek parish, the priest will give out bread at the end of the service instead of kissing the cross [as in Russian churches]. They're really concerned with these little differences, these 'little traditions.'" The lifelong informant admitted that she rarely thought about such issues. "For me, that's just the way that developed. It's just always done that way. I didn't really ask any questions about that. This is the ways the Russians do it. Okay, and that's the end of the subject, you know, if the question was coming from a Greek person. I think that would just kind of be the end of it 'cause they [the lifelong Orthodox] understand more that's kind of just the 'little tradition.'" She continued, "A lot of times people who grow up in the faith, myself included, take for granted all the mysteries of our faith, everything that surrounds Orthodoxy. It just becomes something that our parents did or something that our grandparents did or something that the Russian people did."

These queries highlighted for Marguerite the different ways of knowing that converts and lifelong church members often possessed in regard to the concrete practices of the Orthodox Church. She also described her own attempts to close this gap in knowledge and understanding: "Some of my friends were looking into Orthodoxy and I didn't know how to express in words everything that I believed and that was something that he [the priest] helped me with a little bit. He made me realize that some things, when you grow up in the faith, they're just kinda imprinted on your heart, engrained in you and you may not necessarily know how to express them in words." Conversely, converts possessed more discursive, intellectualized knowledge of the church. "Sometimes people who've converted to the faith are really good about pinpointing everything exactly in words to what they believe, but you notice it takes a little more time for that to be truly imprinted on their hearts." Still, Marguerite saw a gradual mergence of these two ways of knowing over time. "So, while I have to learn more so I can express it, with them being in the Orthodox Church longer, it will just become more a natural part of them. They can express it, but then it has to come inside yet."

Fr. Nicetas maintained a deep belief that liturgical attendance, as intuitive, habitualized knowledge, trumped reading and studying as the most effective channel for learning about the church, for convert and lifelong Orthodox Christians alike. He stressed that persons develop an instinct for liturgical performance and come to unconsciously know what to expect from moment to moment without necessarily possessing the ability to verbalize it. They, like Marguerite, just *know*. Fr. Nicetas explained, "Stay there and simply take it all in. That's the traditional way of attending Liturgy—to take it in and people often know it very, very well indeed and have a sense of ownership." Fr. Nicetas offered his own illustration of this intuitive liturgical knowledge and its resulting sense of lay ownership, in recounting a visit he once made to a weekday Lenten service in Moscow:

> There was a small choir of maybe three old women and there was a priest and a deacon serving and at one stage, somewhere in the middle of Matins or something like that, the priest and deacon must have been in deep conversation with each other in the sanctuary because nothing happened. I mean, there was a pause and you were expecting a little litany, "Again and again let us pray to the Lord." There was a pause. The lady leading the choir said, "*Paki, paki,*" you know, "Again and again." Still no reply. So the woman standing nearest the [icon] screen went and knocked on it. Suddenly there was "*Paki, paki.*" [He laughs] Now that to me very much illustrated that the Orthodox know exactly what's going to happen next even if they're not saying a word. And if you do something out of the ordinary, they say, "Hey," There is that sense of ownership.

Fascinated with such on-the-ground enactments of Orthodox Liturgy, Fr. Nicetas concluded that rituals, in all their performative richness, can never be reduced to the written page, for, as he maintained, "Because things do change in Orthodoxy, but they develop by incremental changes, which is why you can never celebrate *exactly* according to what our liturgical books say. You follow what is the local custom."

The transfer and deepening of Orthodox practices from surface expression to "a natural part" of one's interior life was an important aspect of these conversions. Regardless of whether converts found Orthodox worship initially appealing or distasteful, the necessity of learning and becoming accustomed to the gestures and practices of the church was fundamental. However, a surprising lacuna of Orthodox Christian catechesis as reported by converts and intimated by clerics, with their constant emphasis on the intellectual content of the faith and a discernment of motives and interiorized conversion readiness, was precisely the nuts and bolts of ritual action—how individuals should act Orthodox in Orthodox church settings. Although clerics and lifelong church members were quite willing to answer convert questions about the meaning and performance of ritual actions, converts repeatedly claimed that they had learned to act Orthodox only gradually over time through observation and practice. Brad from Ascension, for instance, answered "just through practice" when asked how he had learned to become Orthodox. He continued, "Just going to the church's services and of course hanging out with the priest. So, yeah, I surround myself with holy people, hoping I can go in on their coattails." Another informant echoed this response when offered the same query:

> It was all through experience. It was all through experience. Yeah, I would love if someone wrote a convert manual that answered all the questions. But I just experienced it and it was through loving help. . . . All these people who came into our [she and her husband's] lives who would explain if I ever had a question. There was always a real, living body to ask, "What's this?" So, I would say through experience and human example. . . . But the burden becomes lighter and lighter and lighter the longer that I feel that I'm Orthodox because your understanding grows and you have the grace and you build stamina. Rome wasn't built in a day.

Furthermore, as in the case of the church's teachings, the assurance that Orthodoxy was theologically true only confirmed, for many informants, that its ritual and practical prescriptions for growth and transformation de facto were wholesome and efficacious. As in the case of its more conceptual components, Orthodox ritual provided converts a perfect blend of choice and structure. Karen, for instance, declared that as a Protestant she had remained spiritually "stagnant" after many years of dedicated Christian living. She felt left "alone to flounder" in her Christian practice, which included, in her view, little more than Bible study attendance and being told to just "try to be a good person." She complained that in Protestantism "there was no method," a situation quite unlike her experience of Orthodox Christianity, which provided a rich plate of different ritual actions for self-improvement. As she observed: "Being an Orthodox [Christian] we have fasting. We have services. We have reception of the Holy Communion. We have repentance. We have Pascha [Orthodox Easter]. We have Lent. You know, we have Bright Week [the week after Orthodox Easter]. I mean, we have a method, a clear method for becoming more Christ-like and for me these are the paths you take when you're in the faith. And I never had that before."

Ken insisted that the elaborate preparations of prayer and fasting he undertook before partaking of the Eucharist in the Orthodox Church enhanced his overall sense of the "holiness" of the occasion and ensured it was never "a mechanical thing" as it once had been during his Roman Catholic days. In describing his overall attraction to the Orthodox Church, he maintained, "And I felt myself drawn to the spirituality, the actual physical awareness I was sensing with the Orthodox faith. The Orthodox faith up close is very interactive whether it be through sight with the icons, through your sense of smell with the incense, just through Communion with actually tasting the Body and Blood of Christ. It is a very interactive, physical experience and I like that." Another informant declared:

> You can find something for everyone. If you're very cerebral and want to look at theology, there's no end to it. And yet, it's often simply enough to go and just listen to the hymns and look at the ornateness and the iconography and sense that there's another world and I know it's right here and it's here now and even though I can't see it, I am in it. So that depth never has disappointed and I can't get to the bottom of it, where I did very soon and quickly in all those other experiences I had [as a Protestant]. I found them wanting in some way or another.

In this way, Orthodox Christianity appears open and accessible to everyone and offers its adherents a host of different methods for accessing the divine.

Informants not only appreciated the "interactive" and "participatory" nature of the church's public worship, but the portable physical accoutrements, the icons, prayer ropes, and momentary gestures such as making the sign of the cross, they could carry about, perform, and use in personal spaces at home or work, sometimes in quite innovative and "unorthodox" ways. Shortly after beginning his inquiries into the Orthodox faith, Carl, in his desire to have an icon of his own, placed an image of Christ as a screensaver on his computer before which he experimented saying written prayers. When Fr. Mark learned of this practice, he advised Carl to acquire some "real icons," which he duly did in the hopes that he "will get more."

Meanwhile, Karen discussed her love for the saints of the church, even exclaiming at one point when I interviewed her at her home, "Saints are family, you know. They're part of my spiritual family. And, oh, I'm so unworthy to even call them part of my family, but they are. They're still alive. The scriptures are clear that people who die are still alive in Christ." This declaration had its visual counterpart in the many icons interspersed with family photos that lined her living room mantel. She excitedly identified for me the family members posed in the photos as well as the meanings the interspersed saints held for her. Even her still Protestant, German-born husband was represented in the saintly panoply by an image of the Russian New Martyr, the former Grand Duchess Elizabeth, who too, the informant reminded me, had once been both German and Protestant and thus perhaps would act as a worthy superhuman aid in effecting her husband's conversion.[8] At the conclusion of her in-home interview, another woman showed me an icon she had recently commissioned of the Virgin Mary bordered by saints. Each saint had a special meaning for the family, as patron saints or figures who were believed to have provided intercession at times of illness or crisis.

The centrality of the ritual practices of the church for converts is evidenced by the fact that fasting, the keeping of the fasts of the Orthodox Church, was one of the most common informant responses to the question of difficulties they had encountered in becoming or being Orthodox Christians.[9] While many, especially lifelong and intermarriage convert church members, admitted to regularly ignoring these prescriptions, seeker converts, even when holding serious reservations about the spiritual or practical efficacy of fasting, seemed to consider it integral to becoming fully Orthodox. One former Roman Catholic woman at St. Michael's declared, for instance, "Fasting was so hard for me to accept at first because I was just used to, like, giving up candy for Lent. That's the only fasting I ever did. [She laughs.] I'm like what do you mean we can't have meat or dairy for, like, days or months? But then I find out later, it's for my own benefit, you know, to make me realize how much I need God, and I find out things are different than I actually thought they were. And it's not so bad after you start doing it." Carl echoed these pre-conversion concerns in his narrative: "The biggest concern on my part was fasting. . . . Oh, my Lord, my mom being the typical Irish-Italian cook, you know, there has to be more meat than anything else on the dish. How am I gonna do that?" Other practices with which convert informants experimented included the wearing of distinctive clothing (especially head coverings for women), pilgrimages to monasteries and holy sites, everyday usage of baptismal for given names, and the learning and practice of sacred arts (iconography, choral singing, and hymnography).

Orthodox Converts as Ritual Critics

The different ways in which convert and lifelong church members imbibed and interpreted Orthodox ritual often served as flashpoints of conflict within the parishes. While converts expressed a desire for their churches to conform to the Orthodoxy encountered in the pages of their theology and history books, lifelong members insisted that their parishes carry on the forms and norms of their childhoods and ancestors. Avidly citing their readings of the Orthodox faith, converts of St. Michael's, for instance, regularly complained to Fr. Mark (and to me) about the many "Western-style," Roman and Byzantine Catholic influenced icons adorning the parish's interior. Often referring to the images as "paintings" rather than icons, a number of converts advocated their replacement with others they deemed more appropriately "Eastern" and Orthodox. Yet, when the parish *did* commission and acquire two new "Eastern" icons to adorn its sanctuary, one elderly lifelong church member took me aside and asked, with clear alarm, about the unfamiliar iconographic depiction of the Mother of God newly set before her in the church.[10] With her intuitive, habitualized way of apprehending her faith, the woman had never before seen the Mother of God depicted without the Christ Child and, thus, expressed concern that the icon was spiritually wrong or tainted in the same way I had heard converts descry the remaining "Western" icons surrounding the new image.

In this respect, lay parishioners, convert and lifelong alike, readily assumed the position of ritual critic in their communities. Although Ronald Grimes wields the notion of ritual criticism as a technical phrase describing scholarly evaluations of the effectiveness of ritual actions, religious insiders regularly assess and offer pointed critiques of what is wrong or misguided in liturgical performances. American converts are certainly entering an ecclesial context highly sensitive to matters of ritual, given the long history of disputes over its enactment and meaning that course through Orthodox church history. The seventeenth-century Old Believer Schism in Russia, for example, erupted in response to liturgical reforms involving seemingly minor practices and gestures such as the number of Alleluias sung in litanies and how to make the sign of the cross. In this respect, Orthodox Christianity can easily be characterized as "orthoprax" in its concern for maintaining "correct practice," in the multiplicity of ways this has historically and culturally come to be defined.[11]

American converts also arrive at the doors of the Orthodox Church with the added marketplace experience of having compared and evaluated the practices and beliefs of any number of confessions during their years or decades of religious seeking. Their narratives overflow with verdicts on the ritual shortcomings and failures of other Christian churches. From the liturgical changes wrought by Vatican II to the postmodern, technologically charged praise services of many evangelical Protestant churches, seeker converts regularly lamented how various "innovations" had robbed Christian worship of its dignity and formality. Impressed with the grand claims made of Orthodoxy's supposed adherence to traditional Christian doctrine, converts were often eager to embrace what they felt to be the immutable quality of its liturgies. They also possessed considerable confidence in their own abilities to, in Grimes's words, "pit texts against performances" in assessing rituals according to a textualized gold standard of rules and norms of performance and voicing concerns over detected deviations.[12]

As previously mentioned, the gold standard to which converts most readily appealed were the writings of twentieth-century Neopatristic theologians and their direct intellectual descendents—figures such as Fr. Alexander Schmemann, Fr. Georges Florovsky, Fr. John Meyendorff, and Vladimir Lossky who, again, emphasized the abstracted, universal nature of the Orthodox Church and its worship. Schmemann, in particular, has been credited with reviving Orthodox theological reflection on liturgy in espousing a "eucharistic ecclesiology," whereby the Eucharist stands as the visible, embodied (incarnational) essence of the church itself. While this theologizing has had practical effects in parish life in encouraging greater lay awareness of and participation in the services of the church (especially through a more frequent partaking of

Communion), it also presents a liturgy far removed from the everyday earthiness of ethnicity, personal taste, and practicality. A number of converts mentioned the significance of Schmemann's classic exposition of the Divine Liturgy, *For the Life of the World*, in shaping their vision of Orthodox worship and the faith as a whole. One informant recalled the profound impact of the text on her conversion: "I started reading *For the Life of the World* and I just couldn't believe it. I found it [true Christianity]. This is it. There couldn't be anything more than this. This is the nitty-gritty of it all."[13]

Certainly, a number of popular English-language Orthodox authors themselves, in addition to extolling the otherworldly nature of the church's liturgies, enumerate many specific points where modern Orthodox practices, especially in the West, depart from both canon law and what they consider to be the true spirit of traditional Orthodox piety. After citing the twentieth canon of the fourth-century Council of Nicaea, which forbids kneeling on Sundays (a practice found in some American Orthodox churches including those in Pittsburgh), Timothy Ware in his influential introduction *The Orthodox Church* goes on to lament, "sadly in recent years there has been an increasing tendency, alike in Greece and in the diaspora [Orthodox Christians living outside of traditionally Orthodox lands] to clutter the entire church with rows of seats." He continues to inform the would-be convert reader that "It is a remarkable thing how great a difference the presence or absence of pews can make to the whole spirit of Christian worship," with the former circumstance necessarily inhibiting what Ware considers the natural "unselfconscious informality" of Orthodox pious expression.[14]

Informed by these characterizations and critiques, converts often saw themselves as informal parish authorities who can in a single stroke discuss the *filioque* and the reasons why icons painted in westernized styles should be removed from parish walls. Converts armed with these concerns also tended to have little sympathy for what they regarded as the more ethnic elements of parish life. Such elements included the use of foreign liturgical languages, as well as church furnishings and gestures such as pews and kneeling on Sunday, which have become deeply engrained features of some ethnic Orthodox communities. These latter developments were often viewed as Americanizations or modernizations contrary to the ethos of authentic Orthodox practice.

Paul, for example, who converted to Orthodoxy at another (predominantly convert) parish before joining St. Michael's, became as avidly concerned with the ritual propriety of his parish as he had been with notions of absolute truth over the course of his conversion to the Church. In regard to the latter, Paul forthrightly proclaimed, "There is one true Christian faith that is a hundred percent correct in beliefs and doctrines and it puts the whole world of Christianity in a different perspective." Relying on Orthodox literatures, Paul claimed the disjunction between his book-derived knowledge of practices and what occurred within the walls of St. Michael's to be one of the most disturbing aspects of his post-conversion life as an Orthodox Christian: "The biggest frustrating thing is to see some things that from my perspective and from what I have read some things that churches are doing that aren't necessarily what they should be doing." When asked to provide an example, Paul responded, "Well, the icons in the church. The fact that they're not real icons, most of them and the fact that they [the lifelong parishioners] have such a strong commitment to keeping them in the church and [are] not willing to admit the fact that when they built the church that was maybe the best thing they had at the time, but if we can make it better and actually use the real thing we should be using, we should do that."

Paul further made a distinction between the newer, aforementioned icons painted in a decidedly more "Eastern," Byzantine style and the others, which were created for St. Michael's in the 1940s and reflect a more realistic "Western" portrayal of sacred events and figures. "They [the westernized icons] are, technically, from what I believe, just paintings. The two new ones that we got on the sides are real, authentic icons. I think the others are just paintings." In addition to the "paintings" posing as icons, Paul was disturbed by the pews that graced the church's nave. "The biggest thing that I saw that I was shocked when I came to St. Michael's was the fact that they had pews. Obviously, it's a lot more difficult to go into already established churches and to tell them that their worship can be even more worthwhile and that they could connect to their worship more if they got rid of the pews. That's obviously a lot harder thing to sell to them."

John, who as we will recall thought the Orthodox Liturgy and ritual practices "weird" prior to his conversion, considered them of central significance five years after his conversion to the Church. While perhaps a little less concerned about the overall correctness of various practices (he never, for example, expressed worries over icons or pews) in parish life, he did have a preference for liturgies that are not "slimmed down" and confessions treated as more than mere formalities. Indeed, he chose to attend St. Michael's despite the fact that at least two other Orthodox parishes were in much closer proximity, and without a car, he had to navigate a complicated series of municipal bus connections to make it to church each Sunday. While he was put off by what he referred to as the "Greek-lish" of one of the two nearby parishes (a Greek church), John found the other, an Antiochian church with a sizable convert population, off-putting due to its lack of rigor in enforcing standards for Communion and confession. John said in this regard:

> What I've read and what I was taught is that you've got to go to confession every six weeks if you want to go to regular Communion every week. And what you see at St. Stephen's [pseudonym for the Antiochian parish] is everybody goes to Communion and you hardly ever see anybody lined up for confession and it seems to be a once a year thing or never. And so it seemed like a friendly, happy church—a let's-get-together kind of church, but not really enough teaching going on, Orthodox teaching.

John also appreciated the fact that, at St. Michael's, "the services are about right as regards to length," with "about right" indicating fuller liturgies of greater length, for, as John observes, "You'll find a number of churches where they just like to cut out a lot and slim it down. You know, 'Orthodoxy Express.' I don't know there's some line at which Americans will just fall asleep. [He chuckles.] Their attention span is gone and a number of Orthodox priests have decided that they shouldn't cross it even if it means cutting the service way down. They don't do that there." As in the case of Paul, John too was critical of ritual accommodations made expressly for the purposes of conforming to American cultural expectations and sought out churches and priests willing to uphold Orthodox teaching unadulterated.

While generally encouraging the intellectual pursuits of (would-be) converts in their pastoral care, Orthodox priests saw dangers with convert concerns over such matters. Beyond Orthodoxy, scholars have noted that converts in other contexts, in their desire to gain competency in their new religious environments, also often express undue concern over the correct enactment of ritual actions. While converts demonstrating high degrees of ritually focused zeal and commitment can receive fanfare and praise from established community members, they can also come to be regarded with suspicion (as in the "all converts are dangerous" verdict of John Henry Newman). Andrew Buckser, for example, observes in his study of Jewish converts in Denmark that the enthusiasm and exactitude with which intermarriage converts to

Judaism often undertake Jewish ritual practices can be met with bewilderment and consternation on the part of less observant spouses and community members. Patrick Allitt notes in his historical treatment of late nineteenth- and early twentieth-century converts to Catholicism that its hierarchs regarded their new charges with as much hostility and suspicion as hospitality and labored to temper their enthusiasm given the large numbers of Anglo-American intellectuals entering the Catholic Church at that time.[15] While issues of convert commitment were overriding for clerics during the processes of catechesis, priests and lifelong church members often viewed convert zeal for maintaining the supposed purity of the Orthodox faith, especially in regard to ritual, with a certain degree of ambivalence and attempted to temper it with heavy doses of realism and practicality.

Fr. Mark, for instance, maintained in this regard: "From my standpoint, some converts can be zealous for the things of the faith and they want to make a thousand changes. They want to get rid of the pews. They want to get rid of all the bad icons—they're paintings [not icons]. They want absolutely no Russian, no Slavonic in the services. Things like that." Fr. Mark continued by commenting on the fact that while such converts may be well-read in Orthodox theology and church history, as community newcomers they had little experience with the realities of parish life:

> They idealize what they read in the books and there is an Orthodoxy of the books, but there's also the Orthodoxy of the parish. Actually, it's the same, but in practice many times it can be different. And they will ask questions, "Well I've read in this book that you should be doing this—like kneeling on Sundays. We shouldn't be kneeling." And I say, "Well, that's right. We shouldn't be kneeling." [The convert responds] "Well, why are they [the other lifelong members] kneeling?" And I say, "Well, because they've been kneeling for 60 years and I'm not going to start this crusade against kneeling because it's just foolish. It's foolish to play with this. You just tell the people this is what the teaching of the Orthodox Church is. The teaching is that we should not kneel on Sunday and then we leave it go.

Other clerics too mentioned receiving similar convert complaints about the "incorrect" rituals, architectures, and iconographies believed to be found and in need of rectification within their parish communities.

Significantly, these issues of ritual enactment held greater importance in the ethnic churches of Pittsburgh than at St. Seraphim's, where converts have predominated throughout its history. The majority convert population of St. Seraphim's has reduced, although not entirely eliminated, clashes over ritual performance since parishioners were able to fashion their temple along what they considered to be correct ritual procedure from its beginning. While their current site is a former Presbyterian church, the members of St. Seraphim's rearranged its interior to conform to their ideal of Orthodox worship by removing pews and commissioning consistently "Eastern" Byzantine icons. Still, according to some parishioners, an influx of new east European immigrants to Jackson since the early 1990s has created some tensions, with newer constituencies requesting liturgical use of Slavonic and celebration of Old Calendar Orthodox Christmas.[16] Fr. Timothy affirmed that he has not been persuaded by these appeals. However, he maintained that he still occasionally contends with the ritual overzealousness of some converts. He explained how concerns over doctrinal verity carried over into the realm of ritual practice. "So many people are put off by what they see as the total anarchy of American Christianity. They [converts] were in some church that didn't have any clear idea of doctrine or morality and so they embraced the Orthodox Church and it's the true church and it has everything. Then, they get more and more into that well, they say, if we had everything right then the women would be on the left side and the men on the right. One guy tried to do that, where they'd [female parishioners] all be wearing veils or whatever. There's no perspective about what's important."

Crossing Ritual Boundaries

Rather than maintaining the ritual correctitude of the Orthodox faith, a few informants situated themselves at the other end of the attitudinal spectrum in displaying an openness to participate in the rituals of non-Orthodox and even non-Christian religions. While not exclusively so, these religious experimenters tended to be intermarriage converts or lifelong Orthodox church members rather than seeker converts drawn to Orthodoxy for theological reasons. Not surprisingly, informants willing to venture beyond the ritual boundaries of the Orthodox Church were also individuals more demure in identifying Orthodoxy as exclusively true and unchanging. Although maintaining official membership in the Orthodox Church, these individuals acknowledged the legitimacy of other religious and worldview options and were much less likely to draw religious distinctions along the lines of truth, since they considered this a relative quality shared among religions rather than the purview of Orthodoxy alone.

While seeker converts typically waxed enthusiastic about the doctrinal and ritual exclusivity of the Orthodox Church, a few informants considered this view ill-founded, uninformed, and the default position religious practitioners tend to take in regard to themselves. One woman, for example, asserted, "It's a personal choice for me to be Orthodox. I could be Catholic or Protestant. There's no one true faith. You know, like in the sermons every religion says that about their faith, 'We are the one true faith. We are the faith closest to God.' And I don't buy that. There is no one true faith. I think all faiths should be valued and considered good in God's eyes." Another man, who had spent several years attending his wife's Roman Catholic church before returning to the Greek Orthodoxy of his youth, considered exclusivist religious stances "parochial" and something he could personally do without. "You know, I get tired of all the parochialism in the church. We're right and everybody else is wrong. I hear that all the time and I just get so tired of it. We all love God, so who cares?" At the same time one convert felt his openness to the adherents of other faiths to be wholly in keeping with the tenets and spirit of the Orthodoxy: "Orthodoxy is about love and doing good to your neighbor because everyone was made in the image and likeness of God. You have Muslim fundamentalism but I don't think *any* fundamentalism, I don't care which group you pick is ever healthy because fundamentalism by its very nature is I'm right and you're wrong. And I don't think Orthodoxy ever looks at everybody else as wrong."

Significantly, attitudes did not always remain just attitudes but often found active expression in ritual practices. While Orthodox church hierarchs strictly forbid Christian intercommunion, this practice along with general lay participation in the worship and observances of other religions were far more common than parish priests or Orthodox observers ever like to assume. One intermarriage convert who proudly proclaimed herself an agnostic and Sagittarius, for instance, made mention of taking Communion along with her daughter at a nearby Episcopal church, which she approvingly referred to as "Orthodoxy lite," given the vague similarities she saw between the churches' liturgies and the fact that it took the Episcopalians forty-five minutes to complete a service that went on for two hours in her home parish. Another parishioner maintained that one's relationship to the divine transcended religious affiliation, for, as he forthrightly declared, "It's what's in your heart," and he regularly partook of Communion in other

Christian settings. He justified his actions: "We're praying for the unity of the faith and I think everybody of all faiths should be allowed to go to Communion." He again dismissed religious boundaries, flatly asserting: "I'd take Communion from a rabbi if he'd give it to me because Communion is the Communion between me and the Lord. It has nothing to do with religion."

At the same time, Pam, who converted to Eastern Orthodoxy in the early 1990s from Pentecostalism, firmly grounded the differences she saw between the two forms of Christianity on the simple notion that different churches just appealed to different temperaments and tastes. She said of Pentecostal worship, "It's just a different form of worship and it's not any worse or any better than anything else, you know. . . . It's how they wish to worship the Lord, but it doesn't mean it's wrong." Pam admitted to having participated in charismatic healings and to having been "gifted" to speak in tongues during her Pentecostal days. Furthermore, in the midst of a series of deep marital and emotional crises she experienced a year before I interviewed her in 2005, Pam admitted having returned to charismatic Protestant services for spiritual healing and support and having called the evangelical television program *700 Club* for prayer. She coupled these non-Orthodox resources with confession, anointing with oil, and counsel from her local Orthodox priest, thus calling upon and intermingling *all* sources of help available to her regardless of their specific origins.

Conclusion

Rituals, however, are only one significant cachet of cultural materials available for the construction of pre- and post-conversion identities within the Orthodox Church. Expressions of ethnicity too, often vitally entwined with ritual performance, served as a critical means for making one's home within local parish communities. Next is a discussion of this final narrative theme.

CHAPTER *Six*

"The Other Side of the Veil"

Convert Responses to Ethnicity

In becoming Orthodox Christians, converts were required to come to terms with more than the theological and liturgical peculiarities of a new faith. They were also called upon to embrace the realities and relationships of everyday parish life, including its ethnic components and the forging of ties with lifelong church members. No less than the aesthetic and sensory aspects of its worship, Eastern Orthodoxy's close association with various ethnic groups from eastern and southeastern Europe and the Middle East has remained central to its popular and scholarly characterizations. Not only are American Orthodox churches organized and divided along ethnic lines (that is, Greek, Ukrainian, Syrian, Carpatho-Rusyn, and the like), but easily consumable expressions of these ethnic affiliations, in the form of foreign cuisines and folk customs (for example, Old World dancing, costumes, and arts often put on community display and sale during various food and folk festivals) continue to be key means by which the general public identifies Orthodox churches. Much of the comedic line of one of the few recent American film portrayals of Orthodoxy, *My Big Fat Greek Wedding* (2002), for example, involves cultural misunderstandings that ensue when a non-Greek convert meets and interacts with the members of his new wife's Greek church.[1]

Despite the fact that Orthodox Christianity is typically coupled with these expressions of ethnicity, the majority of persons populating St. Michael's and Ascension are the second-, third-, and fourth-generation descendents of immigrants. Given this demographic fact, the above examples of ethnic identity and expression more appropriately reflect what sociologist Herbert J. Gans famously described as "symbolic ethnicity," abstracted signs pulled from their original contexts and reinterpreted as representing a culture as a whole.[2] The Pittsburgh field sites offered a number of examples of "symbolic ethnicity." Ascension Church, for instance, regularly held a community-wide Greek food festival each June, and St. Michael's hosted an annual *blini* (Russian pancakes) breakfast before Orthodox Lent and offered church-made pierogies as edible symbols of the parish's Slavic origins for sale throughout the year. Meanwhile, as will be made more clear in chapter seven, ethnicity played a different role at St. Seraphim's, founded and populated as it overwhelmingly was by converts.

The varied ways in which informants utilize the ethnic components of their adopted parishes are explored in this chapter. Theoretical considerations of ethnicity as a category in Orthodox parish life will be offered, followed by examination of three primary reactions of converts to expressions of ethnicity within their communities. First, some converts became more intensely aware of their own familial ethnic heritage as existing, at least nominally, in contrast to that supposedly represented by the parish. Second, individuals sometimes recognized an affinity between their own pre-conversion ethnic identity and Orthodox Christianity, such as individuals with east European backgrounds raised in non-Orthodox environments, a fairly common situation in Pittsburgh. Finally, a few converts, regardless of background or sense of ethnic affiliation, adopted the material effects, behaviors, or symbols believed to be emblematic of the ethnic identity of the wider Orthodox parish. In each of these instances, the labels "convert" and "ethnic" do not indicate distinct social groupings within the parish (as suggested in other studies of American converts) but overlapping categories, arising through on-the-ground circumstance and relationship. We will then conclude with reflections on converts and conversion from a cradle Orthodox perspective.

Convert Responses to Ethnicity in Orthodox Church Life

Symbolic or otherwise, ethnicity stands as a central organizing principle among contemporary American Orthodox churches and informs
the ways in which converts and their experiences are conceptualized.
In recent academic studies, a line has often been drawn between so-
called ethnic Orthodox Christians, lifelong Orthodox church members
who supposedly claim fealty to parochial ethnic affiliations, and converts who are portrayed as lacking ethnic ties and interests. Scholars
commonly describe these as distinct groups standing in opposition,
even antagonism, to one another. Phillip Charles Lucas, for example,
has focused on the challenge nonethnic converts pose to "ethnic Orthodox parishes," and Paisios Bukowy Whitesides explores the tensions
wrought between former evangelical Protestant converts and ethnic
Orthodox Christians in his 1997 article.[3]

The categories of "convert" and "ethnic" Orthodox Christians are
potent precisely in presenting a narrative of ordinary Americans embracing an exotic, immigrant form of Christianity, of encountering a
foreign other in their own backyard. Furthermore, choice-making
and its relative instrumentality in establishing ecclesial affiliation were
coded into the very usage of these categories in everyday life. Converts
were not simply or even primarily considered transformed persons or
new church members but, rather, individual choice-makers who had
consciously studied and "read their way to the Orthodox Church" and,
in the end, freely chosen apart from familial or social constraints to
become Orthodox Christians.[4] The convert, as a category of person,
thus provided an alternative vision of Orthodox identity in which an
individual's choice to become Orthodox took precedence over church
affiliation through one's birth or heritage. By and large, lifelong Orthodox church members both clerical and lay appreciated these efforts and
considered them indicative of Orthodoxy's increased "capital" in the
spiritual marketplace.

Significantly, convert and ethnic Orthodox Christians do not represent reified groups but, rather, boundaries of recognized similarity
and difference constantly created and re-created in the course of social
interaction. For one thing, fully aware of and engaged with contemporary American culture including its spiritual marketplace, lifelong
Orthodox Christians also engaged in religious choice-making. Yet, the
choice-making of the cradle Orthodox either received little recognition
in parish discussions or was negatively perceived as representing a net

population loss for local communities, since many exercised the option to abandon Orthodoxy for other churches or religions. Additionally, distinctions between convert and ethnic Orthodox Christians were only relevant at certain junctures of parish life. While they were a staple of informal social interaction, readily wielded during coffee hours or after-church meet-and-greets, they carried no official sacramental importance. During confession or distribution of the Eucharist, converts and their fellow lifelong parishioners were wholly indistinguishable from one another, although converts' stories of discovering and entering the Orthodox Church were occasionally mentioned by priests in Sunday homilies as a means of inspiring the faithful.

Certainly, the fluid quality of ethnicity as found in Orthodox parishes reflects wider scholarly assessments of ethnicity as a category of analysis. Indeed, as scholars of ethnicity have maintained, beginning with Fredrik Barth's landmark introduction to the essay collection *Ethnic Groups and Boundaries*, ethnicity is malleable and situational in its everyday deployments in social interaction rather than objectively residing in external features such as language and customs. Following on Barth's work, most recent theorizing on ethnic identity stresses its contingent, process-oriented rather than static and objectified character. As Stuart Hall writes: "Cultural identity . . . is a matter of 'becoming' as well as 'being.' . . . Far from being eternally fixed in some essentialized past [it is] subject to the continuous play of history, culture and power." Meanwhile, Mary Waters observes that specifically in the American context persons are generally free to choose and alter their ethnic affiliations and expressions at will and according to circumstance: "An individual may change ethnic identification over time, for various reasons. At various times and places, one is more or less at ease dropping or inventing a self-identification."[5]

In this way, ethnicity cannot be considered an attribute of lifelong Orthodox Christians alone, for it also arises as an important aspect of converts' self-perceptions and experiences within the Orthodox Church. Although Whitesides acknowledges that converts themselves do not lack ethnic affiliations and heritages, he does not explore the ramifications of this in his article. Sociologist Ashley W. Doane has noted in his research that scholars generally have ignored the significance of "dominant group" ethnicity, which in the United States has "expanded beyond Anglo-Americans to include, successively, Protestant European Americans and Euro-Americans in general." Indeed, according to this definition, most of the ethnic Orthodox worshiping in Pittsburgh churches, themselves hailing from European descent, would also be considered non-minority members of American society. Yet, even in the most symbolic and lighthearted wielding of the accoutrements of foreign cultures (the use of foreign words and phrases and the practice of Old World customs), lifelong Orthodox Christians and their churches appear more closely tied to ethnicity than the many white American converts of northern and western European ancestry who are "the most likely of any group to be unable or unwilling to identify with an ethnic group." Doane observes that the normalization of dominant group (or "plain American") inability or unwillingness to overtly identify with ethnicity and its expressions "is significant in that it enhances a sense of culturelessness and of 'being the same as everybody else.'" Despite this perceptual state of affairs, dominant groups do not lack ethnicity but, as Doane argues, an ongoing consciousness of it. In the case study under consideration here, the process of accepting a form of Christianity deemed "ethnic" can throw this previously "hidden" ethnicity into sharp relief.[6]

Among convert informants, the provisional, ever-flexible nature of ethnic identity, emerging through social interactions and symbolic utilizations in parish life, was made manifest in informant words and actions in three ways. Informants reported standing apart from, feeling a deep affinity with, or appropriating the ethnic features of the adopted parish. What follows is an examination of each of these in turn.

Entering a context perceived as ethnic, the Pittsburgh Orthodox converts commonly demonstrated a heightened awareness of and sensitivity towards this aspect of Orthodox church life. From their pre-conversion readings and studies of the Orthodox Church, informants often reported delaying their initial visits to local parishes out of a concern that they would not understand its ethnic features, especially foreign liturgical languages, or that they would be shunned by xenophobic parishioners. Karen, for instance, only ventured a visit to St. Michael's after receiving Fr. Mark's e-mailed assurance that his parish was indeed "seeker friendly," especially as evidenced in the predominance of the use of English in its worship services. Meanwhile, despite his early acquaintanceship with Fr. Joseph and ardent self-propelled studies of Orthodox theology, Fred refused to attend a Sunday service at Ascension for over two years, plagued as he was by fears of how he and his wife would be received. He recalled his apprehension at the time: "I knew it was going to be hyper-ethnic, because that's the way the understanding is. I expected a fairly hostile return."

Even if they did not receive a "hostile return" from lifelong Orthodox priests and parishioners, many informants found the easy coupling
of Orthodoxy with expressions of ethnic identity difficult to accept and
understand. As Doane maintains: "If ethnicity is viewed as attachment
to a 'foreign' culture—an attribute not possessed by the dominant
group—then the ethnic identity of the subordinate groups becomes an
undesirable quality that must be shed in order to claim full membership."[7] Ironically, the "full membership" into which ethnicity served
as an inhibitor, at least in the estimation of many converts, was the
fullness of the Orthodox faith itself, which as one convert maintained,
"is Christianity itself, not baklava or pierogies or needlework." Even
years after living and worshiping at the Greek church where he was
"welcomed warmly" rather than hostilely upon his first visit, Fred referenced the Apostle Paul in extolling the ideal of a Christianity unsullied
with ethnic expressions: "You read the scripture and you see what Paul
is saying and Paul is saying that, you know, in Christ, he has created
this new humanity that is the church, the body of the new covenant
that is to undo Babylon and undo the separation that was created at
the Fall, where humanity comes together as one new humanity, not
Greek and Jew, certainly not Greek and Russian, certainly not Greek
and American. Not Greek. Not American, but Christian, who happen
to be in America."

These sentiments are echoed in the writings of modern Orthodox
theologians in the West who too have been careful to differentiate Orthodoxy's Holy Tradition from temporal ethnic attitudes and practices.
John Meyendorff, for example, wrote in this regard: "To disengage Holy
Tradition from the human traditions which tend to monopolize it is in
fact a necessary condition of its preservation, for once it becomes petri-
fied into the forms of a particular culture, it not only excludes others
and betrays the catholicity of the Church, but it identifies itself with a
passing and relative reality and is in danger of disappearing with it."
Orthodox commentators regularly denounce the tendency to conflate
Orthodoxy with nationalism or ethnic aspirations, known as ethno-
phyletism, as a sharp distortion of the proper relationship of the church
to the particularities of human cultures.[8]

Regardless of whether they considered ethnic divisions indicative
of living in a fallen world, converts, especially at Ascension where
expressions of Greek language and culture remained important, had to
contend with them as aspects of their everyday experience. It was in the
midst of such activities that Brad recalled hearing fellow parishioners

apply the Greek word *xenie* or "foreigner" to him in the early days of his conversion. He explained, "There were lots of times when ethnic groups and parts of the church would be like why is the *xenie*—the stranger, the foreigner—here? I would hear that in their Greek language. I would hear them say, '*Xenie*' and in a derogatory way. 'He's *xenie*. He's *Americanie*. And I'm like, 'Yeah, so what?'" The man quickly discovered, however, a way to connect with many of the parishioners: "But there were others that as soon as you made any attempt—if you said a word of Greek to them—they would immediately warm to you. Look, he's trying to be like us."

Meanwhile, Dee, a woman in her late 30s who had converted at Ascension in the mid-1990s, after spending several years attending a Greek parish in Wisconsin, felt radically out of place in both churches, at least initially. She describes here the lifelong members she knew at the Wisconsin parish before expanding her discussion to include those whom she met later at Ascension:

> They were really ethnic. I didn't meet a lot of people who were real self-aware. I think they grow up with the faith and it's just the way it is and their family and feasting and their lives are so full and rich and that's the one thing I really always saw—it's the same thing I saw here [at Ascension]. I felt like there was this invisible veil around these people—that they were so blessed and they were just used to living this huge blessing and they didn't understand what it was like to be on the other side of the veil and I felt like it was this protection for them and they didn't understand. They don't quite understand because they've always lived it and then I walk across. Like I said, I got that bridge through to the other side. I came into that too.

The notion that the conversion process conferred a wider, more far-ranging vision into the internal circumstances of the Orthodox Church and the condition of the Orthodox-born was a common narrative theme. Here, based on her panoramic experience of having lived outside the Orthodox Church and having struggled to attain its membership, Dee, specifically *as a convert*, situated herself in a narrative position of seeing and identifying the "invisible veil" surrounding her fellow ethnic Orthodox Christians whose experience of the church rather cozily resided in "family and feasting" rather than movement into new ecclesial terrains. In this way, converts regularly and unhesitatingly moved beyond their own biographical circumstances to furnish authoritative versions of the collective life of the Orthodox-born. As persons who had negotiated and mastered what they believed to be the disparate idioms of a former non-Orthodox confession (or perhaps several over the years), the American religious marketplace, and Orthodox Christianity, converts often considered themselves as culturally multilingual, the ready articulators, translators, and interpreters of experiences that were, by their own admission, difficult to comprehend and foreign from their own.

While the sense of ethnic alienation was more pronounced at Ascension, a few converts reported encountering similar incidents and feelings at St. Michael's as well. With its more recent influx of east European immigrants (mostly from Russia and Ukraine), tensions occasionally arose between the Russian or Ukrainian and American-born contingents of the parish. One convert commented on the negative attitudes she had witnessed among the Russians who attended the church: "When you go to coffee hour, you see the Russians sitting on one side of the church meeting hall and the Americans on the other side. The Russians act like we're invading *their* church. I mean, they just have this attitude like, 'Why are you in *our* church?' I don't have anything against Russians, but it's just really uncomfortable." As this woman identified recent immigrants as the source of intra-parish tensions, Carl found the lifelong, American-born parishioners occasionally aloof and unhelpful: "It's like the cradle Orthodox, they just look at us [the converts] and say, 'What are you doing here?' This church is for our children. We built it for them. You're not Russian or whatever, what are you doing here?"

Even in the most amicable of situations, cradle Orthodox embrace of converts did not directly translate into a disavowal or whitewashing of ethnicity from parish life. Rather, a kind of ethnic parsing, whereby external features such as surnames or physical characteristics were believed to act as signposts of Orthodox identity, was a staple of church life. As one example of the many to be cited of this phenomenon, Sarah, a lifelong Orthodox Christian who today attends St. Michael's church, recalled her disappointment in learning her future husband was Roman Catholic rather than Eastern Orthodox, an assumption she had initially made given his "very Ukrainian last name." Certainly, converts learned these signs and the larger taxonomy of ethnic stereotyping to which they pointed from lifelong church members, for whom such features could prove significant for intra- and inter-parish boundary maintenance. This tacit, habitualized knowledge could only be gained through the everyday experience of parish life—books do not convey such information. Upon my own arrival at these research sites, converts as well as lifelong members attempted to discern my own ethnic identity as indicative of possible Orthodox affiliation or not. For example, Alex, to whom I was introduced on my very first visit to St. Michael's, immediately asked if I myself was an Orthodox Christian, quickly adding, "You look Greek" as a rationale for the question.

Converts at Ascension, in particular, appealed to physical features in articulating their distinctness from the surrounding ethnic community. Although Mary agreed with her husband, Fred, that she and her family had been warmly welcomed to Ascension, she also evinced a keen awareness that they would always remain somewhat apart from the community. For Mary, this point was underscored by her sense of being "one of the blonds" of the parish. "I don't feel excluded but at the same time I don't have expectations that I'm a real Greek here. I know I'm not. I know I'm blond and I don't fit and that's okay. We're fairly integrated into the community. I feel like we are to a certain degree and maybe this is my paranoia, but I guess I'm aware that I'm one of the blonds."

However, the sense of standing apart from the ethnic background of the adopted parish as a whole did not always translate into alienation or discomfort. Often, the ethnic heritages of converts were positively highlighted as an aspect of post-conversion identity worthy of exploration or display. Expressions of convert ethnic and familial heritages, as points of differentiation, frequently emerged in the course of social interactions and were a significant means by which the lines between convert and ethnic identities became blurred and porous. During the course of my fieldwork at St. Michael's in the spring of 2005, I attended a luncheon held in honor of a visiting OCA church official. After lunch, the honored priest made his way among the parishioners, making introductions and engaging them in conversation. When he happened upon a convert family, the father spontaneously exclaimed in the course of their short exchange, "We're Italian," to which, with a conspiratorial look, the official laughed and responded, "I'm 51 percent Italian." In the midst of this lighthearted exchange, the convert wielded nominal ethnic identity as a boundary, a mark of differentiation between himself and a wider "Slavic" parish community perceived as ethnically other. In the above instance, the creation and fomentation of such an ethnic boundary in no way placed the convert outside the Orthodox Church but further substantiated his place *within* it by expanding Orthodoxy's traditional ethnic orbit to include his own.

While some converts were interested in asserting their own familial ethnic affiliations as valuable and worthy of note in parish life, others occasionally considered their own ethnic distinctiveness as less attractive than expressions they observed in Eastern Orthodox and other Christian settings. Brad, for instance, observed that the closely knit character of ethnic churches only underscored the relative poverty of his own fragmented "WASP-ish" identity: "I was as much drawn by the ethnic part of it as anything. I mean, I remember even being in grade school and admiring the Italians because they had this familial bond and this strong sense of the Old World that I didn't have any of. I was a WASP and a fractured one at that. So there were lots of elements that drew me and I found my niche in many ways." Brad's admiration for the ethnic "otherness" of his parish was so strong that he defended this component of church life from its detractors. "When people say, 'Well, we shouldn't be so ethnic,' I say, 'Well, let's be careful about that because sometimes that's the richest part of the church, the family and everything. You can't just separate one without ripping out these other good things, I don't think.'"

Another parish convert, Christine, who embraced Orthodox Christianity through intermarriage, expressed a heightened awareness of her own ethnic background given the wider context of having married a man whom she considered an "ethnic" Orthodox Christian, given his Greek heritage. In casual conversation during church coffee hour, she described her background as "very Anglo-Saxon" since her ancestors had emigrated from England to America in the seventeenth century and she had spent her early childhood in Massachusetts. Although never a practitioner of the religion itself, for her parents were avid religious skeptics, this woman counted a number of New England Christian Scientists among her ancestors and present relations. The informant teasingly noted: "Here I am an Anglo-Saxon and I go off and marry this Greek man." A further point of joking in her family revolved around the fact that her own maternal grandfather was both Greek and Orthodox, hence the observation that she was indeed "a quarter Greek."

This last remark provides a glimpse into a second way in which ethnic identity was significant to Orthodox converts. Rather than experiencing a sense of disparity, however good-naturedly framed, between the convert's own family background and the parish context, many converts reported a wider convergence between the two. Given the historical significance of Pittsburgh as a center attracting central, eastern, and southeastern European immigrants and the relative ease with which these immigrants and their descendents drifted from Eastern Christianity, in either its Eastern Orthodox or Greek Catholic varieties, to Roman Catholicism and Protestantism, it is not surprising that a handful of convert informants, especially native Pittsburghers of central and east European descent, considered their conversions an affirmation of these familial and ethnic backgrounds.

While clearly attributing her eventual conversion to the Orthodox Church to an intellectual desire for patristically formulated, absolute truth, Karen also considered her embrace of Orthodoxy as a positive expression of her Slovak heritage. Although Karen maintained that her Byzantine Catholic, Slovak-born grandmother had "really pushed Roman Catholicism" on her as a child, the woman had also been a positive influence on the young girl's sense of "Slovak-ness." Not only did she fondly recall Slovak Christmas traditions celebrated in her grandmother's home, but her grandmother would often verbally identify her as "Slovak." Such exchanges only strengthened Karen's sense of self as indeed possessing a strong ethnic component, which continued in adulthood and found a religious outlet in her embrace of Orthodox Christianity. Karen discussed the significance of ethnic self-identity as a factor motivating her attendance at St. Michael's: "Why would I choose this particular church as opposed to a Greek church? Well, I would choose a church that was Russian because I have a Slavic background, you know, as opposed to choosing to go to an Antiochian church. Of course, if the Greek or Antiochian church were the only church in town I would go there. So, it mainly has to do with the doctrine. Then my choice of Orthodox churches has to do with my heritage." Her initial concerns about finding a "seeker-friendly," English-speaking parish notwithstanding, Karen experienced a comfortable convergence between her Slovak identity and what she perceived as the Russian or Slavic character of St. Michael's church.

Other convert informants, too, framed their conversions to Orthodoxy as a return to their ethnic roots. Of self-proclaimed "Carpatho-Russian" heritage, Fr. Andrew of Ascension parish, for instance, considered Eastern Orthodoxy to be a more original and authentic expression of his roots than the Byzantine Catholicism in which he was raised. "All my family were Byzantine Catholics, although if you go back far enough as a Carpatho-Russian there's always at some point, way back, there is a familial split between Orthodoxy and the Byzantine Catholic church and I was interested in that." Although aware of this split from childhood, Fr. Andrew did not begin his search for Orthodoxy until briefly attending a Byzantine Catholic seminary, where he described himself "as a part of those individuals who really wanted to learn more about their Orthodox roots." Yet, this desire to learn more about such matters only aroused the suspicions of the seminary faculty: "Now, during the time that I was a student there [in the mid-1970s] it was very much frowned upon for individuals to search out their Orthodox roots, to learn more about the Byzantine Catholic Church vis-à-vis Orthodoxy, so I left [the seminary]." Within two years, Fr. Andrew had sought out a local Orthodox priest and been received into the Orthodox Church.

James and Olivia too found a resonance between their ethnic backgrounds and the Orthodox Church they had come to embrace. Although his paternal grandparents hailed from Italy, James admitted to having a far greater interest in the "Carpatho-Rusyn and Slovak heritage" of his maternal relations and begged his still Eastern Orthodox maternal grandfather (most of his other relatives had converted to Roman Catholicism) to take him to church. Despite his dismay at the liturgical changes wrought by the Second Vatican Council, James situated his late adolescent embrace of Eastern Orthodoxy within the general "roots fever" that he took to be part of the general milieu of the mid-1970s. From his first exposure to church life, James related the general enthusiasm he felt for Orthodoxy's ethnic attributes:

> Boy, if you want to be ethnic, go get yourself attached to an Orthodox Church. My hometown had a great big, four-day ethnic festival. So, you could feel you were a part of something. But even then I think that was one of the things I've always found to be such a strength of Orthodoxy. Forget the fact that people will criticize its ethnicity, but with that ethnicity comes a set of values which are so focused on valuing the individual and making people inclusive that if you want to be part of us, we take you.

Even James's wife, Olivia, who described herself as "Irish and German," considered the Orthodox Church a significant venue for exploring aspects of her background in its historical light. Conducting research at a local Episcopal seminary in preparation for a Sunday school lesson, Olivia mentioned her delight in the many books on "Celtic things, Celtic history and St. Patrick" the seminary library possessed and in discovering "that although they [the early Celts] did not call themselves Orthodox. . . . Their practices were Eastern. They were not Western. They were not Roman Catholic practices."[9] Convinced that "the original Irish faith wasn't even like Roman Catholicism," Olivia and her husband established an informal three-member "Celtic Orthodox Society" and staffed a booth at a local Irish festival to pass out literature and engage passersby in historical and theological discussion. Under the watchful eyes of Irish Saints Patrick and Brigid, Orthodox icons of whom adorned the dining room where our interview took place, Olivia explained: "We never tried to, like, change people's minds. We just offered them information. But we blew up a little icon of St. Patrick and had it there, you know, in the booth so that people could see it. And we explained how, you know, if [the Celts] were always Roman Catholic, then how is it that this and this and this changed them to be more Roman in their rite than Eastern? And people were amazed." Whereas James embraced Orthodox Christianity with the conscious knowledge that in doing so he was harking back to his roots, Olivia was clearly pleased years after her conversion to stumble upon an Orthodox affirmation of and affinity with her own background, which only further substantiated an already deep devotion to Orthodoxy.

A third pattern of overlapping convert and ethnic identities emerged through convert appropriation of the material effects or behaviors thought emblematic of the church's ethnic identity. Simultaneously, the adoption of such emblems, Gans's symbols of ethnicity, underscored the permeability of ethnic boundaries and substantiated the perception of the Orthodox Church as, indeed, fundamentally Slavic, Greek, or more generally ethnic. Additionally, in a context where ethnicity serves as a fundamental organizing principle of ecclesial life, converts, without familial or ethnic ties to the said groups, often expressed preferences for one ethnic affiliation over another in their choice of parishes. For example, informants with pre-conversion exposure to elements of Russian or Greek cultures, through formal language or historical study, frequently gravitated to parishes with these affiliations. Having spent two years working in Ukraine for the Peace Corps, John noted his strong affinity for Slavic Orthodox churches since his return to the United States. At the same time, over the course of my fieldwork, one convert family had departed St. Michael's to join a nearby Greek Orthodox parish, a move taken partly in response to the son's fervent desire to learn liturgical Greek as a supplement to the ancient Greek he was already studying as a university classics major.

Convert informants, again, often admitted a fascination with exploring the emblematic and physical accoutrements of ethnicity accompanying their entry into local Orthodox parish life. With particular relish, some informants set upon exploring folk customs believed indicative of

the ethnic particularity of their parishes such as painting *pysanky*, preparing Greek or Slavic foods, or learning Old World dances for festivals
or cultural events.[10] From his high school study of Russian and deep
admiration for Russian liturgical music, Carl evinced an enthusiasm
for all things Russian at St. Michael's and rather comically considered
vodka an important means of demonstrating his support for the supposed "Russian character" of his beloved parish. He noted that since his
conversion, he customarily includes three bottles of vodka in his "Easter
basket," to be blessed by the priest after the Paschal Liturgy. Afterwards,
he shares a bottle with other parishioners in the church meeting hall to
celebrate the feast, an occasion that arouses general amusement in the
community. In this practice, the convert simultaneously substantiated
a view of this church as "Russian" and extended the boundaries of this
identity to include himself.

Even in instances where they were unable to access or understand
expressions of ethnic identity within their communities, especially
with the continued usage of foreign liturgical languages, converts could
appear as their most fervent supporters. Convert informants at Ascension commented more extensively and frequently on the liturgical use
of Greek, which was much less an immediate issue at St. Michael's.
While some converts found the language alienating, others defended
its use as a vital link to ancient Christian traditions. Brad, for example,
was wary of parting with the Greek language precisely for this reason:
"I didn't find Greek to be the hurdle some do. I mean, some part of
me was drawn to the Greek. It just seemed a more holy language or
something. Remember, it's the language of the New Testament. It just
had an appeal to me. It was a beautiful language so that didn't give me
hurdles and I think we need to be careful when we talk about replacing
it." Meanwhile, fellow convert and parishioner Kay considered the specific language (whether Greek or English) used in prayer and worship
irrelevant given that, in her view, these were activities that ultimately
transcended language. As she observed: "I understand quite a bit and
I know key words and if I don't know everything that's going on in the
Liturgy, I know that it's all just praising God, so you don't have to know
all the Greek in order to comprehend it."

While ethnicity itself remained a fluid category in parish life, so
too did parochial understandings of what it meant to be American.
Certainly, some converts set "American" in firm opposition to "ethnic,"
with "American" appearing as a kind of vanilla identity transcending
expressions and recognitions of cultural particularity, as Doane points

out in his work. In describing the role ethnicity plays in church life at Ascension, one convert juxtaposed "ethnic" and "American" as potent, deeply engrained marks of identity that cannot be easily discarded at will. "So, when people say, 'Well, we shouldn't be so ethnic,' I say, 'Well, let's be careful about that.' Because it's like me saying, 'I'm not American.' It's as much a part of me and it certainly makes a difference wherever I go, especially in other parts of the world where I'll stand out, you know what I mean? So, it—you can't separate one without ripping out the other I don't think." Meanwhile, Fred (who described himself as a "social conservative") identified the actor John Wayne as epitomizing a homogenized American culture he considered worthy of respect and emulation. "I would argue if anyone just sits down and watches four or five John Wayne movies you get what it means to be an American very quickly. You know, fair play, doing what's right, being willing to sacrifice, you know—all these things were inculcated through John Wayne movies. Not to say I walked with a swagger or talked like that—it's just to say that you learn certain values." Given the fact that their parish lacked specific immigrant roots, the informants at St. Seraphim's in Jackson (as we shall see in chapter seven) more readily identified "American" in precisely this way, as an identity distinct from that reflective of "ethnic" heritages.

Interestingly, when reflecting on what a specifically American Orthodoxy would look like, many informants outlined a vision of cultural inclusivity and affirmation reminiscent of American liberal ideas of multiculturalism, even if informants (as noted in chapter four) considered multiculturalism, as such, corrosive to traditional Christianity. Informants generally did not want to see an Orthodoxy whitewashed of ethnic expressions but, rather, a more expansive embrace and recognition of cultures beyond those of their particular ethnic parishes. One informant, Sam, as an iconographer discussed his conscious attempts to produce icons of saints drawn from across the globe—western Europe, Africa, and Asia—to reflect the multiplicity of backgrounds and heritages found among converts entering Orthodoxy today.[11] Beyond providing individuals access to the divine (again, as icons are theologically understood), Sam commented on the social significance these images serve as mirrors of multicultural inclusivity. As he imagines it, the heavenly realms do not erase national and ethnic distinctions but showcase them precisely through the iconography of the church. As he maintains: "The purpose of icons is not to have pretty pictures, but it's also to form connections—that all these people [depicted on the icons] are praying with me right now and they're Greek. They're Russian. They're Ethiopian. They're Chinese. They're Vietnamese. They're South American. They're all praying with you and it's a powerful way of making sure people understand that the saints are just like you and me. It makes it so real." Despite the fact that Sam forthrightly maintained "I don't really believe in multicultural diversity," he was enthusiastic about the "multiculturally diverse" iconographic schema (including Chinese, Japanese, North American, and African saints) his priest implemented in the OCA parish he attended for many years. Significantly, Sam considered this schema a model for American Orthodoxy as "it should be," and he hoped to see local parishes regularly and increasingly exemplify this diversity among their church members in the coming years. He characterized his parish as already well on its way to embodying this iconographic (and heavenly) model: "So in the parish there are Greeks, Russians, Serbs. There are Texans. There are Germans. There are Irish. It's almost like a view into the future of what Orthodox parishes a hundred years from now will look like." Even if ordinarily disdainful of multiculturalism, this informant presents a warm fuzzy picture of different cultures living side by side in peace and harmony within the walls of the Orthodox Church, for, as he concludes, "And the church is kinda like that because you have people of all different cultures and we're all able to come together and it's a very tight-knit, very loving, very embracing community and there are a whole lot of converts there." In this way, the Orthodox faith does not transcend ethnic affiliation and background but, rather, provides a spiritualized backdrop for their display.

Converts through Cradle Orthodox Christian Perspective

While converts reported a variety of encounters with lifelong Orthodox Christians over the course of their conversions, the cradle Orthodox Christians with whom I spoke generally considered converts beneficial to their communities both for adding extra pairs of hands to parish tasks and for infusing their churches with a sense of spiritual renewal and enthusiasm. Brad recalled the expectations of renewal he heard from lifelong parishioners upon his conversion: "I had people coming up to me and saying, 'You're gonna be a light here.' I'm like going, 'Stop. I'm looking for the light. I'm no light myself.' They think that you're gonna be the life-changing force here, and I'm not."

Thus, parish clergy were not alone in considering converts more zealous and fervent for "things of the faith," for lifelong lay parishioners often expressed to me a genuine personal interest in converts and looked for ways to reach out to them as well. Deacon Morris, of Ascension church, described his own "fascination" with the otherness of converts. He noted, "I'm curious. I'm just fascinated from the standpoint of converts because I mean I'm cradle Orthodox. I've never really known what it's like to be not [Orthodox]." At both St. Michael's and Ascension, lifelong members regularly stood as sponsors for converts and established deep emotional, family-like ties with them. In the aftermath of her miscarriage, for example, Mary from Ascension discussed the support and informal counseling she received from a lifelong Orthodox Christian couple of Ascension who had lost a child many years before. The couple stood as her sponsors at her chrismation and her family regularly partook in their Easter dinner celebrations.

A nurse and mother of four children, Sarah of St. Michael's church was a lifelong Orthodox church member whose parents and grandparents were devout, practicing Orthodox Christians. To emphasize the "innate" quality of her church affiliation, Sarah described herself as an "Orthodox thoroughbred," who nonetheless developed an abiding attachment to the church of her childhood. As she recalled: "I somehow fell in love with the church and at an early age I knew I would never leave the church. It was just something that I always knew." Despite her pride at having been born and raised in the Orthodox Church (as she stated, "I've never been anything else"), Sarah carefully distanced herself from other lifelong Orthodox Christians who stressed ethnicity rather than the "truth of the faith," which she had tried to instill in her own children. She discussed the habitual church affiliation that marked the words and actions of many of her fellow lifelong parishioners: "They just do what they do. They do what they do because they're Greek or this is what Baba [colloquial term for grandmother] told them or whatever, not because it's the teaching of the church or because it's Orthodoxy." As a point of contrast, Sarah said of her own family: "Like in my family, we try to put the religion, the faith, the dogma first—the teachings of Christ, being connected to Christ, God and Christ and so forth." She continued with emphasizing this distinction between herself and other cradle Orthodox Christians: "And in all of these [Orthodox] churches people are there not because of Christ or the teachings of the church, but because this is my ethnic background. This is where my parents went. This is what I've always been. This is the way it is. And that's first and not the teachings of the church. So they don't understand the church." Rather than seeing the Orthodox Church in exclusivist terms, as indicative of "my ethnic background," Sarah emphasized the universality of Orthodoxy. "You need to put the beauty of the faith first—the teachings of Christ. You need to say, 'This is the church from its inception, this is the ancient church.' Therefore, everybody should embrace it."

In assessing conversion from her "Orthodox thoroughbred" standpoint, Sarah admired the effort inquirers expended in discovering and investigating the church. Just as vehemently as any clerical informant, Sarah emphasized the care and deliberateness interested individuals must take in deciding whether conversion to Orthodoxy is, indeed, the right course of action. She maintained that conversion to Orthodoxy involved the acceptance of an entire way of life, for, in her words, Orthodoxy "is not a religion, it's not joining a church or a country club. I think of the Amish and if you understand the Amish, it's their way of life. And that's really what Orthodoxy is if you're really willing to accept it as your life. A lifestyle is what it is." In Sarah's view, the complexity and richness of this Orthodox lifestyle could only be understood by potential converts through rigorous, deliberate study and experience far outpacing the general education expected from and granted to the Orthodox-born. She continued, "I think converts should really experience a whole life cycle of the church for a complete year, you know, really learn and study and read and have questions answered and not just on Sunday, but really understand these fasting periods and these holy days and what we do. Be here for this holy day and understand this and grasp the catechism. *Then*, after all this, make the decision if this is what you want."

Sarah remarked that she often held her breath when reading the published narratives of Orthodox converts out of concern that the protagonist might embrace the faith without adequate preparation. "As I said, I like to read [conversion] stories and sometimes I'm thinking, 'Woooh, stop. Wait, wait, wait, this is something you really have to think about, not just for you, but if they have a spouse or whatever. They have to really think about this.'" Despite the innumerable caveats surrounding conversion articulated by priests in their narratives, Sarah worried that lack of pastoral vigilance and oversight might result in persons entering the church ill prepared to embrace its "lifestyle": "I think some clergy have the way of thinking that it's like a fishnet. You just throw it out there and catch and bring everybody in maybe prematurely. I think it's really a danger when you jump in too quickly before you understand what you're getting into."

Conclusion

In keeping with the situational, socially constructed character of ethnicity, as formulated in recent theories, converts also choose, appropriate, or acquire a heightened awareness of ethnicity as a fundamental expression of post-conversion identity in the church. Through the three patterns of ethnic differentiation, affinity, and appropriation, converts play with cultural elements, thus blurring and expanding the boundaries of American Orthodoxy's ethnic categories. As this case study illustrates, ethnic identity is not the simple domain of a supposedly immigrant church but a powerful vehicle for self-reflection among American-born converts eager to position themselves within it. Thus, the standard categories of "convert" and "ethnic" Orthodox Christian, so often held as distinct in scholarly and popular literatures, can appear as fluid, overlapping identities when viewed through an ethnographic lens.

CHAPTER *Seven*

Orthodox Christianity in Mississippi

Although my fieldwork at St. Seraphim's was much less extensive than that carried out among the churches in Pittsburgh, it is important for raising the question of the impacts of U.S. regional differences on the development of Orthodox churches and the perspectives of their members. As Edwin S. Gaustad notes, regionalism has been a significant theme in analyses of American religions as a whole, with a number of historical and ethnographic studies exploring the regional particularities of the experiences of Roman Catholics, Jews, and Protestants from a vast array of denominations.[1] While most scholarship on American Orthodoxy has focused on the experiences of different ethnic or immigrant constituencies, little attention has been paid to the ways that Orthodox Christians differ from one area of the United States to the next. An examination of conversions to Orthodoxy in Jackson, Mississippi, a city and state culturally and historically distinct from Pittsburgh, Pennsylvania, thus provides an important perspective on the potency of the spiritual marketplace and its interplay with Orthodox belief and practice. It also allows for the charting of thematic variations among diverse populations of Orthodox converts.

Certainly, a fundamental parity of conversion experiences and methods can be discerned between converts in Jackson and Pittsburgh. As in the case of the Pittsburgh converts, the Mississippi informants tended to be highly educated, well traveled, and prone to religious experimentation and seeking. Many of the Jackson informants too had made their way through a number of religious traditions before settling upon Orthodoxy. As Fr. Timothy remarked of the many inquirers who had come to him over the years: "They're just general searching youth as well as older people who've been through all that. These people are just from all over the place. They've tried three or four churches. I had one who's been a Bahai. You know, a lot of things they've tried."

In this regard, the Pittsburgh and Jackson informants accessed the same sources of information—print and electronic media as well as personal and social contacts—in the course of their religious explorations. In keeping with characterizations of American converts as being intellectual and bookish in their approaches to Orthodoxy, Fr. Timothy concurred that most of the persons coming to his church doors had initially encountered the faith through reading and studying: "Well, obviously, in Mississippi nobody's ever heard of the Orthodox Church so the person who gets interested typically is somebody who's come in through books, who's read about it in history or in Dostoevsky or something. Or people who are intellectual and spiritually oriented and kind of looking for something." Yet, personal contacts and friendships also served as key channels for learning about the faith. Joan, for example, explained how she first learned about Orthodox Christianity: "Well, I got a job at the local United Way and Fr. Timothy's wife was an employee here and she and I formed a quick friendship and she's just a wonderful person. And they [St. Seraphim's] were gonna have an infant baptism and I was invited to the infant baptism so I made sure I got a coworker to come with me. And when I came into that church, I knew that very moment that I was in a holy place."

The Pittsburgh and Jackson converts also shared motivations for converting to Orthodoxy. They claimed the Orthodox Church as unchanging and steadfast, as well as a site for personal growth and transformation. As far as the former motivating factor was concerned, one informant maintained that in becoming Orthodox she had "gone home to where it all [Christianity] started," to what she considered to be the ecclesial source of the Christian faith. Meanwhile, Harold, who joined St. Seraphim's in 2005 at the age of 71, was impressed that Eastern Orthodoxy remained, in his view, the "unbroken line" of original Christianity from which all other churches deviated. He asserted: "I had seen history lines on Christianity. There was the Catholic Church and then the Episcopal Church broke off and the Presbyterian and the

Calvinist and all the rest of them. I could see the Orthodox kept going straight and really the Catholics broke off from them and all of
them, if you will, spinning off into what—twenty-six hundred different
denominations now? Something like that."

At the same time, the spiritual dynamism of Orthodoxy was attractive
and compelling. As another woman maintained of her post-conversion
"journey" of living and worshipping within the Church: "It's such a
great journey to be an Orthodox Christian. It's just such a great journey
and you just want everybody to have it too, you know?" Furthermore,
like their northern counterparts, the Jackson informants drew upon
the same cultural elements of Orthodox Christian belief and practice
in constructing post-conversion identities and lives within the church.
Regardless of regional distinctions, converts found themselves working within a complicated religious system where the negotiation and
maintenance of quite specific ritual and theological boundaries remain
critically important.

Despite the commonalities linking Orthodox converts in Pittsburgh
and Jackson, they did differ in some respects in their attitudes towards
ethnicity and the place of Orthodoxy in American culture more generally as well as in the ways and means they came to be integrated into
church life. There were also subtle differences in the way they described
Orthodox Christianity and spoke of their conversions. Although I do
not claim these differences to be necessarily representative of distinct
"southern" and "northern" perspectives, since Orthodoxy varies considerably within these regions, they do reflect the impacts history and
demographics can have on conversion as well as the attitudinal and
experiential diversity present among seeker converts in particular.
There follows in this chapter a brief overview of the thematic nuances
and differences found in the narratives of the Mississippi informants.

Themes of Ethnicity and Americanness

While Pittsburgh stands as the "Holy Land" of American Orthodoxy, few observers naturally associate Eastern Orthodoxy with the
Deep South, this despite the fact that New Orleans was home to one
of the first Orthodox churches established in the "lower 48" and that
Orthodox immigrant communities dotted their churches throughout
the region in the early portions of the twentieth century. Indeed, as
mentioned, the earliest Orthodox parishes established in Mississippi
were those of Syrian/Lebanese and Greek immigrants who settled in

Vicksburg and Jackson, respectively, over the first half of the twentieth century. In this regard, Fr. Timothy clearly considered the Greek Orthodox church in Jackson an ethnic community catering to individuals of Greek heritage rather than converts per se. He observed from his experience: "I mean the Greeks in this country aren't very mission-oriented. I don't even know of a church they've founded in the South since I've been here [since the late 1970s]." When Orthodox Christians (predominantly non-Greeks) first banded together in the late 1970s to start St. Seraphim's, the local Greek parish complained to diocesan officials that the new church threatened their membership rolls. After Fr. Timothy convinced the then Greek Orthodox priest that St. Seraphim's appealed to an entirely different "market" (namely, converts and non-Greeks), relations between the churches settled to their present state of peace and amicability.

Without the direct pull of an immigrant past where foreign liturgical tongues and customs can still hold sway such as at St. Michael's and Ascension, St. Seraphim's has eschewed any specific Old World ethnic coloration. From its very inception, its services have been conducted entirely in English, and Fr. Timothy forthrightly maintained that he did little to "cater" to ethnic constituencies within his parish. In reference to the increased numbers of east Europeans arriving in his parish over the last five to six years, he asserted: "I don't do anything to cater to these Russians. I don't do Old Calendar Christmas. I don't know any Slavonic." He also romanticized little the religious pieties of traditional Orthodox lands, which he often considered as more form than substance. "I often kind of wish there was a way to have a catechumenate for people who come in here who are already Orthodox because a lot of these Russians don't know a thing about Orthodoxy."

While acknowledging and expressing interest in the cultural diversity contained within Orthodox Christianity, the convert informants of St. Seraphim's considered their church fundamentally American in orientation and a model for how Orthodoxy should develop within the United States. One informant—Charlie, a man in his early 20s who had come to Orthodoxy after a childhood spent in the Roman Catholic Church—appreciated St. Seraphim's for being specifically "an American church," a community that, in his view, seemed authentic in having stopped "trying to be something else culturally." The notion that to be "fully Orthodox," one must be culturally "Greek or Russian" was wrongheaded, this informant declared: "Most of those people have the best of intentions but they're mistaking cultural nuances for religious observances." He continued, "I like the concept of an American church a lot more than I like the concept of keeping to something which was built to preserve the culture of an immigrant community. And it's nothing against anybody's culture or anything. It's just that my culture is American and I felt like this church [St. Seraphim's] after just a lot of personal searching would be better for me to belong to nationally first and foremost as an American." When asked what was "American" about the parish, he immediately chimed, "Very much the people, very much just the general atmosphere."

As affirmed by other converts, this "general atmosphere" involved a genial familiarity with the apprehension and confusion newcomers to Orthodox settings can experience. Conversion was not the select experience of a minority within the parish, but the common denominator experience for most of St. Seraphim's church members. Therefore, parishioners attempted to smooth out the rough edges of unfamiliarity for visitors and inquirers. Fr. Timothy, for example, took time to explain basic components of Orthodox services, especially ritual gestures such as prostrating during Lent that may make visitors uncomfortable, and converts themselves often reported being taken in hand and guided through the intricacies of Orthodox worship by parishioners from their very first step into the church.

Orthodoxy in Mississippi

In addition to the experience of conversion so many church members shared, Orthodoxy's minority status within Mississippi also contributed to the tight-knit social cohesiveness of St. Seraphim's. Not only had most of the parishioners freely chosen to enter the church as adults, they were keenly aware of their distinct "otherness," as an island of Eastern Christians amidst a sea of mostly (evangelical) Protestants.[2] As in other contexts, the converts of St. Seraphim's readily swapped their stories of discovering the Orthodox Church, not as "an ego thing," as one woman asserted, but out of surprise and gratitude for the rarity of the event. The woman continued to enthuse, "But just the joy and the thankfulness that I have and some of my friends seem to have to find ourselves where we are is just remarkable. We don't have very many Orthodox churches around, so we know the odds, literally. They're slim. The odds are real slim to find yourself as an Orthodox in Mississippi. All the churches are basically right here and scattered one or two around. It's so remarkable to me."

Intensely aware that the Orthodox Church could appear exotic and foreign to Bible Belt southerners, the converts of St. Seraphim's emphasized the compatibility of their newly chosen faith with southern life and sensibilities. Indeed, in this way, the Mississippi informants, many of whom were lifelong inhabitants of the state, regularly drew upon another "toolkit" of cultural materials foreign to their Pittsburgh counterparts—southern manners, ethos, and heritage. The informants readily identified themselves as "southerners" in the course of their interviews and conversations, a category that seemed to denote a body of shared experience and understanding cutting across religious, ethnic, racial, and class boundaries. As Lorraine maintained, Mississippi was like "one big little town." She continued, "You get Mississippi people all aggravated and then they are all of one mind. And race and economic barriers and all of that just vanish as they form a group together. And I don't think that that is something that many outsiders understand—I can talk about my brother, but you can't. I mean, that is very engrained in us. It's like we can form a group real fast against some situation that we don't like." Another informant too maintained that southerners shared a common culture that transcended racial and class distinctions. "If you take two people from the South—black and white—and you stick them in a place like Germany they're gonna find each other and they're all gonna enjoy turnip greens and cornbread and black-eyed peas because we have the same roots and the same experiences in many ways."

In characterizing southern religious sensibilities, the Jackson informants considered southerners more openly willing to discuss God and Christ than persons in other regions of the United States. Having traveled extensively both within the United States and abroad, Lorraine, for instance, maintained that the general openness to religious faith shared by many Mississippians bodes well for the future of Orthodox Christianity in the state. "Mississippi people already have, in general, strong spiritual beliefs. You're dealing with a basis of people who say they love God and love Christ and truly believe that God exists and that Christ came as a human and died on the cross. That's something that's in place. So, Orthodoxy would be the fullness of that faith as it was for me." In contextualizing the prominent place of religion in Mississippi public life, Lorraine continued, "The other thing is that when you come here the first thing somebody's gonna ask you is 'Where do you go to church?' And people will speak about God and not be embarrassed to do it. And it's not a no-no subject like it is in a lot of other areas."

Living and working in Mississippi, I too observed that questions about the location and frequency of church attendance were perfectly acceptable conversation starters among new acquaintances and that public expressions of Christian affiliation and sympathy were part and parcel of everyday life. Not only were church billboards common, advertising worship services and encouraging public morality (for example, sexual abstinence), but religious expressions could appear in unexpected places, such as the Bible verses that frequently grace bank marquees.

Interestingly, this was a view articulated by the Orthodox bishop in Pittsburgh as well who had served in Texas for a time and found southerners more receptive to discussions of the religious life than their northern counterparts. He said:

> In most places in the South, it's not a question of do you go to church, it's where you go to church. People go to church and they have a serious interest in talking about their salvation. You go to other parts of the United States, that's not their immediate focus. I mean, if you go to New York City, I think you would see—it'd be somewhat different. I'm not saying that New Yorkers don't have any concern about their salvation, but I think you'd see that there's other temptations and concerns.

For the church members of St. Seraphim's, therefore, Orthodox Christianity simply represented an alternative means of expressing this natural, homegrown Christian piety. According to this view, Mississippians were already familiar with and serious about Christ. They simply lacked a theologically and experientially robust Christianity to match their commitment and interest. Orthodoxy was in no way antithetical to southern sensibilities and forms of religious life; it only needed to be made better known and accessible to Mississippians. Not surprisingly, the Jackson informants considered the establishment of additional parishes vital to the spreading of Orthodox Christianity in their state. Commute times for Pittsburgh parishioners were considerably shorter than those of their southern counterparts, many of whom traveled over a hundred miles one way to Jackson from other areas of Mississippi in order to attend church. While Pittsburgh informants occasionally considered their city "overchurched" in possessing too many physical buildings to be sustained by the Orthodox population there, the Mississippi informants were keenly aware that additional structures and priests were needed to meet increased demand for and interest in the Orthodox faith.

A number of converts from the Delta, for example, expressed a desire to see a parish built in the region some day. One convert maintained that the area contains an untapped population receptive to learning about the Orthodox Church: "I have many friends that I would like to see have an opportunity to experience the Orthodox Church. I feel, based on what I hear them tell me about where they are spiritually and what their needs are that they might respond to Orthodoxy. But, there's nowhere for them to go to experience it and I wish there were. I wish that there was an Orthodox church in the Delta, for instance, in that area of the state. There's not." Another informant responded similarly when asked about Orthodoxy's prospects in the state: "Orthodoxy in Mississippi? Everybody should be Orthodox. I want to preach to the Delta. The fields are ripe for harvest. We have this Christ-haunted culture in the South. Orthodoxy can fill so many needs." One man who drove over an hour and a half each way to attend St. Seraphim's each Sunday maintained: "My heart's desire is that there would be an Orthodox church at least within 40 miles of everybody if that were possible in Mississippi. I think, in general, it seems to me that this is just very important because of the society that we're living in."

Not only did the Mississippi converts characterize southerners, in general, as more open to discussing God and religious faith, they themselves more frequently referenced classic elements of Christian life and cosmology—such as heaven, hell, and salvation—than their Pittsburgh counterparts. Significantly, the Jackson informants described their relationships to the church and the divine also in much more emotionally diffuse and open terms. For example, a much higher percentage of the Mississippi converts (40 percent) wept in the course of relating their conversion stories, as compared to 10 percent of the northern informants. In discussing their newfound Orthodox faith, the converts were often clearly drawing upon the conceptual frameworks and vocabularies of former confessions and evangelical sensibilities. One informant, for example, remarked that, if nothing else, her "Baptist heritage" had taught her that "there will be an accounting," an accounting wholly compatible with her present Orthodox church membership. She explained, "There will be an accounting for people for what they do, say, and justify. Am I making sense? Do you know where I'm coming from? There will be an accounting. There will be a Judgment Day and I'm so glad to be Orthodox. I'm sure there will be things I'll answer for like everybody. I'm not a perfect person by any means. But, I want to be in my shoes on Judgment Day."

In addition to emphasizing the compatibility of Orthodox Christianity with southern religious sensibilities, the Jackson converts generally spoke of Orthodoxy's distinctiveness when compared to other religions and American culture in softer, less polemically divisive terms than many of the more ardent Pittsburgh converts. While in no sense absent from the Pittsburgh narratives, the notion that Orthodoxy somehow completed or fulfilled one's pre-conversion faith, rather than erasing or correcting it, was a narrative emphasis common to the Jackson informants. Although certainly preferable to the religions of one's pre-conversion experience, Orthodoxy stood more consistently in superlative rather than oppositional terms to them. Orthodox Christianity deepened earlier religious experiences and feelings rather than calling them into complete moral question and served as an important flashpoint of dialogue and engagement with others.

Charlie, for example, displayed a deep appreciation for his Roman Catholic upbringing as a foundation for the Christian life, for, as he explained: "Religion was always a very prevalent part of my life growing up. My parents are very good, pious, practicing Catholics. So, they did their very best to bring me up with a good and true knowledge of what it's like to live a Christian life and they did, in my opinion, an excellent job." Finding Catholicism's "scholastic theology" as evidenced in its penchant "to rationalize things too much" distasteful, Charlie distanced himself from Catholic theology but never, he argued, from the loving, humble piety of his family. According to Charlie, Orthodox Christianity simply expanded and made "more tangible" the firm foundation of Christian practice and belief already acquired as a Catholic: "Growing up Catholic made life in Christ a reality for me. But becoming Orthodox, going through the process and worshipping with the Orthodox helped make the life *of* Christ—the historical Jesus—a reality for me. And it seemed like rather than just something I could take as a lesson learned and just go on living my life, this was something that drew me in even deeper and something which made me really determined to keep going in spite of a lot of questioning on my part." Although cognizant that, in his words, "There was still a lot that was different about Orthodoxy from Catholicism," Charlie asserted that he "still kept the moral and spiritual life that I had been raised with" as a matter of course.

Meanwhile, Lorraine recalled that she had grown dissatisfied with the lack of spiritual depth that her years first as a Baptist and then as a Presbyterian had afforded her. Rather than being concerned over issues of doctrine (as she asserted, "I never looked at Baptist or Presbyterian in any way as the doctrine. God knows everything anyway. I figured God is God and he knows. I'm not going to worry about these things"), she maintained that the faiths never brought her "the unity with God, communion with God," for which she so ardently yearned. However, she remained intensely aware and appreciative of the different ways her Baptist and Presbyterian backgrounds had shaped her Christian faith. Lorraine explained, "The reality of God and the reality of Christ and all of this came from that [Baptist] part of my background. And so I carried that with me. But, as a Presbyterian, the Bible training and the classes and the history really impressed me. That was a real important period in my life." Lorraine's experiences with these churches had been largely positive, but, in her words, "I felt like there was more to all of this than I knew . . . neither one of these go further than that [what they had contributed to her life] as the Orthodox do. In Orthodoxy, there is the Liturgy. There's confession. There's repentance. There is Communion and it's all one thing. And it's body and soul. It's all the completeness. I felt like that was what I needed but I didn't know that's what I needed." In the end, Orthodoxy provided Lorraine "the fullness of the faith," the missing pieces of physical worship and theological speculation bringing her into a more intimate and sustained relationship with the divine.

Another informant was hesitant to criticize specific doctrines of his former Baptist faith, for, as he remarked, "They believe in Christ's death, burial, and resurrection just like it would be with the Orthodox Church." Furthermore, he found the judgmental attitude many Protestants held of other faiths, especially Roman Catholicism and Eastern Orthodoxy, unsavory: "I didn't like the anti-Catholic bias because when you collectively unify to judge something—someone, some faith, I think that's immensely bad. I just think that that's so bad that people as a congregation agree to judge something."

The Jackson informants employed at least one important dichotomy in their characterizations of southern Christianity—that of church attendance and participation as either a "social" or "spiritual" affair. Interestingly, the social/spiritual dichotomy carried connotations similar to the ethnic/convert categorization of Pittsburgh Orthodox life. Many converts complained about what they considered to be the country-club atmosphere of Mississippi Protestantism, in which displays of social prominence and contacts seemed to take precedence over the deepening of one's relationship with God. As Pittsburgh converts often cast ethnic Orthodox Christians as lackadaisical in their religious lives, especially in what they supposed to be the ready coupling of church affiliation with familial or ethnic heritages, so too the Jackson informants considered convention rather than conviction to be the true motivation for much southern Protestant churchgoing. One informant remarked of his experience growing up in the Episcopal Church, "There's a tendency for it to be more social than it is religious and I think that goes way back. There's a lot of social to it. People just wanting to get together and meet and greet every Sunday." Joan described her brief childhood attendance at a Methodist church in a similar manner: "There was a Methodist church down the street and I had friends who went there. But, I think to a certain degree that was more a social attendance than a spiritual attendance."

By contrast, according to this assessment, the Orthodox Church presented its members with an unparalleled degree of "holiness" and spiritual depth, especially as conveyed through its worship. While Orthodoxy provided its members with religious communion and community, the core of their expression was presented as far deeper than that typically experienced in the social, program-oriented milieu of southern Protestantism. Certainly, the Jackson informants offered critiques of Protestantism similar to those articulated in Pittsburgh, most notably Fred from Ascension. Joan, for example, remarked upon the stark differences she experienced between the "holiness" of Orthodoxy and the constant need for being "entertained" in the Protestant churches she had attended. "I love the holiness of the [Orthodox] church. The first time I came and even now when you walk in, you just know. One of the main things I love about Orthodoxy is when you come to church you're not being entertained. When you come to church, it's not about the programs your church has. It's not about the ladies' group or this or that or the other thing." For Joan, Orthodox Christianity highlighted the essentials of the Christian life: "What it is about when you walk in an Orthodox church is that you're coming in to worship. That's what church is about. It's not about who can sing the best. It's not about the class you go to and what it can offer you. It's about the fact you're walking in to worship God. Period." Furthermore, she maintained, Orthodoxy was "too deep thinking" for most people, even the most religiously versed, in general to comprehend. "You just have to be open-minded. But if people aren't gonna open their mind and open their heart, then they're just not going to understand that. They're not going to accept that. It's too foreign. I wish everybody could understand that there is something so much deeper. If everybody could see that, it would be fantastic."

In addition to its general congruity with southern religiosity, Orthodox Christianity was presented as a religion that could transcend and heal the racial divisions marking the historical and contemporary experience of Mississippi. As one informant remarked, "Orthodoxy could be an intensely healing experience because, what, over 40 percent or more of our population is African American and certainly this group of people have their own experience of Christianity."

Interestingly, these references to Orthodoxy as a salve for the deep wounds of racism and discrimination spoke to a fundamental feature setting Eastern Orthodoxy apart from other non-Protestant southern religions, including Roman Catholicism and Judaism—that its appearance was a wholly post–Civil War, post-Reconstruction phenomenon. No Orthodox churches dotted the landscape of the "Old South," and they played no institutional role in the fomenting of slavery. Orthodoxy only arrived in Mississippi decades after Reconstruction. While historical research on the experiential contours and social placement of Orthodox Christians (again, primarily immigrants) in southern life over the first half of the twentieth century needs to be undertaken, Eastern Orthodoxy's relative novelty and absence from these critical events may contribute to the natural linkage a couple of informants saw between their newfound faith and its potential to reconcile persons divided by race and class.

In this vein, Veronica, who entered the Orthodox Church in 2007, underscored the importance Orthodoxy's cultural and racial inclusivity held for her as she investigated the Church before her conversion:

> I came here [to St. Seraphim's] and I saw that most of the people here are white converts and I wanted to make sure that there was nothing in the documents that said that these people are better than those people and we don't like those people—that we want everybody in. And when I found that as a matter of fact—historical fact—that the greatest of our church fathers are from Egypt and Africa and that the African continent was evangelized by the Apostles and when you realize the Apostolic origins of African Christianity as well as the Eastern—when you go to China or wherever—you see that the Apostles really got around and you see that Christianity really isn't a white man's religion, that it is multiethnic and multicultural and multiracial and that this richness is very much present is part of my attraction [to Orthodoxy].

For Veronica, the overcoming of racial divides was not an abstract concern for social justice but a deeply personal yearning for "repentance and reconciliation" based on her own family history: "I'm from the South and I have a lot of issues around being southern and I still have a lot of issues of being white and southern and I'd love to suddenly discover some white person in my family who stood up for liberation but it isn't gonna happen. You know, that person was in hiding or whatever. But, anyway, all of this Orthodox Christianity incorporates everybody and it has the mechanism of repentance and reconciliation that could make a genuine reconciliation across very painful lines. The divide of hurt is terrible but Orthodox Christianity has the medicine for that and if we wanted to we could give that medicine out. I'd like to see that happen."

Still, Veronica acknowledged that on-the-ground difficulties remained in bringing larger numbers of southern African Americans into the Orthodox faith. She explained:

> I've heard people say, "Black people aren't interested in Orthodoxy." I don't think that's true. I don't believe they understand it. And there's lots of good reasons for them to be resistant. I was suspicious. An African American who has their church that they've had for years and years and years—why would they leave that? I mean, unless there's a real good reason. There has to be a really good reason for somebody to give up something that's meant a lot to their families through the generations. But I don't believe that black people aren't interested in Orthodoxy.

While this convert interest in the multiracial and cultural character of Orthodox Christianity carries a historical poignancy in Mississippi, it also reflects the fact that the Orthodox Church has received increasing, although still small, numbers of African American converts in recent years. One of the informants, for instance, mentioned Fr. Moses Berry, a black convert who pastors a church in Ash Grove, Missouri, and founded the Brotherhood of St. Moses the Black, an Orthodox organization dedicated to making the African roots of early Christianity better known.[3] Fr. Moses served as a model for the mission and outreach some converts felt necessary to African American communities in Mississippi and beyond.

Conclusion

The eight interviews featured here represent only the faintest glimmerings of the more extensive research needed on Eastern Orthodox Christianity in Mississippi and other areas of the Deep South. While

Pittsburgh stands, in the eyes of many, as the "Holy Land" of American Orthodoxy, Jackson indicates the demographic vigor and expansiveness of the Orthodox Church as it grows and develops in areas of the United States with little historical Orthodox presence. The ways in which Orthodox Christianity adds to the religious culture and diversity of the "Bible Belt" as well as the impacts the religiosity of this region can exercise on Orthodoxy itself are questions ripe for future research. Unfortunately, they are beyond the scope of the present study.

Conclusion

As narrated in the 48 interviews sitting at the heart of this book, conversion to Eastern Orthodoxy remains a fluid and variegated phenomenon. The fundamental coexistence and entwinement of America's ongoing and omnipresent "culture of choice" with the doctrinal, liturgical, and experiential richness of Orthodox Christianity ensures that these conversions defy simple characterizations. Just as Orthodoxy itself cannot be considered an Old World relic, unchanged in its social and demographic contours over the course of its two centuries in North America, so too these conversions cannot be viewed as an unmitigated turn from modernity to tradition or from American culture to what many converts claim to be the early church. Certainly, recent scholarly and popular assessments of the increasing numbers of Americans interested in Orthodox Christianity over the past 30 years often suggest such a scenario. Rather than indicating the wholesale change and transformation so often presented in theological, psychological, and popular understandings of conversion, the events and perspectives outlined in the everyday experience of Americans discovering, entering, and situating themselves within the Orthodox Church yield a strategic, context-specific interplay of diverse cultural elements. The women and men from Pittsburgh and Jackson with whom I spoke drew upon the methods, language, and assumptions of both the spiritual marketplace and Orthodox Christianity over the course of their pre- and post-conversion experiences.

Although rather critical of modern individualism and pluralism in their embrace of traditional Christianity, the persons whose lives and experiences have unfolded over the course of these pages took for granted their freedom and ability to compare and decide between a vast array of religious options. Certainly, the overarching spiritual marketplace stood as the first cultural repertoire providing informants with rich sets of methodologies and vocabularies for making sense of and enacting their religious lives. Predominantly baby boomers or their children, the informants came into contact early in their lives with the expansive religious diversity and choice increasingly available and normative to post–World War II American culture. Frequently exposed from childhood to multireligious and multicultural households, neighborhoods, and educational settings, informants, including many cradle Orthodox parishioners, often embarked upon their own religious quests as young adults. While some informants, such as Alex, discovered Orthodox Christianity in rather short order as a college student, others, such as Karen, devoted years to the single-minded pursuit of finding the "true church" or the "true faith."

Given the modern choice-making imperative for individuals to rely on their own abilities to gather information and compare options, informants devoted a considerable amount of time in their narratives to outlining the various resources—reading, studying, social contacts, visits to religious sites—consulted in the course of their religious searches. Despite the fact that investigations usually involved a combination of these sources, most converts first learned about the Orthodox faith in the course of reading church history or theology or through family and friends. Meanwhile, despite common parochial characterizations of being less committed or "on fire" for the Orthodox faith than their seeker counterparts, intermarriage converts also regularly utilized the language of personal autonomy and choice-making in describing their own decisions to become Orthodox. A constituency rarely featured in academic studies of conversion to Orthodoxy, intermarriage converts stressed their own desires and affinities to join the church over social or marital expectations for domestic religious unity.

The spiritual marketplace affects not only the contours of converts' pre-conversion searches but also the means of catechesis once they arrive at church doorsteps. Just as commitment rises as the primary means of holding relationships together under conditions of late modernity, so too demonstrations of one's seriousness and staying power become key criteria for determining when and whether conversion to the Orthodox Church should occur. In addition to imparting fundamental information about the doctrines and history of the church, priests assumed a "gatekeeping" function in the control of conversion processes and determining commitment levels of inquirers. Concerned about the free exchange of religious venues that is increasingly common in American culture and religious life, clerics often devoted considerable time to one-on-one spiritual counseling in order to discern conversion motives and earnestness. This care not only reflected concerns over potential convert fickleness but also raised the "spiritual capital" of Eastern Orthodoxy in underscoring that the church could not be entered simply on personal whim.

However, the significance of this research to our understanding of this field cannot be limited to the "marketplace" alone. Despite the subjectivity and individualism driving these conversions to Orthodoxy, we must never lose sight that they are fundamentally about the finding of community, as an ecclesial dwelling and nexus of complex social relationships. Robert Bellah's fears of an American landscape comprised solely of Sheila Larsons practicing their "Sheilaisms" has in no way come to pass, if one takes into account this case study of Orthodox converts, a group bent on finding concrete brick-and-mortar, flesh-and-blood communities. While much has been made of the "spiritual, but not religious" model of individuals, eschewing organized religion in favor of a fluid bricolage of self-appropriated beliefs and practices, these converts exemplify an alternative pattern of what we may consider "spiritual *and* religious," persons who consider religious institutions, even those with robed, jewel-bedecked bishops and dogmatic formulae, the vehicles for personal growth and transformation as discussed in chapter four. They desire truth and moral certainty *and* opportunities for personal self-expression and on-the-ground strategizing. With few exceptions, the informants rarely questioned the importance of organized, institutional religion to their spiritual lives and even the most ardent of seeker converts described concrete churches, in the form of denominations and congregations, as the objects of their sundry searches. However propelled to begin searching for deeper meaning in their lives, nearly all informants began and ended their searches rather soberly with church on Sunday morning. This book, thus, offers a valuable glimpse into the continued presence and power of institutional, organized religion as an outlet for "spiritual" interests.

Furthermore, the shift in units of analysis from the denomination as a whole (Eastern Orthodoxy) to the local parish (St. Michael's, Ascension, and St. Seraphim's) brings to light fundamental processes of religious change that are barely perceptible from the perspective of theological discourse or hierarchical pronouncements alone. It was only by living and working in local Orthodox churches that I came into contact with priests engaged in techno-evangelism, and parishioners eager in (near) equal measure to attend morning liturgies and afternoon Steelers' games (or as one parishioner declared, the "church of St. Art"—for the franchise owner, Art Rooney). Congregations are the sites where competing religious and secular interests are at their most acute, where the ideal of theological formulae gives way to the reality of human interaction and the messiness of actual lives lived.[1] They are where variability of form, norm, and openness to change and transformation far outstrip that of the ecclesial entity as a whole. St. Michael's, Ascension, and St. Seraphim's are peculiar in their histories and demographic compositions, but so too is each Orthodox parish in the United States. It is through the lens of the local that one sees Orthodox Christianities rather than Orthodox Christianity, multiplicity rather than singularity. While the Orthodoxy "of the books" may seem impervious to historical change, its parishes decidedly are not.

If religious communities have not been rendered obsolete under the conditions of late modernity, the motives for individual affiliation with them have altered. With a population on the geographical move and the weakening of old familial and religious bonds, American congregations, including Orthodox churches, are voluntary communities that must strategize to retain and attract membership; hence the new significance of Orthodox evangelism and technological acumen in reaching inquirers. The perceptual fault lines between "convert" and "ethnic" Orthodox Christians as well as the categories of intermarriage and seeker converts in parish life provide a lens by which to observe the shift in these meanings within a community that continues to be cast as ethnic and marginal to American religious mainstreams. The clerical valorization of seeker converts as model Orthodox Christians worthy of emulation by the community as a whole signals an intraparish acceptance of, rather than a resistance to, this voluntarism. In essence, ecclesial membership by birth, nature, familial, or national heritages as ideals of church affiliation have been supplanted by voluntary, conscious, and emotionally driven associations such as those represented by seeker converts. Clerics wanted all their parishioners, regardless of birth affiliations, to become the functional equivalents of seeker converts, to be Orthodox church members by choice rather than through natal or familial tradition or accident.

Still, the stage for these powerful macro-processes remains the lives of the individual converts. Despite the wider themes their stories share, each person felt her discovery and acceptance of the Orthodox faith as a singular event resonating at its deepest and most profound within the confines of her own biography. For Karen, Orthodox Christianity stood as more than a marketplace choice, for, as she related, "My conversion is the chief conclusion of my life, my search, my hope. It's such a huge thing. I'm just so thankful that I'm only 36 when I'm converting. I have, hopefully God willing, 30 or 40 years to be Orthodox. I want to go as deeply into this as I can." Even more broadly Karen, rather paradoxically, envisioned her discovery of the Orthodox Church as the greatest legacy she had to bequeath to her children, whom she hoped to spare the doubt and effort attendant to setting out to find a religion of one's own. She concluded, "I want *really* to pass it [Orthodoxy] on to my kids. I want to give them the opportunity of not having to search around to find a teacher, that they're just in it. And I can tell them all about my search and what Protestantism and Catholicism is like and this is how you be a Christian."

However, mixed with this yearning was the realization that her children may one day reject the Orthodox faith, as she once had the Roman Catholicism of her parents: "Now, of course, my daughter may grow up and say, 'I want to be a Protestant like Papa.' Fine, go ahead on your own search, but at least I'm providing them what I've learned over my whole life. I'm able to pass it on in some way. They'll make their own decisions once they get older, but at least I'm giving them the best that I can."

It remains to be seen whether the infant kicking and cooing in Karen's homey living room the afternoon of our interview will be an exception to the trend of Americans leaving their childhood faiths by age 24. It remains to be seen whether most of the adult converts here featured will remain Orthodox over the course of the coming years and decades.[2] Many converts, even those of the seeker variety, leave the Orthodox Church for other religious options. Still, for the moment, the women and men whom I was honored to meet and converse with have found Eastern Orthodoxy to be the culmination of their faith, a faith carefully refined and shaped through the assumptions and experiences of a context of religious multiplicity.

APPENDIX *A*

Demographic Overview of Informants

Although all the interviews began with a collection of more generalizable demographic data, I designed and utilized different interview guides reflective of the varied social groupings represented in Eastern Orthodox parish life (see Appendix B for interview guides). Occasionally, I interviewed persons who belonged to multiple social groupings, for example, priests who were also converts to Orthodox Christianity. In these cases, I utilized the clerical interview guide in addition to sections three and four from the interview guide for converts. While armed with these guides, I encouraged interview subjects to formulate their answers and conversion stories as freely, spontaneously, and naturally as possible, and informants responded to this desire in different ways. Some informants were so eager and articulate in their narrative renderings that I could barely engage them with my demographic queries, while other informants were heavily reliant on my direct questioning. I received permission from all informants to tape record the interviews, which ranged in length from forty-five minutes to four hours and which I then kept under lock and key and transcribed in full over the summers of 2006 and 2009. I then used NVIVO, a computerized data analysis program, to code the collected interviews.

Informants chose interview settings most preferable and convenient to them with interview sites ranging from the churches themselves (in pews, libraries, and offices) to homes, restaurants, and cafes as well as my university departmental offices. The interviews themselves usually proceeded in a very conversational manner and were augmented with additional conversations and social exchanges occurring before and after the formal interviews took place. While most parishioners were positively responsive to my interview requests, some individuals, including clerics, whom I would have liked to have formally interviewed, flatly refused to participate or ignored specific requests for interview scheduling. However, I was often able to record more casual conversations with these individuals in my written field notes.

Of the Pittsburgh interviews, eighteen of the informants hailed from St. Michael's (four interviews were conducted with lifelong lay members, four with intermarriage converts, nine with seeker converts, one with a cleric), thirteen from Ascension (one interview was with a lifelong church member, four with intermarriage converts, five with seeker converts, and three with clerics, one of whom was a convert); and nine from additional parishes and jurisdictions (two interviews were conducted with intermarriage converts, two with seeker converts, and five with clerics, two of whom were converts to Orthodox Christianity). Twenty-four of these informants (60%) were male and sixteen (40%) were female; the higher number of male informants can be attributed to the many clerical interviews conducted, since the Orthodox Church only ordains men into its clerical ranks (deacon, priest, and bishop). Interview subjects tended to be highly educated (48% of the total number of informants had completed BA or BS degrees; 43% had completed MA, MS, MBAs, or M.Div degrees; 5% held doctorates; and 5% had only a high school diploma at the time of the interview).

Although I endeavored to obtain as diverse a sample as possible, I was limited by informants' availability and willingness to participate in the study. Some peculiarities of this population reflect those of the Pittsburgh area more generally, since approximately 40 percent of study informants hailed from its environs. For example, according to statistical work completed by the Glenmary Research Center and published in *Religious Congregations and Membership in the United States in 2000,* approximately 50 percent of the population of the Pittsburgh metropolitan area (a total of 2.4 million) was Roman Catholic with nearly 25 percent belonging to mainline Protestant groups such as the United Methodist, Presbyterian, and Evangelical Lutheran Church of America.[1] These religious groupings comprised the majority of informants' childhood confessions (57% were Roman Catholic; 35% were Protestant, in which I include the Episcopal/Anglican, Lutheran, United Methodist, Presbyterian, Baptist, and various Pentecostal and non-denominational churches as well as unspecified Protestant churches; 4% were Byzantine Catholic; 4% were unchurched). Approximately 46 percent of the total number of converts were seeker converts, individuals who had investigated different religious options with or without officially becoming members of one or another religious group. Meanwhile, 25 percent of the total number of informants could be classified as "serial converts," persons who had officially taken membership in one or more religious groups before entering the Orthodox Church.

Again, a total of eight interviews were conducted with converts from St. Seraphim's in Jackson, Mississippi. Four men, including the parish priest, and four women ranging in age from 23 to 74 years were formally interviewed. The educational backgrounds of the Jackson informants were more varied than those of their northern counterparts, with five of the eight holding BA or BS degrees and two of these five completing advanced degrees (a PhD and master's degree respectively). Three of the eight informants did not possess college degrees but had some postsecondary college or vocational training.

Five informants had undertaken extensive pre-Orthodox religious seeking, investigating a wide swath of differing religious options. Interestingly, the Jackson informants had experimented with a wider range of religious alternatives including specifically non-Christian religious options such as the Bahai and New Age spiritualities, than the Pittsburgh converts featured in this book. In characterizing his present flock, Fr. Timothy observed that he regularly received persons he referred to as "hippies," persons deeply interested in alternative lifestyles and modes of dress. While the vast majority of informants had spent the entirety of their pre-conversion lives in specifically Christian venues, one woman had belonged to the Bahai faith for a number of years before successively joining the Baptist and Episcopal churches. In this vein, five of the eight Jackson informants were serial converts, having affiliated themselves with one or more religions before becoming Orthodox Christians. As far as religious affiliations of the Jackson converts at the time of their entries into the Orthodox Church were concerned, 38 percent had been Episcopalian directly before converting to Orthodoxy, 50 percent Protestant (again, including the Baptist, Presbyterian, and non-denominational charismatic churches), and 12 percent Roman Catholic.

APPENDIX *B*

Interview Guides

Interview Guides for Convert Informants

I—Demographic Information

Age, birthplace, education, current occupation, marital status (if married, divorced, or separated, how long?), children (sex and age), siblings (sex, age, birth order), how long a member of one's current parish, other Orthodox parish affiliations

II—Pre-Conversion Religious Life

1—Can you tell me a little bit about your religious life growing up?

2—What was your previous religious affiliation?

3—How would you characterize the religious life of your family while growing up?

4—With what other religious groups have you been affiliated in adulthood?

5—Why did you join these groups? Why did you leave?

III—Conversion to Orthodoxy

1—Please tell me about your conversion to Orthodox Christianity.

2—When did you convert to Orthodoxy?

3—Where, when, and how did you first learn about Orthodoxy?

(If any literary sources, what are they?) What originally attracted you to the Orthodox Church?

4—Could you describe for me your first visit to an Orthodox Church? Where was the church? Was there anything you liked or disliked about the service?

5—How did you learn about Orthodox doctrine and practice?

6—What ultimately convinced you to convert? What did it mean for you to convert? Did anything in your life change as a result of your conversion?

7—What has been the most difficult thing for you in converting to Orthodoxy?

IV—Conversion Narrative (Channels of Narrative Self-Reflection)

1—Have you ever discussed your conversion before? With whom? Where? Through what media: written or oral accounts?

Thank you for taking the time to speak with me today.

Interview Guides for Clerical Informants

I—Demographic information

Age, birthplace, education, marital status, children (ages and sexes), length of time in the priesthood, number of parishes served, length of time as pastor of the current parish

II—Spiritual/vocational life of the priest

1—Can you tell me a little bit about your religious life growing up?

2—Who or what influenced you to become a priest? Why did you enter the priesthood?

3—What have you found most difficult/most fulfilling about your life as a priest?

III—Conversion

1—In your view, what is conversion? What is its role in the life of the Orthodox Church?

2—What are the key motivating factors leading individuals to come to the Orthodox Church? Have you identified any patterns in conversion experiences and/or processes?

3—When individuals come to you interested in the Orthodox Church, what advice/suggestions do you provide? How do you guide interested individuals in their exploration of Orthodoxy?

4—What are the most effective ways for converts to learn about the church?

5—In your experience, what is most difficult for converts to accept about Orthodoxy? Can you identify any common pitfalls that emerge among converts as they begin and continue their lives within the Church?

IV—Conversion within individual parish

1—What is the history of conversion within your parish? Has it changed over the past two decades?

2—Have conversions affected your parish and its life in any way? If so, how?

Thank you for taking the time to speak with me today.

Interview Guide for Lifelong Church Members
I—Demographic information

Age, birthplace, educational background, current occupation, current marital status (if married, divorced, or separated, how long?), children (sex and age), siblings (sex, age, birth order). How long have you been a member of your current parish? What other parishes have you been a member of? How long were you a member of each of these parishes?

II—Religious life in childhood and early adulthood

1—Can you tell me a little bit about your religious life growing up?

2—How would you characterize the religious life of your family growing up?

3—What events, persons, or ideas were significant in your early religious development?

4—Have you ever questioned the Orthodox Church or your religious faith?

5—Did you ever consider joining another religion (Christian or non-Christian)? If yes, which ones and why?

6—How many members of your immediate family (the family in which you grew up) have remained Orthodox?

III. Parishioner's life in and opinion of the Orthodox Church today

1—Is there anything you find difficult about being an Orthodox Christian?

2—Do you read books on Orthodoxy? Attend Bible study? Visit Orthodox websites?

3—Have you visited many other Orthodox churches?

4—Why have you continued to stay at St. Michael's or Ascension church? (Or if the individual came from another parish) What attracted you to Ascension or St. Michael's?

5—Over the course of time you have been affiliated with this parish, do you think parish life or the character of the parish has changed in any way? If so, how?

6—Overall, how has the Orthodox Church changed since you were a kid?

7—(If the informant has children) Do you expect your children will remain Orthodox? How have you tried to pass the Orthodox faith down to them?

8—What does the Orthodox Church mean to you and to your life?

Thank you for speaking with me today.

Dramatis Personae

(List of informants who appear by name in the text)

St. Michael's Orthodox Church (OCA)—Pittsburgh, Pennsylvania

Fr. Mark (cradle Orthodox Christian)

Karen (seeker convert; raised Roman Catholic, but attended various Protestant churches as an adult)

Carl (seeker convert from the Presbyterian Church)

Alex (seeker convert; raised in a number of Protestant churches)

John (seeker convert, unchurched)

Paul (seeker convert, Brethren)

Christine (intermarriage convert, unchurched)

Sarah (cradle Orthodox Christian)

Marguerite (cradle Orthodox Christian)

Ascension Greek Orthodox Church—Pittsburgh, Pennsylvania

Fr. Joseph (cradle Orthodox Christian)

Fr. Andrew (seeker convert from Byzantine Catholicism)

Deacon Morris (cradle Orthodox Christian)

Fred and Mary (seeker converts; both were raised Roman Catholic, but both attended various Protestant churches as adults)

Brad (seeker convert, attended various Protestant churches as a child and adult)

Ken (intermarriage convert from Roman Catholicism)

Kay (intermarriage convert from Roman Catholicism)

Various other Orthodox churches in Pittsburgh and Cleveland

Fr. Nicetas (seeker convert from Anglicanism and Roman Catholicism; British-born): priest of a Ukrainian Orthodox church near Cleveland, Ohio)

James (seeker convert from Roman Catholicism) and Olivia (intermarriage convert from Roman Catholicism); attend Carpatho-Rusyn church in Pittsburgh

Sam (seeker convert from Roman Catholicism); attends an OCA parish near Cleveland

Renee (intermarriage convert from Roman Catholicism); attends a Carpatho-Rusyn church in Pittsburgh

St. Seraphim's Orthodox Church (OCA)—Jackson, Mississippi

Fr. Timothy (seeker convert from the Episcopal Church)

Lorraine (seeker convert from the Presbyterian Church)

Joan (seeker convert from a Southern Baptist church)

Harold (seeker convert from the Episcopal Church)

Charlie (seeker convert from Roman Catholicism)

Veronica (seeker convert from the Episcopal Church)

Notes

Introduction

1. Informant as well as all field site names in this book are pseudonymous. See Appendix C for a list of informants along with their mode of entry into Orthodoxy and the parishes to which they belonged during the course of my fieldwork.

2. Peter L. Berger, *The Sacred Canopy: Elements of a Sociological Theory of Religion* (New York: Anchor Books, 1967), 135 and 138.

3. Philip E. Hammond, *Religion and Personal Autonomy: The Third Disestablishment in America* (Columbia: University of South Carolina Press, 1992), 5; for additional discussion of this context, see also Richard Cimino and Don Lattin, *Shopping for Faith: American Religion in the New Millennium* (San Francisco: Jossey-Bass, 2002), 12–13; Will Herberg, *Protestant, Catholic, Jew: An Essay in American Religious Sociology* (Garden City, NY: Doubleday, 1955); Robert N. Bellah, *Habits of the Heart: Individualism and Commitment in American Life* (Berkeley: University of California Press, 1985), 221; *Faith in Flux: Changes in Religious Affiliation in the United States*, Executive summary of a study conducted by the Pew Forum on Religion and the Public Life (April 27, 2009), available at http://pewforum.org/Faith-in-Flux.aspx.

4. Dean M. Kelley, *Why Conservative Churches Are Growing: A Study in Sociology of Religion* (New York: Harper & Row, 1977).

5. Laurence R. Iannaccone, "Why Strict Churches Are Strong," *American Journal of Sociology* 99, no. 5 (March 1994): 1180–211; Roger Finke, "An Orderly Return to Tradition: Explaining Membership Growth in Catholic Religious Orders," *Journal for the Scientific Study of Religion* 36 (1997): 218–30; Rodney Stark and Roger Finke, *The Churching of America, 1776–2005: Winners and Losers in Our Religious Economy*, 2nd ed. (New Brunswick, NJ: Rutgers University Press, 2005); Colleen Carroll, *The New Faithful: Why Young Adults Are Embracing Christian Orthodoxy* (Chicago: Loyola Press, 2002). The Second Vatican Council (1962–1965) reevaluated Roman Catholic belief and practice in light of modernity. The council revised the mass and replaced the traditional Latin in which it had been celebrated with local vernacular languages. Richard P. McBrien, "Vatican Council

II," in *The HarperCollins Encyclopedia of Catholicism*, ed. Richard P. McBrien (New York: HarperCollins, 1995), 1299–306.

6. Jean and John Comaroff, *Of Revelation and Revolution: Christianity, Colonialism, and Consciousness in South Africa*, vol. 1 (Chicago: University of Chicago Press, 1991), 198, as quoted in Diane Austin-Broos, "The Anthropology of Conversion: An Introduction," in *The Anthropology of Conversion*, ed. Andrew Buckser and Stephen D. Glazier (Lanham, MD: Rowman & Littlefield Publishers, 2003), 2

7. For a sampling see Sydney Ahlstrom, *A Religious History of the American People*, 2nd ed. (New Haven, CT: Yale University Press, 2004), 985–94; Edwin S. Gaustad and Leigh E. Schmidt, *A Religious History of America*, rev. ed. (San Francisco: HarperSanFrancisco, 2002), 285–86 and 392–93; Catherine Albanese, *America: Religions and Religion*, 2nd ed. (Belmont, CA: Wadsworth Publishing Company, 1992), 286–92.

8. For more information on the experience of these "New Immigrants" and their impacts on American Orthodoxy, see John H. Erickson, *Orthodox Christians in America* (New York: Oxford University Press, 1999), especially chapters 3–5.

9. Alexei D. Krindatch, "Eastern Christianity in North American Religious Landscape: Ethnic Traditionalism versus Civic Involvement and Social Transformations," report for project *Research on Orthodox Religious Groups in the United States* (Hartford Institute for Religion Research, http://hirr.hartsem.edu/research/krindatch.pdf), 2.

10. See Peter E. Gillquist, *Becoming Orthodox: A Journey to the Ancient Christian Faith*, rev. ed. (Ben Lomond, CA: Conciliar Press, 1992) for an insider's account of these evangelical Protestant conversions in the mid-1980s.

11. See Mark Stokoe and Very Rev. Leonid Kishkovsky, "The Emerging American Mission: Evangelization," in *Orthodox Christians in North America, 1794–1994* (http://www.oca.org/MVorthchristiansnamerica.asp?SID=1&Chap=CH9).

12. See Nancy T. Ammerman, *Bible Believers: Fundamentalists in the Modern World* (New Brunswick, NJ: Rutgers University Press, 1987); Brenda Brasher, *Godly Women: Fundamentalism and Female Power* (New Brunswick, NJ: Rutgers University Press, 1998); R. Marie Griffith, *God's Daughters: Evangelical Women and the Power of Submission* (Berkeley: University of California Press, 1997); Lynn Davidman, *Tradition in a Rootless World: Women Turn to Orthodox Judaism* (Berkeley, CA: University of California Press, 1991); Robert Orsi, *The Madonna of 115th Street: Faith and Community in Italian Harlem, 1880–1950*, 2nd ed. (New Haven, CT: Yale University Press, 2002); Thomas Tweed, *Our Lady of the Exile: Diasporic Religion at a Cuban Catholic Shrine in Miami* (New York: Oxford University Press, 1997); Anna Mansson McGinty, *Becoming Muslim: Western Women's Conversions to Islam* (New York: Palgrave Macmillan, 2006).

13. Alexei D. Krindatch, "Eastern Christianity in North American Religious Landscape: Ethnic Traditionalism versus Civic Involvement and Social Transformations," report for project *Research on Orthodox Religious Groups in the United States* (Hartford Institute for Religion Research, http://hirr.hartsem.edu/research/krindatch.pdf), 5; Alexander Agadjanian and Victor Roudometof, "Introduction: Eastern Orthodoxy in a Global Age—Preliminary Considerations," in *Eastern Orthodoxy in a Global Age: Tradition Faces the Twenty-First Century*, ed. Victor Roudometof, Alexander Agadjanian, and Jerry Pankhurst (Walnut Creek, CA: AltaMira Press, 2005), 9.

14. Elizabeth H. Prodromou, "Religious Pluralism in Twenty-First-Century America: Problematizing the Implications for Orthodoxy [sic] Christianity," *Journal of the American Academy of Religion* 72, no. 3 (September 2004): 751–52.

15. Paisios Bukowy Whitesides, "Ethnics and Evangelicals: Theological Tensions within American Orthodoxy," *St. Vladimir's Theological Quarterly* 41, no. 1 (1997): 19–35; Phillip Charles Lucas, *The Odyssey of a New Religion: The Holy Order of MANS from New Age to Orthodoxy* (Bloomington: Indiana University Press, 1995); Phillip Charles Lucas, "*Enfants Terribles*: The Challenge of Sectarian Converts to Ethnic Orthodox Churches in the United States," *Nova Religio: The Journal of Alternative and Emergent Religions* 7, no. 2 (2003): 5–23.

16. H.B. Cavalcanti and H. Paul Chalfant, "Collective Life as the Ground of Implicit Religion: The Case of American Converts to Russian Orthodoxy," *Sociology of Religion* 55, no. 4 (1994): 451 and 453; Richard P. Cimino, *Against the Stream: The Adoption of Traditional Christian Faiths by Young Adults* (Lanham, MD: Religion Watch: University Press of America., 1997).

17. David D. Hall, "Introduction," in *Lived Religion in America: Toward a History of Practice*, ed. David D. Hall (Princeton: Princeton University Press, 1997), vii–xiii; Robert Orsi, "Everyday Miracles: The Study of Lived Religion," in *Lived Religion in America: Toward a History of Practice*, ed. David D. Hall (Princeton: Princeton University Press, 1997), 3–21; Nancy T. Ammerman, "Introduction," in *Everyday Religion: Observing Modern Religious Lives*, ed. Nancy T. Ammerman (New York: Oxford University Press, 2007), 3–18. Vera Shevzov argues for the need to bridge the gap between "popular" and "institutional" religion in the study of Russian Orthodoxy in her essay, "Letting the People into Church: Reflections on Orthodoxy and Community in Late Imperial Russia," in *Orthodox Russia: Belief and Practice under the Tsars*, ed. Valerie A. Kivelson and Robert H. Greene (University Park: Pennsylvania State University Press, 2003).

18. See Ann Swidler, "Culture in Action: Symbols and Strategies," *American Sociological Review* 51, no. 2 (April 1986): 273–86, and Ann Swidler, *Talk of Love: How Culture Matters* (Chicago: University of Chicago Press, 2001), especially 11–26 (24). Similarly, Lynn Davidman discusses the importance of Swidler's work for understanding the religious expression of unsynagogued American Jews in her essay "The New Volunteerism and the Case of Unsynagoged Jews," appearing in *Everyday Religion: Observing Modern Religious Lives*.

19. See M.M. Bakhtin, *The Dialogic Imagination: Four Essays*, trans. Caryl Emerson and Michael Holmquist (Austin: University of Texas Press, 1981), 351–52; Jean and John Comaroff, *Of Revelation and Revolution: Christianity, Colonialism, and Consciousness in South Africa*, vol. 1 (Chicago: University of Chicago Press, 1991), 8; Gauri Viswanathan, *Outside the Fold: Conversion, Modernity, and Belief* (Princeton: Princeton University Press, 1998), 43.

20. See John H. Erickson, "The Reception of Non-Orthodox into the Orthodox Church: Contemporary Practice," *St. Vladimir's Theological Quarterly* 41, no. 1 (1997): 1–17, for a discussion of the varied diocesan and parochial administration of these initiation rites across Orthodox churches in the United States.

Chapter One

1. Peter E. Gillquist, *Becoming Orthodox: A Journey to the Ancient Christian Faith*, rev. ed. (Ben Lomond, CA: Conciliar Press, 1992), 179.

2. Paul Valliere, "Introduction to the Modern Orthodox Tradition," in *The Teachings of Modern Orthodox Christianity on Law, Politics, and Human Nature*, ed. John Witte, Jr., and Frank S. Alexander (New York: Columbia University Press, 2007), 1; John Anthony

McGuckin, *The Orthodox Church: An Introduction to Its History, Doctrine, and Spiritual Culture* (Malden, MA: Wiley-Blackwell, 2008), 1.

3. McGuckin, 3.

4. Dimitri Obolensky, *The Byzantine Commonwealth: Eastern Europe 500–1453* (London: Weidenfeld & Nicholson, 1971). See Warren Treadgold, "The Persistence of Byzantium," *The Wilson Quarterly* 22, no. 4 (1998): 66–91 for a valuable reevaluation of misconceptions about and the continued cultural and religious significance of the Byzantine Empire. See Marshall Poe, "Moscow, the Third Rome: The Origins and Transformations of a 'Pivotal Moment,'" *Jahrbücher für Geschichte Osteuropas* 49, no. 3 (2001): 412–29 for a discussion of the development of the "Third Rome" ideology.

5. McGuckin, 30.

6. See John Binns, *An Introduction to the Christian Orthodox Churches* (New York: Cambridge University Press, 2002), 201–31; McGuckin, 20–23; and Timothy Ware, *The Orthodox Church,* 2nd edition (New York: Penguin Books, 1993), 43–72, for different perspectives on the causes and outcomes of the Great Schism.

7. Ware, 2.

8. Ware, 1–2; McGuckin, 2.

9. Ware, 1.

10. McGuckin, 28; see Donald Fairbairn, *Eastern Orthodoxy through Western Eyes* (Louisville: Westminster John Knox Press, 2002), 11–21.

11. See Fairbairn, 24–25; Binns, 40–43; McGuckin, 90–100 for various discussions and perspectives on *sobornost.*

12. Paul Valliere, *Modern Russian Theology: Bukharev, Soloviev, Bulgakov: Orthodox Theology in a New Key* (Grand Rapids, MI: William B. Eerdmans Publishing Company, 2000), 373–403.

13. Fr. John Meyendorff, *Living Tradition: Orthodox Witness in the Contemporary World* (Crestwood, NY: St. Vladimir's Seminary Press, 1978), 373–403.

14. Ware, 264. See McGuckin, 288–306; Binns, 39–59; and Fairbairn, 39–47 for additional discussions of the Orthodox Divine Liturgy.

15. Meyendorff, 25 and 22.

16. Mark Stokoe and Leonid Kishkovsky, *Orthodox Christians in North America, 1794–1994* (Syosset, NY: Orthodox Christian Publications Center, 1995), 24–25; John H. Erickson, *Orthodox Christians in America* (New York: Oxford University Press, 1999), chapters 3–5. For a historical overview of the Alaskan missions, see [Bishop] Gregory Afonsky, *A History of the Orthodox Church in Alaska, 1794–1917* (Kodiak, AK: St. Herman's Theological Seminary, 1977).

17. Erickson, 118.

18. See Erickson, 62–65, and James Jorgenson, "Father Alexis Toth and the Transition of the Greek Catholic Community in Minneapolis to the Russian Orthodox Church," *St. Vladimir's Theological Quarterly* 32, no. 2 (1988): 119–37, for discussions of Fr. Alexis Toth; and see Erickson, 96, for a treatment of the formation of the Orthodox Carpatho-Rusyn Archdiocese.

19. "Table 4: Religious Congregations by County and Group: 2000—Pennsylvania, Allegheny County," in *Religious Congregations and Membership in the United States 2000: An Enumeration by Region, State and County Based on Data Reported for 149 Religious Bodies,* compiled by Dale E. Jones, Sherri Doty, Clifford Grammich, James E. Horsch,

Richard Houseal, Mac Lynn, John P. Marcum, Kenneth M. Sanchagrin, Richard H. Taylor (Nashville, TN: Glenmary Research Center, 2002), 389–90.

20. The major feast days of the Orthodox Church are the Nativity of the Mother of God (the Theotokos/Virgin Mary), Exaltation of the Cross, Presentation of Mary in the Temple, the Nativity of Christ (Christmas), Theophany, Presentation of Christ in the Temple, Annunciation, Palm Sunday, Easter (Pascha), Ascension, Pentecost, Transfiguration, Dormition (the death or falling asleep) of the Mother of God. The liturgical year in the Orthodox Church begins on September 1.

21. An akathist is a special hymn in the Orthodox Church written and sung in honor of Christ, the Theotokos, or a saint. A moleben is a short prayer service.

22. A *Paraclesis* service is sung for the intercession of a saint, usually the Theotokos.

23. H. Russell Bernard, *Research Methods in Anthropology: Qualitative and Quantitative Approaches*, 4th edition (Lanham, MD: AltaMira Press, 2006), 492–93.

24. Victor Turner, "Symbolism, Morality, Social Structure," in *The Forest of Symbols: Aspects of Ndembu Ritual* (Ithaca, NY: Cornell University Press, 1967), 50–51.

Chapter Two

1. Patricia Caldwell, *The Puritan Conversion Narrative: The Beginnings of American Expression* (New York: Cambridge University Press, 1983), 45–48. When comparing the conversion narratives of evangelical Protestant women in the nineteenth and twentieth centuries, Virginia Lieson Brereton too observed a general desacralization of the "search" motif, whereby conversion as essentially the product of individual convert agency supplanted earlier themes of God finding and changing the heart of lost sinners. Virginia Lieson Brereton, *From Sin to Salvation: Stories of Women's Conversions, 1800 to the Present* (Bloomington: Indiana University Press, 1991), 55.

2. A number of scholars have also explored the application of "shopping" and other consumerist metaphors to contemporary religion. In this regard, see Wade Clark Roof, *Spiritual Marketplace: Baby Boomers and the Remaking of American Religion* (Princeton, NJ: Princeton University Press, 1999); Richard Cimino and Don Lattin, *Shopping for Faith: American Religion in the New Millennium* (San Francisco: Jossey-Bass, 2002); Robert Wuthnow, *America and the Challenges of Religious Diversity* (Princeton: Princeton University Press, 2005), 106–29.

3. Roof, 101–2. See also Kelly Besecke, "Beyond Literalism: Reflexive Spirituality and Religious Meaning" in *Everyday Religion: Observing Modern Religious Lives*, ed. Nancy T. Ammerman (New York: Oxford University Press, 2007), 79, for an additional discussion of "reflexive spirituality."

4. Anthony Giddens, *Modernity and Self-Identity: Self and Society in the Late Modern Age* (Stanford: Stanford University Press, 1991), 75; Ulrich Beck and Elisabeth Beck-Gernsheim, *Individualization: Institutionalized Individualism and Its Social and Political Consequences* (London: Sage Publications, 2002), 5; see also Roof, 101–3, for additional discussion of the "leveling effect" that has occurred in the religious language utilized in many American denominations.

5. William James, *The Varieties of Religious Experience: A Study in Human Nature*, foreword by Jacques Barzun (New York: New American Library, 1958), 169, 177, 170, and 157.

6. Ibid., 170; Paula Fredriksen, "Paul and Augustine: Conversion Narratives, Orthodox Traditions, and the Retrospective Self," *Journal of Theological Studies* n.s., 37 (April

1986), 3–34; Talal Asad, "Comments on Conversion," in *Conversion to Modernities: The Globalization of Christianity*, ed. Peter van der Veer (New York: Routledge, 1996), 263–64; Rudolf Otto, *The Idea of the Holy: An Inquiry into the Non-Rational Factor in the Idea of the Divine and Its Relation to the Rational*, trans. John W. Harvey (New York: Oxford University Press, 1958). See Andrew Buckser for an overview of conversion studies in the twentieth century in his preface to *The Anthropology of Religious Conversion*, ed. Andrew Buckser and Stephen D. Glazier (Lanham, MD: Rowman & Littlefield, 2003), xi.

7. See James V. Downton, Jr., *Sacred Journeys: The Conversion of Young Americans to Divine Light Mission* (New York: Columbia University Press, 1979); Francine J. Daner, *The American Children of Krsna: A Study of the Hare Krsna Movement* (New York: Holt, Rinehart and Winston, 1976); Harriet Whitehead, *Renunciation and Reformation: A Study of Conversion in an American Sect* (Ithaca, NY: Cornell University Press, 1987); Lorne L. Dawson, "Cult Conversions: Controversy and Clarification," in *Religious Conversion: Contemporary Practices and Controversies*, ed. Christopher Lamb and M. Darrol Bryant (New York: Cassell, 1999), 284–87.

8. Jean and John Comaroff, *Of Revelation and Revolution: Christianity, Colonialism, and Consciousness in South Africa*, vol. 1; Gauri Viswanathan, *Outside the Fold: Conversion, Modernity, and Belief* (Princeton: Princeton University Press, 1998); Christopher Queen, "Ambedkar, Modernity, and the Hermeneutics of Buddhist Liberation," in *Dr. Ambedkar, Buddhism and Social Change*, ed. A.K. Narain and D.C. Ahir (Delhi: B.R. Publishing, 1994).

9. Viswanathan, 145.

10. Ibid., 43 and 4.

11. For discussions of features of baby boomer religiousness, see Roof; Wuthnow, especially 106–29; Dean Hoge, Benton Johnson, and Donald Luidens, *Vanishing Boundaries: The Religion of Mainline Protestant Baby Boomers* (Louisville, KY: Westminster/John Knox Press, 1994); Robert S. Ellwood, *The Sixties Spiritual Awakening: American Religion Moving from Modern to Postmodern* (New Brunswick, NJ: Rutgers University Press, 1994). For differing perspectives on the religious lives of Generation Xers, see Tom Beaudoin, *Virtual Faith: The Irreverent Spiritual Quest of Generation X* (San Francisco: Jossey-Bass, 1998); Colleen Carroll, *The New Faithful: Why Young Adults Are Embracing Christian Orthodoxy* (Chicago: Loyola Press, 2002); Richard P. Cimino, *Against the Stream: The Adoption of Traditional Christian Faiths by Young Adults* (Lanham, MD: Religion Watch: University Press of America, Inc., 1997); Robert Wuthnow, *After the Baby Boomers: How Twenty- and Thirty-Somethings Are Shaping the Future of American Religion* (Princeton: Princeton University Press, 2007).

12. Wuthnow, 115–16; Catherine Bell, *Ritual: Perspectives and Dimensions* (New York: Oxford University Press, 1997), 100–101; Bradd Shore, "American Middle-Class Families: Class, Social Reproduction, and Ritual," in *Family Transformed: Religion, Values, and Society in American Life*, ed. Steven M. Tipton and John Witte, Jr. (Washington, DC: Georgetown University Press, 2005), 194–95.

13. Alex's use of the term "lifestyle" conveys the moral uncertainty and urgency underscored in Anthony Giddens's theoretical treatment of the concept and to Zygmunt Bauman's roughly analogous, ever provisional "life strategies." See Giddens, 80–87, and Zygmunt Bauman, *Life in Fragments: Essays in Postmodern Morality* (Oxford: Blackwell Publishers, 1995), 8–9.

14. Wuthnow, 115–16.

15. See Peter Berger, *The Heretical Imperative: Contemporary Possibilities of Religious*

Affirmation (Garden City, NY: Anchor Press, 1979), 19–20; Edward C. Rosenthal, *The Era of Choice: The Ability to Choose and Its Transformation of Contemporary Life* (Cambridge, MA: MIT Press, 2005), xi; and Beck, 5 for discussions of choice-making methodologies.

16. Richard P. Cimino notes this in his work *Against the Stream*, 68–71; Paisios Bukowy Whitesides, "Ethnics and Evangelicals: Theological Tensions within American Orthodoxy," *St. Vladimir's Theological Quarterly* 41, no. 1 (1997): 19–35.

17. Frederica Mathewes-Green, *Facing East: A Pilgrim's Journey into the Mysteries of Orthodoxy* (San Francisco: HarperCollins Publishers, 1997); Frank Schaeffer, *Dancing Alone: The Quest for Orthodox Faith in an Age of False Religion* (Brookline, MA: Holy Cross Orthodox Press, 1994).

18. Timothy W. Luke, "Identity, Meaning and Globalization: Detraditionalization in Postmodern Space-Time Compression," in *Detraditionalization: Critical Reflections on Authority and Identity*, ed. Paul Heelas, Scott Lash, and Paul Morris (Cambridge, MA: Blackwell Publishers, 1996), 109–21; Barbara Adam, "Detraditionalization and the Certainty of Uncertain Futures," in *Detraditionalization*, 134–37. The literature on the impact of the media, especially electronic, on contemporary religions is immense. See Steward M. Hoover and Knut Lundby, eds., *Rethinking Media, Religion, and Culture* (Thousand Oaks, CA: Sage Publications, 1997); Brenda E. Brasher *Give Me that Online Religion* (San Francisco, CA: Jossey-Bass, 2001); Stephen O'Leary, "Cyberspace as Sacred Space: Communicating Religion on Computer Networks," *Journal of the American Academy of Religion* 64, no. 4 (Winter 1996): 781–806.

19. Rodney Stark and William Sims Bainbridge, "Networks of Faith: Interpersonal Bonds and Recruitment to Cults and Sects," *American Journal of Sociology* 85, no. 6 (May 1980): 1376–95. See, for example, Lynn Davidman, *Tradition in a Rootless World: Women Turn to Orthodox Judaism* (Berkeley: University of California Press, 1991), and, more recently, Carolyn Chen, *Getting Saved in America: Taiwanese Immigration and Religious Experience* (Princeton: Princeton University Press, 2008).

20. Wuthnow, 260–61; Barbara Dafoe Whitehead, "The Changing Pathway to Marriage: Trends in Dating, First Unions, and Marriage among Young Adults," in *Family Transformed: Religion, Values, and Society in American Life*, ed. Steven M. Tipton and John Witte, Jr. (Washington, DC: Georgetown University Press, 2005), 176 and 177.

21. However, even this allowance for inter-Christian unions is an interpretation made in light of practical considerations, for the canons of the Orthodox Church themselves forbid marriages between church and nonchurch members of any sort. See Canon LXXII of the Quinisext Council (692) for the original prohibition of intermarriage between church and nonchurch members, in *The Seven Ecumenical Councils of the Undivided Church: Their Canons and Dogmatic Decrees, together with the Canons of All the Local Synods Which Have Received Ecumenical Acceptance*, ed. Henry R. Percival. Nicene & Post-Nicene Fathers (Grand Rapids, MI: Eerdmans Publishing Company, reprint 1997), 397. For other contemporary Orthodox understandings on intermarriage, see *Intermarriage: Orthodox Perspectives*, ed. Anton C. Vrame (Brookline, MA: Holy Cross Orthodox Press, 1997), and Charles J. Joanides, *Ministering to Intermarried Couples: A Resource for Clergy and Lay Workers*, foreword by Demetrios Trakatellis (New York: Greek Orthodox Archdiocese of America, 2004).

22. See Jane Kaplan, *Interfaith Families: Personal Stories of Jewish-Christian Intermarriage* (Wesport, CT: Praeger, 2004), xiii; Anna Mansson McGinty, *Becoming Muslim: Western Women's Conversions to Islam* (New York: Palgrave MacMillan, 2006), 115.

Chapter Three

1. "Ask Father," *Again* 26, no. 4 (Winter 2004): 28.

2. M. Darrol Bryant and Christopher Lamb, "Introduction: Conversion in a Plural World," in *Religious Conversion: Contemporary Practices and Controversies*, ed. M. Darrol Bryant and Christopher Lamb (New York: Cassell, 1999), 7. Here, Bryant and Lamb discuss the "gatekeeping" function of the priest in Roman Catholicism. The priest plays a similar role in Eastern Orthodoxy.

3. Wade Clark Roof, *Spiritual Marketplace: Baby Boomers and the Remaking of American Religion* (Princeton: Princeton University Press, 1999), 312; Pierre Bourdieu, *Distinction: A Social Critique of the Judgment of Taste*, trans. Richard Nice (Cambridge, MA: Harvard University Press, 1984); David Swartz, "Bridging the Study of Culture and Religion: Pierre Bourdieu's Political Economy of Symbolic Power," *Sociology of Religion* 57, no. 1 (Spring 1996): 71–85.

4. For an overview of the development of the catechumenate in these early centuries see Robert M. Grant, "Development of the Christian Catechumenate," in *Made, Not Born: New Perspectives on Christian Initiation and the Catechumenate*, Liturgical Studies from the Murphy Center for Liturgical Research (Notre Dame, IN: University of Notre Dame Press, 1976), 39–46.

5. See Article 64 of "Constitution on the Sacred Liturgy" (Sacrosanctum Concilium) in *The Documents of Vatican II* (New York: Guild Press, 1966), 159, for official Roman Catholic reinstatement of the catechumenate for adults in response to increased conversions to the Roman Catholic Church. See also Karen Ward, "Making Adult Disciples: Rite for Our Times—Adult Baptism," *Christian Century* 116, no. 10 (March 24, 1999), 348–50 for a discussion of renewed Protestant interest in adult catechesis and initiation rituals.

6. The Orthodox Divine Liturgy is divided into two sections. The first half of the Liturgy, known as the "Liturgy of the Catechumens," was overtly dedicated to teaching the baptized faithful as well as persons preparing for baptism/chrismation the tenets of the Christian faith through Gospel and Epistle readings as well as sermons. The "Litany of the Catechumens" is a petitionary prayer offered on behalf of catechumens concluding this half of the Liturgy before, in centuries past, they were ushered out of the "Liturgy of the Faithful," when the Eucharistic gifts would be distributed to baptized church members. Today, catechumens as well as non-Orthodox church visitors are usually present for the entire Liturgy.

7. The liturgical scholar Daniel B. Stevick offers a fascinating history of the development and proliferation of catechetical texts in post-Reformation Europe in "Christian Initiation: Post-Reformation to the Present Era," in *Made, Not Born*, 99–117.

8. See Ann Swidler, *Talk of Love: How Culture Matters* (Chicago: University of Chicago Press, 2001), 26–28; Anthony Giddens, *Modernity and Self-Identity: Self and Society in the Late Modern Age* (Stanford: Stanford University Press, 1991), 6.

9. Gauri Viswanathan, *Outside the Fold: Conversion, Modernity, and Belief* (Princeton: Princeton University Press, 1998), 244–46; Zygmunt Bauman, *Modernity and Ambivalence* (Ithaca, NY: Cornell University Press, 1991), 78; Ian Ker, *John Henry Newman: A Biography* (Oxford: Clarendon Press, 1988), 473, as quoted in Patrick Allitt, *Catholic Converts: British and American Intellectuals Turn to Rome* (Ithaca, NY: Cornell University Press, 1997), 7; Allitt, 7.

10. Grace Davie, "Vicarious Religion: A Methodological Challenge," in *Everyday Religion: Observing Modern Religious Lives*, ed. Nancy T. Ammerman (New York: Oxford

University Press, 2007), 29–30; Enzo Pace, "Religion as Communication: The Changing Shape of Catholicism in Europe," in *Everyday Religion*, 46–48. Wuthnow also discusses the changing models and meanings of clerical life in contemporary America in *America and the Challenges of Religious Diversity* (Princeton: Princeton University Press, 2005), 266–68.

11. See John Binns, *An Introduction to the Christian Orthodox Churches* (New York: Cambridge University Press, 2002), 107–34 for an overview of Orthodox monasticism and the role of the elder. See also Irenee Hausherr, *Spiritual Direction in the Early Christian East*, trans. Anthony P. Gythiel (Kalamazoo, MI: Cistercian Publications, 1990); and *The Sayings of the Desert Fathers: The Alphabetical Collection*, rev. ed., trans. Benedicta Ward (Kalamazoo, MI: Cistercian Publications, 1984).

12. Fyodor Dostoevsky, *The Brothers Karamazov: A Novel in Four Parts with Epilogue*, trans. Richard Pevear and Larissa Volokhonsky (San Francisco: North Point Press, 1990); Archimandrite Sophrony, *St. Silouan the Athonite*, trans. Rosemary Edmonds (Crestwood, NY: St. Vladimir's Seminary Press, 1999); *The Way of a Pilgrim*, trans. Olga Savin (Boston: Shambhala, 1996), 43–45.

Chapter Four

1. Phillip Charles Lucas, "*Enfants Terribles*: The Challenge of Sectarian Converts to Ethnic Orthodox Churches in the United States," *Nova Religio: The Journal of Alternative and Emergent Religions* 7, no. 2 (2003): 5; Richard P. Cimino, *Against the Stream: The Adoption of Traditional Christian Faiths by Young Adults* (Lanham, MD: Religion Watch: University Press of America, Inc., 1997), 81.

2. Philip Rieff, *The Triumph of the Therapeutic: Uses of Faith after Freud* (New York: Harper & Row, 1966). Wade Clark Roof discusses the roles and importance of this "process-oriented" language in contemporary American culture in *Spiritual Marketplace*, 101–3; Cimino makes a similar observation of Orthodox converts and reverts in *Against the Stream*, 82.

3. H.B. Cavalcanti and H. Paul Chalfant, "Collective Life as the Ground of Implicit Religion: The Case of American Converts to Russian Orthodoxy," *Sociology of Religion* 55, no. 4 (Winter 1994): 453.

4. Patrick Allitt, *Catholic Converts: British and American Intellectuals Turn to Rome* (Ithaca, NY: Cornell University Press, 1997), 162–63. For another account of these prominent converts to Catholicism, see Adam Schwartz, *The Third Spring: G.K. Chesterton, Graham Greene, Christopher Dawson, and David Jones* (Washington, DC: Catholic University of America Press, 2005). For discussions of the prevalence and strength of fundamentalism across religions, see Gilles Kepel, *The Revenge of God: The Resurgence of Islam, Christianity, and Judaism in the Modern World*, trans. Alan Braley (University Park: Pennsylvania State University Press, 1994), and Bruce B. Lawrence, *Defenders of God: The Fundamentalist Revolt against the Modern Age* (San Francisco: Harper & Row, 1989). For an ethnographic case study, see Nancy T. Ammerman, *Bible Believers: Fundamentalists in the Modern World* (New Brunswick, NJ: Rutgers University Press, 1987).

5. John Meyendorff, *Living Tradition: Orthodox Witness in the Contemporary World* (Crestwood, NY: St. Vladimir's Seminary Press, 1978), 16, quoted in Paul Valliere, *Modern Russian Theology: Bukharev, Soloviev, Bulgakov: Orthodox Theology in a New Key* (Grand Rapids, MI: William B. Eerdmans Publishing Company, 2000), 377. Ignatius is an apostolic father martyred in Rome in the second century. Maximus the Confessor and Symeon the New Theologian are church fathers from the sixth–seventh and the tenth centuries,

respectively. St. Tikhon (of Zadonsk) lived in Russia in the eighteenth century, as did St. Theophan (the Recluse) in the nineteenth.

6. Lucas, 5–23. As suggested by Lucas, see Richard T. Hughes and C. Leonard Allen, *Illusions of Innocence: Protestant Primitivism in America, 1630–1875* (Chicago: University of Chicago Press, 1988) for a discussion of the theme of Christian origins in American religious history. For examples of these concerns as expressed in American Orthodox convert literatures, see for example Peter E. Gillquist, *Becoming Orthodox: A Journey to the Ancient Christian Faith*, rev. ed. (Ben Lomond, CA: Conciliar Press, 1992), especially 45–58, and Frederica Mathewes-Green, *Facing East: A Pilgrim's Journey into the Mysteries of Orthodoxy* (San Francisco: HarperCollins Publishers, 1997), xvii–xx.

7. A number of studies have noted the continued importance of community and communities to modern religious seekers and adherents. See Nancy T. Ammerman, *Pillars of Faith: American Congregations and Their Partners* (Berkeley: University of California Press, 2005); Richard P. Cimino and Don Lattin, *Shopping for Faith: American Religion in the New Millennium* (San Francisco: Jossey-Bass, 2002), 55–94. In their works, Cavalcanti and Chalfant, 441–54, and Cimino, 71–76, discuss the importance of community to Orthodox converts.

8. Christopher Lasch, *Haven in a Heartless World: The Family Besieged* (New York: Basic Books, 1977), as noted in Robert Wuthnow, "The Family as Contested Terrain," in *Family Transformed: Religion, Values, and Society in American Life*, ed. Steven M. Tipton and John Witte, Jr. (Washington, DC: Georgetown University Press, 2005), 193. See Barbara Dafoe Whitehead and David Popenoe, "Who Wants to Marry a Soulmate?" in *The State of Our Unions 2001* (Piscataway, NJ: National Marriage Project, Rutgers University, 2001), 13; Ann Swidler, *Talk of Love: How Culture Matters* (Chicago: University of Chicago Press, 2001), 201–2. See also Uma Narayan and Julia J. Bartkowiak, "Introduction," in *Having and Raising Children: Unconventional Families, Hard Choices, and the Social Good*, ed. Uma Narayan and Julia J. Bartkowiak (University Park: Pennsylvania State University Press, 1999), 1–14.

9. Wuthnow, 77.

10. See Nancy T. Ammerman, *Bible Believers: Fundamentalists in the Modern World* (New Brunswick, NJ: Rutgers University Press, 1987), 196; R. Marie Griffith, *God's Daughters: Evangelical Women and the Power of Submission* (Berkeley: University of California Press, 1997), 1–23; Frederick Bird, "The Pursuit of Innocence: New Religious Movements and Moral Accountability," *Sociological Analysis* 40: no page number provided, quoted in Ammerman, *Bible Believers*, 196.

11. Cimino makes a similar observation of the language used by the young people in his study in *Against the Stream*, 82.

12. In apophatic theology, also known as negative theology, the basic incomprehensibility of the divine to human thought is emphasized. This variety of theologizing is considered by some commentators, such as Vladimir Lossky, to be more pronounced in Eastern than Western Christianity. See Valliere, *Modern Russian Theology*, 299–300. See also Lossky's classic discussion of apophatic theology in *The Mystical Theology of the Eastern Church* (Crestwood, NY: St. Vladimir's Seminary Press, 1976).

Chapter Five

1. *The Russian Primary Chronicle: Laurentian Text*, trans. and ed. Samuel Hazzard Cross and Olgerd P. Shobowitz-Wetzor (Cambridge, MA: The Medieval Academy of

America, 1953), 110–11; Valerie A. Kivelson and Robert H. Greene, "Introduction," in *Orthodox Russia: Belief and Practice under the Tsars* (University Park: Pennsylvania State University Press, 2003), 10. For an example of how American conversions to Eastern Orthodoxy are often portrayed as aesthetically driven in popular media portrayals of the phenomenon, see Amy Johnson Frykholm, "Smells and Bells: Turning to Orthodoxy," in *Christian Century* 121, no. 26 (December 28, 2004): 18–20.

2. See Ronald L. Grimes, *Reading, Writing, and Ritualizing: Ritual in Fictive, Liturgical, and Public Places* (Washington, DC: The Pastoral Press, 1993); Tom F. Driver, *Liberating Rites: Understanding the Transformative Power of Ritual* (Boulder, CO: Westview Press, 1998); and Catherine Bell, *Ritual: Perspectives and Dimensions* (New York: Oxford University Press, 1997) for differing perspectives on the lack of ritual in modern life; Richard Cimino, 96.

3. Lynn Davidman, *Tradition in a Rootless World: Women Turn to Orthodox Judaism* (Berkeley: University of California Press, 1991), 136–37 and 224. For other studies discussing the ritual experimentation of modern converts, see Mary Jo Neitz, *Charisma and Community: A Study of Religious Commitment within the Charismatic Renewal* (New Brunswick, NJ: Transaction Books, 1987); James V. Downton, Jr., "An Evolutionary Theory of Spiritual Conversion and Commitment: The Case of the Divine Light Mission," *Journal for the Scientific Study of Religion* 19 (September 1980): 381–96; Georges Florovsky, quoted in Bishop Kallistos Ware, "The Witness of the Orthodox Church in the Twentieth Century," *Sourozh* 80 (May 2000), 9.

4. See my article, "Imagined Aesthetics: Constructions of Aesthetic Experience in Orthodox Christian Conversion Narratives," in *Aesthetics as a Religious Factor in Eastern and Western Christianity: Selected Papers of the International Conference held at the University of Utrecht, the Netherlands, in June 2004*, ed. Wil van den Bercken and Jonathan Sutton (Leuven, Belgium: Peeters, 2005), 53–63, for a critique of this common coupling of Orthodox conversion experiences with aesthetics.

5. Alex is here referring to the triple-barred, Eastern cross common to Eastern Christian churches, both Eastern Orthodox and Byzantine Catholic, of Slavic orientation. See LeRoy H. Appleton and Stephen Bridges, *Symbolism in Liturgical Art* (New York: Charles Scribner's Sons, 1959), 21–22.

6. Ann Swidler, "Culture in Action: Symbols and Strategies," *American Sociological Review* 51, no. 2 (1986), 278; Zygmunt Bauman, *Modernity and Ambivalence* (Ithaca, NY: Cornell University Press, 1991), 75.

7. Swidler, 279.

8. The Grand Duchess Elizabeth was originally a German princess and sister to the last empress of Russia, Alexandra, who married into the Russian imperial family and converted from Lutheranism to Russian Orthodoxy. She became a nun after her husband's assassination in 1905 and was herself murdered by the Bolsheviks in 1918. She was glorified as a saint by the Russian Orthodox Church in 1992.

9. Orthodox fasting, at its most rigorous, requires abstention from meat and dairy products. Wednesdays and Fridays are weekly fast days, while the church recognizes four major fasting periods over the course of its liturgical year.

10. The icon that was installed in the church is known as the "Mother of God, Joy of All Who Sorrow" and depicts the Virgin surrounded by angels and people in need. This is an image of specifically Russian, rather than Greek Byzantine, provenance.

11. Ronald L. Grimes, "Ritual Criticism and Infelicitous Performances," *Readings in*

Ritual Studies, ed. Ronald L. Grimes (Upper Saddle River, NJ: Prentice Hall, 1996), 279–93. For an overview of the liturgical changes precipitating the Old Believer Schism, see Paul Meyendorff, *Russia, Ritual, and Reform: The Liturgical Reforms of Nikon in the Seventeenth Century* (Crestwood, NY: St. Vladimir's Seminary Press, 1991).

12. Grimes, 281.

13. John Binns, *An Introduction to the Christian Orthodox Churches* (New York: Cambridge University Press, 2002), 42.

14. Timothy Ware, *The Orthodox Church*, 2nd edition (New York: Penguin Books, 1993), 269.

15. Andrew Buckser, "Social Conversion and Group Definition in Jewish Copenhagen," in *The Anthropology of Religious Conversion*, ed. Andrew Buckser and Stephen D. Glazier (Lanham, MD: Rowman & Littleman Publishers, 2003), 75; Patrick Allitt, *Catholic Converts: British and American Intellectuals Turn to Rome* (Ithaca, NY: Cornell University Press, 1997), 7.

16. Old Calendar Christmas, based on the Julian Calendar, is on January 7 in contrast to the celebration of Christmas on December 25, which is the norm in Orthodox churches (for example, the OCA) that mark the liturgical year according to the Gregorian Calendar. The Russian Orthodox Church uses the Julian Calendar.

Chapter Six

1. See Alexei D. Krindatch, "Orthodox (Eastern Christian) Churches in the United States at the Beginning of a New Millennium: Questions of Nature, Identity, and Mission," *Journal for the Scientific Study of Religion* 41, no. 3 (September 2002): 533–63, for a current discussion of the ethnic configurations and demographics of American Orthodoxy; *My Big Fat Greek Wedding*, dir. Joel Zwick (Hollywood, CA: Warner Brothers, 2002).

2. Herbert J. Gans, "Symbolic Ethnicity: The Future of Ethnic Groups and Cultures in America," in *Theories of Ethnicity: A Classical Reader*, ed. Werner Sollors (Basingstoke: Macmillan, 1996), 435.

3. Phillip Charles Lucas, "*Enfants Terribles*: The Challenge of Sectarian Converts to Ethnic Orthodox Churches in the United States," *Nova Religio: The Journal of Alternative and Emergent Religions* 7, no. 2 (2003), 5–23; Paisios Bukowy Whitesides, "Ethnics and Evangelicals: Theological Tensions within American Orthodoxy," *St. Vladimir's Theological Quarterly* 41, no. 1 (1997), 19–35. While Whitesides footnotes an awareness that "evangelicals" (former Protestants) too may have familial ethnic attachments, he never explores this in his work.

4. Cimino, 69.

5. Fredrik Barth, "Introduction," in *Ethnic Groups and Boundaries: The Social Organization of Culture Difference*, ed. Fredrik Barth, reissued ed. (Prospect Heights, IL: Waveland Press, Inc., 1998), 9–38; [Stuart Hall], *Identity, Community, and Cultural Difference*, ed. Jonathan Rutherford (London: Lawrence & Wishart, 1990), 225; Mary C. Waters, *Ethnic Options: Choosing Identities in America* (Berkeley: University of California Press, 1990), 19. See Richard Jenkins, *Social Identity*, 2nd ed. (New York: Routledge, 2004), for an overall discussion of the malleability of identity.

6. Whitesides, 19; Ashley W. Doane, Jr., "Dominant Group Ethnic Identity in the United States: The Role of 'Hidden' Ethnicity in Intergroup Relations," *Sociological Quarterly* 38, no. 3 (Summer 1997): 377 and 378.

7. Doane, 384.

8. John Meyendorff, *Living Tradition: Orthodox Witness in the Contemporary World* (Crestwood, NY: St. Vladimir's Seminary Press, 1978), 26; John Anthony McGuckin, *The Orthodox Church: An Introduction to its History, Doctrine, and Spiritual Culture* (Malden, MA: Wiley-Blackwell, 2008), 26–27.

9. The notion that early Celtic Christianity was essentially "Eastern" in its practices has been a common point of discussion among modern Orthodox Christians in the West. A number of church practices are cited in support of this view. For example, many early Christians of the British Isles calculated the date for Easter in the same manner as did the Greek East. Thomas O'Loughlin, however, disputes that a distinctive "Celtic church" radically departing from the rest of Latin Christendom existed. See Thomas O'Loughlin, *Celtic Theology: Humanity, World, and God in Early Irish Writings* (New York: Continuum, 2000), 17–21.

10. Pysanky are especially decorated keepsake eggs usually given at Easter. The painting of these eggs is a Ukrainian folk tradition.

11. Veneration of pre-schism Western saints (such as Patrick, Brigid, and Boniface) and those outside historically Orthodox cultures such as China and Native North America, many of whom have only been added to the rolls of the saints in the course of the twentieth century, is a recent phenomenon. The bishop, missionary, and now saint himself, John Maximovich of the Russian Orthodox Church Outside Russia (ROCOR), championed these figures as something of a hidden cachet of Orthodox sanctity in the West. Appointed Bishop of Western Europe in 1951 before arriving in San Francisco in 1962, John Maximovich was a strong advocate of official veneration of local Western saints. He collected information about the lives of these pre-schism figures and supported the composing of services, hymns, and icons to their honor.

Chapter Seven

1. Edwin S. Gaustad, "Regionalism in American Religion," in *Religion in the South*, ed. Charles Reagan Wilson (Jackson: University Press of Mississippi, 1985), 155–72. General studies of religion in the South include Samuel S. Hill, ed., *Religion in the Southern States: A Historical Study* (Macon, GA: Mercer University Press, 1983); Ruel W. Tyson, James L. Peacock, and Daniel W. Patterson, eds., *Diversities of Gifts: Field Studies in Southern Religion* (Urbana: University of Illinois Press, 1988); Beth Barton Schweiger and Donald G. Mathews, eds., *Religion in the American South: Protestants and Others in History and Culture* (Chapel Hill: University of North Carolina Press, 2004); Corrie E. Norman and Don S. Armentrout, eds., *Religion in the Contemporary South: Changes, Continuities, and Contexts* (Knoxville: University of Tennessee Press, 2005). For discussions of southern Roman Catholicism and Judaism, see Randall M. Miller and Jon L. Wakelyn, eds., *Catholics in the Old South: Essays on Church and Culture* (Macon, GA: Mercer University Press, 1983); Leonard Dinnerstein and Mary Dale Palsson, eds., *Jews in the South* (Baton Rouge: Louisiana State University Press, 1973).

2. For a religious history of Mississippi, see Randy J. Sparks, *Religion in Mississippi*, Heritage of Mississippi Series, vol. 2 (Jackson: University Press of Mississippi, 2001).

3. The Brotherhood of St. Moses the Black hosts an annual conference and provides additional information on Orthodox Christianity at its official website http://www.moses-theblack.org.

Conclusion

1. See James P. Wind and James W. Lewis, eds., *American Congregations*, vol. 1, *Portraits of Twelve Religious Communities* (Chicago: University of Chicago Press, 1994), 7; and James P. Wind and James W. Lewis, *American Congregations*, vol. 2, *New Perspectives in the Study of Congregations* (Chicago: University of Chicago Press, 1994) for a discussion of the importance of the "congregation" as a unit of historical and ethnographic research and analysis.

2. Although it is beyond the scope of the present study, Fr. Timothy suggested that future ethnographic research on the children of converts would be important and useful to gauge religious attitudes and responses to parental conversions. He said from his own pastoral experience, "You can't make people do anything. There will always be some children who won't take to it. But, I think we need to work harder to reach them."

Appendix A

1. Dale Jones, "Fifteen Largest [Religious] Groups in Metropolitan Areas of the United States, 2000," report for project *Religious Congregations and Membership in the United States 2000: An Enumeration by Region, State and County Based on Data Reported by 149 Religious Bodies*, compiled by Dale E. Jones, Sherri Doty, Clifford Grammich, James E. Horsch, Richard Houseal, Mac Lynn, John P. Marcum, Kenneth M. Sanchagrin, Richard H. Taylor (Nashville, TN: Glenmary Research Center, http://ext.nazarene.org/rcms).

Bibliography

Books and Essays

Adam, Barbara. "Detraditionalization and the Certainty of Uncertain Futures." In *Detraditionalization: Critical Reflections on Authority and Identity*, ed. Paul Heelas, Scott Lash, and Paul Morris. Cambridge, MA: Blackwell Publishers, 1996.

Afonsky, Gregory. *A History of the Orthodox Church in Alaska, 1794–1917*. Kodiak, AK: Saint Herman's Theological Seminary, 1977.

Agadjanian, Alex, and Victor Roudometof. "Introduction: Eastern Orthodoxy in a Global Age—Preliminary Considerations." In *Eastern Orthodoxy in a Global Age: Tradition Faces the Twenty-First Century*, ed. Victor Roudometof, Alexander Agadjanian, and Jerry Pankhurst. Walnut Creek, CA: AltaMira Press, 2005.

Ahlstrom, Sydney. *A Religious History of the American People*. 2nd edition. New Haven: Yale University Press, 2004.

Albanese, Catherine. *America, Religions and Religion*. 2nd edition. Belmont, CA: Wadsworth Publishing Company, 1992.

Allitt, Patrick. *Catholic Converts: British and American Intellectuals Turn to Rome*. Ithaca, NY: Cornell University Press, 1997.

Ammerman, Nancy T. *Bible Believers: Fundamentalists in the Modern World*. New Brunswick, NJ: Rutgers University Press, 1987.

——. "Introduction." In *Everyday Religion: Observing Modern Religious Lives*, ed. Nancy T. Ammerman. New York: Oxford University Press, 2007.

——. *Pillars of Faith: American Congregations and Their Partners*. Berkeley: University of California Press, 2005.

Appleton, LeRoy H., and Stephen Bridges. *Symbolism in Liturgical Art*. New York: Charles Scribner's Sons, 1959.

Asad, Talal. "Comments on Conversion." In *Conversion to Modernities: The Globalization of Christianity*, ed. Peter van der Veer. New York: Routledge, 1996.

"Ask Father." *Again* 26, no. 4 (Winter, 2004): 28.

Augustine, Saint. *Confessions*. Translated with notes by Henry Chadwick. New York: Oxford University Press, 1998.

Austin-Broos, Diane. "The Anthropology of Conversion: An Introduction." In *The Anthropology of Conversion*, ed. Andrew Buckser and Stephen D. Glazier. Lanham, MD: Rowman & Littlefield Publishers, 2003.

Bakhtin, M.M. *The Dialogic Imagination: Four Essays*. Edited by Michael Holmquist. Translated by Caryl Emerson and Michael Holmquist. Austin: University of Texas Press, 1981.

Barth, Fredrik. "Introduction." In *Ethnic Groups and Boundaries: The Social Organization of Culture Difference*, ed. Fredrik Barth. Reissued edition. Prospect Heights, IL: Waveland Press, 1998.

Bauman, Zygmunt. *Life in Fragments: Essays in Postmodern Morality*. Oxford: Blackwell, 1995.

———. *Modernity and Ambivalence*. Ithaca, NY: Cornell University Press, 1991.

———. *Postmodernity and Its Discontents*. New York: New York University Press, 1997.

Beaudoin, Tom. *Virtual Faith: The Irreverent Spiritual Quest of Generation X*. San Francisco: Jossey-Bass, 1998.

Beck, Ulrich, and Elisabeth Beck-Gernsheim. *Individualization: Institutionalized Individualism and Its Social and Political Consequences*. London: Sage Publications, 2002.

Bell, Catherine. *Ritual: Perspectives and Dimensions*. New York: Oxford University Press, 1997.

Bellah, Robert N. *Beyond Belief: Essays on Religion in a Post-traditional World*. New York: Harper & Row, 1970.

Bellah, Robert N., et al. *Habits of the Heart: Individualism and Commitment in American Life*. Berkeley: University of California Press, 1985.

Berger, Peter L. *The Heretical Imperative: Contemporary Possibilities of Religious Affirmation*. Garden City, NY: Anchor Press, 1979.

———. *The Sacred Canopy: Elements of a Sociological Theory of Religion*. New York: Anchor Books, 1967.

Besecke, Kelly. "Beyond Literalism: Reflexive Spirituality and Religious Meaning." In *Everyday Religion: Observing Modern Religious Lives*, ed. Nancy T. Ammerman. New York: Oxford University Press, 2007.

Billerbeck, Franklin, ed. *Anglican-Orthodox Pilgrimage*. Ben Lomond, CA: Conciliar Press, 1993.

Binns, John. *An Introduction to the Christian Orthodox Churches*. New York: Cambridge University Press, 2002.

Bird, Frederick. "The Pursuit of Innocence: New Religious Movements and Moral Accountability." *Sociological Analysis* 40.

Bobango, Gerald J. *The Romanian Orthodox Episcopate of America*. Jackson, MI: Romanian-American Heritage Center, 1979.

Bogolepov, Alexander. *Toward an American Orthodox Church: The Establishment of an Autocephalous Orthodox Church*. Crestwood, NY: St. Vladimir's Seminary Press, 2001.

Bourdieu, Pierre. *Distinction: A Social Critique of the Judgment of Taste*. Translated by Richard Nice. Cambridge, MA: Harvard University Press, 1984.

Brasher, Brenda. *Give Me that Online Religion*. San Francisco: Jossey-Bass, 2001.

———. *Godly Women: Fundamentalism and Female Power*. New Brunswick, NJ: Rutgers University Press, 1998.

Brereton, Virginia Lieson. *From Sin to Salvation: Stories of Women's Conversions, 1800 to the Present.* Bloomington: Indiana University Press, 1991.

Bruce, Steve. *Choice and Religion: A Critique of Rational Choice Theory.* Oxford: Oxford University Press, 1999.

Bryant, M. Darrol, and Christopher Lamb. "Introduction: Conversion in a Plural World." In *Religious Conversion: Contemporary Practices and Controversies*, ed. M. Darrol Bryant and Christopher Lamb. New York: Cassell, 1999.

———, eds. *Religious Conversion: Contemporary Practices and Controversies.* New York: Cassell, 1999.

Buckser, Andrew. "Social Conversion and Group Definition in Jewish Copenhagen." In *The Anthropology of Religious Conversion,* ed. Andrew Buckser and Stephen D. Glazier. Lanham, MD: Rowman & Littlefield, 2003.

Buckser, Andrew, and Stephen D. Glazier, eds. *The Anthropology of Religious Conversion.* Lanham, MD: Rowman & Littlefield, 2003.

Bunyan, John. *The Pilgrim's Progress.* Edited with an introduction and notes by W.R. Owens. New York: Oxford University Press, 2003.

Bernard, H. Russell. *Research Methods in Anthropology: Qualitative and Quantitative Approaches.* 4th edition. Lanham, MD: AltaMira Press, 2006.

Caldwell, Patricia. *The Puritan Conversion Narrative: The Beginnings of American Expression.* New York: Cambridge University Press, 1983.

Carroll, Colleen. *The New Faithful: Why Young Adults Are Embracing Christian Orthodoxy.* Chicago: Loyola Press, 2002.

Catechism of the Catholic Church. Chicago: Loyola University Press, 1994.

Cavalcanti, H.B., and H. Paul Chalfant. "Collective Life as the Ground of Implicit Religion: The Case of American Converts to Russian Orthodoxy." *Sociology of Religion* 55, no. 4 (Winter 1994): 441–54.

Chen, Carolyn. *Getting Saved in America: Taiwanese Immigration and Religious Experience.* Princeton, NJ: Princeton University Press, 2008.

Cimino, Richard P. *Against the Stream: The Adoption of Traditional Christian Faiths by Young Adults.* Lanham, MD: Religion Watch: University Press of America, 1997.

Cimino, Richard P., and Don Lattin. *Shopping for Faith: American Religion in the New Millennium.* San Francisco: Jossey-Bass, 2002.

Clendanin, Daniel B. *Eastern Orthodox Christianity: A Western Perspective.* 2nd edition. Grand Rapids, MI: Baker Academic, 2003.

Comaroff, Jean, and John Comaroff. *Of Revelation and Revolution: Christianity, Colonialism, and Consciousness in South Africa.* Volume 1. Chicago: University of Chicago Press, 1991.

"Constitution on the Sacred Liturgy" (*Sacrosanctum Concilium*), Article 64. Vatican II. In *The Documents of Vatican II.* New York: Guild Press, 1966.

Daner, Francine J. *The American Children of Krsna: A Study of the Hare Krsna Movement.* New York: Holt, Rinehart and Winston, 1976.

Davidman, Lynn. "The New Volunteerism and the Case of the Unsynagoged Jew." In *Everyday Religion: Observing Modern Religious Lives*, ed. Nancy T. Ammerman. New York: Oxford University Press, 2007.

———. *Tradition in a Rootless World: Women Turn to Orthodox Judaism.* Berkeley: University of California Press, 1991.

Davie, Grace. "Vicarious Religion: A Methodological Challenge." In *Everyday Religion:*

Observing Modern Religious Lives, ed. Nancy T. Ammerman. New York: Oxford University Press, 2007.

Dawson, Lorne L. "Cult Conversions: Controversy and Clarification." In *Religious Conversion: Contemporary Practices and Controversies*, ed. Christopher Lamb and M. Darrol Bryant. New York: Cassell, 1999.

Dinnerstein, Leonard, and Mary Dale Palsson, eds. *Jews in the South*. Baton Rouge: Louisiana State University Press, 1973.

Doane, Ashley W., Jr. "Dominant Group Ethnic Identity in the United States: The Role of 'Hidden' Ethnicity in Intergroup Relations." *Sociological Quarterly* 38, no. 3 (Summer 1997): 375–97.

The Documents of Vatican II. New York: Guild Press, 1966.

Dostoyevsky, Fyodor. *The Brothers Karamazov: A Novel in Four Parts with Epilogue*. Translated by Richard Pevear and Larissa Volokhonsky. San Francisco: North Point Press, 1990.

Doulis, Thomas, ed. *Journeys to Orthodoxy: A Collection of Essays by Converts to Orthodox Christianity*. Minneapolis, MN: Light & Life Publishing, 1986.

———. *Toward the Authentic Church: Orthodox Christians Discuss Their Conversion: A Collection of Essays*. Minneapolis, MN: Light & Life Publishing, 1996.

Downton, James V., Jr. "An Evolutionary Theory of Spiritual Conversion and Commitment: The Case of the Divine Light Mission." *Journal for the Scientific Study of Religion* 19 (September 1980).

———. *Sacred Journeys: The Conversion of Young Americans to Divine Light Mission*. New York: Columbia University Press, 1979.

Driver, Tom F., *Liberating Rites: Understanding the Transformative Power of Ritual*. Boulder, CO: Westview Press, 1998.

Efthimious, Miltiades G., and George A Christopoulos, eds. *History of the Greek Orthodox Church in America*. New York: Greek Orthodox Archdiocese of North and South America, 1984.

Ellwood, Robert S. *The Fifties Spiritual Marketplace: American Religion in a Decade of Conflict*. New Brunswick, NJ: Rutgers University Press, 1997.

———. *The Sixties Spiritual Awakening: American Religion Moving from Modern to Postmodern*. New Brunswick, NJ: Rutgers University Press, 1994.

Erickson, John H. *Orthodox Christians in America*. New York: Oxford University Press, 1999.

———. "Reception of Non-Orthodox Clergy into the Orthodox Church." *St. Vladimir's Theological Quarterly* 19, no. 2 (1985): 115–32.

———. "The Reception of Non-Orthodox into the Orthodox Church: Contemporary Practice." *St. Vladimir's Theological Quarterly* 41, no. 1 (1997): 1–17.

Fairbairn, Donald. *Eastern Orthodoxy through Western Eyes*. Louisville, KY: Westminster John Knox Press, 2002.

Faith in Flux: Changes in Religious Affiliation in the United States. Executive summary of a study conducted by the Pew Forum on Religion and the Public Life (April 27, 2009). Available at http://pewforum.org/Faith-in-Flux.aspx.

Finke, Roger. "An Orderly Return to Tradition: Explaining Membership Growth in Catholic Orders." *Journal for the Scientific Study of Religion* 36 (1997): 218–30.

Fitzgerald, Thomas. "The Development of the Orthodox Parish in the United States." In *The Orthodox Parish in America: Faithfulness to the Past and Responsibility for the Future*, ed. Anton C. Vrame. Brookline, MA: Holy Cross Orthodox Press, 2003.

Fitzgerald, Thomas E. *The Orthodox Church*. Westport, CT: Greenwood Press, 1995.

Florovsky, Georges, quoted in Bishop Kallistos Ware. "The Witness of the Orthodox Church in the Twentieth Century." *Sourozh* 80 (May 2000).

Fredriksen, Paula. "Paul and Augustine: Conversion Narratives, Orthodox Traditions, and the Retrospective Self." *Journal of Theological Studies* n.s., 37 (April 1986): 3–34.

Frykholm, Amy Johnson. "Smell and Bells: Turning to Orthodoxy." *Christian Century* 121, no. 26 (December 28, 2004): 18–20.

Gans, Herbert J. "Symbolic Ethnicity: The Future of Ethnic Groups and Cultures in America." In *Theories of Ethnicity: A Classical Reader*, ed. Werner Sollors. Basingstoke: Macmillan, 1996.

Gaustad, Edwin S. "Regionalism in American Religion." In *Religion in the South*, ed. Charles Reagan Wilson. Jackson: University Press of Mississippi, 1985.

Gaustad, Edwin S., and Leigh E. Schmidt. *A Religious History of America*. Revised edition. San Francisco: HarperSanFrancisco, 2002.

Geertz, Clifford. "Religion as a Cultural System." In *The Interpretation of Cultures: Selected Essays*. New York: Basic Books, 1973.

Giddens, Anthony. *The Consequences of Modernity*. Stanford: Stanford University Press, 1990.

———. *Modernity and Self-Identity: Self and Society in the Late Modern Age*. Stanford: Stanford University Press, 1991.

———. *The Transformation of Intimacy: Sexuality, Love, and Eroticism in Modern Societies*. Stanford: Stanford University Press, 1992.

Gillquist, Peter E. *Becoming Orthodox: A Journey to the Ancient Christian Faith*. Revised edition. Ben Lomond, CA: Conciliar Press, 1992.

———. *Coming Home: Why Protestant Clergy Are Becoming Orthodox*. 2nd edition. Ben Lomond, CA: Conciliar Press, 1995.

———. *Making America Orthodox*. Brookline, MA: Holy Cross Orthodox Press, 1984.

Grant, Robert M. "Development of the Christian Catechumenate." In *Made, Not Born: New Perspectives on Christian Initiation and the Catechumenate*. Liturgical Studies from the Murphy Center for Liturgical Research. Notre Dame, IN: University of Notre Dame Press, 1976.

Griffith, R. Marie. *God's Daughters: Evangelical Women and the Power of Submission*. Berkeley: University of California Press, 1997.

Grimes, Ronald L. *Reading, Writing, and Ritualizing: Ritual in Fictive, Liturgical, and Public Places*. Washington, DC: Pastoral Press, 1993.

———. "Ritual Criticism and Infelicitous Performances." In *Readings in Ritual Studies*, ed. Ronald L. Grimes. Upper Saddle River, NJ: Prentice Hall, 1996.

Haddad, Yvonne Yazbeck. "The Quest for Peace in Submission: Reflections on the Journey of American Women Converts to Islam." In *Women Embracing Islam: Gender and Conversion in the West*, ed. Karin van Nieuwkerk. Austin: University of Texas Press, 2006.

Hall, David D. "Introduction." In *Lived Religion in America: Toward a History of Practice*, ed. David D. Hall. Princeton, NJ: Princeton University Press, 1997.

Hammond, Philip E. *Religion and Personal Autonomy: The Third Disestablishment in America*. Columbia: University of South Carolina Press, 1992.

Hausherr, Irenee. *Spiritual Direction in the Early Christian East*. Translated by Anthony P. Gythiel. Kalamazoo, MI: Cistercian Publications, 1990.

Heelas, Paul, Scott Lash, and Paul Morris, eds. *Detraditionalization: Critical Reflections on Authority and Identity.* Cambridge, MA: Blackwell Publishers, 1996.

Herbel, Oliver, Fr. "A Catholic, Presbyterian, and Orthodox Journey: The Changing Church Affiliation and Enduring Social Vision of Nicholas Bjerring." *Journal for the History of Theology* 14, no. 1 (2007): 49–80.

Herberg, Will. *Protestant, Catholic, Jew: An Essay in American Religious Sociology.* Garden City, NY: Doubleday, 1955.

Hill, Samuel S., ed. *Religion in the Southern States: A Historical Study.* Macon, GA: Mercer University Press, 1983.

Hoge, Dean, Benton Johnson, and Donald Luidens. *Vanishing Boundaries: The Religion of Mainline Protestant Baby Boomers.* Louisville, KY: Westminster/John Knox Press, 1994.

Hoover, Steward M., and Knut Lundby, eds. *Rethinking Media, Religion, and Culture.* Thousand Oaks, CA: Sage Publications, 1997.

Hughes, Richard T., and C. Leonard Allen. *Illusions of Innocence: Protestant Primitivism in America, 1630–1875.* Chicago: University of Chicago Press, 1988.

Iannaccone, Laurence R. "Why Strict Churches Are Strong." *American Journal of Sociology* 99, no. 5 (March 1994): 1180–211.

James, William. *The Varieties of Religious Experience: A Study in Human Nature.* Foreword by Jacques Barzun. New York: New American Library, 1958.

Jenkins, Richard. *Social Identity.* 2nd edition. New York: Routledge, 2004.

Joanides, Charles J. *Ministering to Intermarried Couples: A Resource for Clergy and Lay Workers.* Foreword by Demetrios Trakatellis. New York: Greek Orthodox Archdiocese of America, 2004.

Jones, Dale E. "Fifteen Largest [Religious] Groups in Metropolitan Areas of the United States, 2000." Report for project *Religious Congregations and Membership in the United States, 2000: An Enumeration by Region, State, and County Based on Data Reported by 149 Religious Bodies.* Compiled by Dale E. Jones, Sherri Doty, Clifford Grammich, James E. Horsch, Richard Houseal, Mac Lynn, John P. Marcum, Kenneth M. Sanchagrin, Richard H. Taylor. Nashville, TN: Glenmary Research Center. Accessed at http://ext.nazarene.org/rcms.

Jones, Dale E., Sherri Doty, Clifford Grammich, James E. Horsch, Richard Houseal, Mac Lynn, John P. Marcum, Kenneth M. Sanchagrin, Richard H. Taylor, "Table 4: Religious Congregations by County and Group: 2000—Pennsylvania, Allegheny County." In *Religious Congregations and Membership in the United States, 2000: An Enumeration by Region, State and County Based on Data Reported for 149 Religious Bodies.* Nashville, TN: Glenmary Research Center, 2002.

Jorgenson, James. "Father Alexis Toth and the Transition of the Greek Catholic Community in Minneapolis to the Russian Orthodox Church." *St. Vladimir's Theological Quarterly* 32, no. 2 (1988): 119–37.

Kaplan, Jane. *Interfaith Families: Personal Stories of Jewish-Christian Intermarriage.* Westport, CT: Praeger, 2004.

Karner, Christian. *Ethnicity and Everyday Life.* New York: Routledge, 2007.

Kelley, Dean M. *Why Conservative Churches Are Growing: A Study in Sociology of Religion.* New York: Harper & Row, 1977.

Kepel, Gilles. *The Revenge of God: The Resurgence of Islam, Christianity, and Judaism in the Modern World.* Translated by Alan Braley. University Park: The Pennsylvania State University Press, 1994.

Ker, Ian. *John Henry Newman: A Biography*. Oxford: Clarendon Press, 1988.

Kivelson, Valerie A., and Robert H. Greene, "Introduction." In *Orthodox Russia: Belief and Practice under the Tsars*, ed. Valerie A. Kivelson and Robert H. Greene. University Park: Pennsylvania State University Press, 2003.

Krindatch, Alexei D. "'American Orthodoxy' or 'Orthodoxy in America'? Profiling the Next Generation of Eastern Christian Clergy in the USA." Research report for *Research on Orthodox Religious Groups in the United States*. Hartford Institute for Religion Research. http://hirr.hartsem.edu/research/orthodoxarticle2.html.

———. "Eastern Christianity in North American Religious Landscape: Ethnic Traditionalism versus Civic Involvement and Social Transformations." Research report for *Research on Orthodox Religious Groups in the United States*. Hartford Institute for Religion Research. http://hirr.hartsem.edu/research/krindatch.pdf.

———. "Orthodox (Eastern Christian) Churches in the United States at the Beginning of a New Millennium: Questions of Nature, Identity, and Mission." *Journal for the Scientific Study of Religion* 41, no 3 (September 2002): 533–63.

———. "The Realities of Orthodox Parish Life in the Western United States: Ten 'Simple' Answers to Ten 'Not Too Easy' Questions." Research report for *Research on Orthodox Religious Groups in the United States*. Hartford Institute for Religion Research. http://hirr.hartsem.edu/research/krindatchart3.pdf: 1–24.

———. "What Makes the Orthodox Churches Strangers to American Mainstream Christianity." Research report for *Research on Orthodox Religious Groups in the United States*. Hartford Institute for Religion Research. http://hirr.hartsem.edu/research/orthodoxarticle1.html.

Lamb, Christopher, and M. Darrol Bryant, eds. *Religious Conversion: Contemporary Practices and Controversies*. New York: Cassell, 1999.

Lasch, Christopher. *Haven in a Heartless World: The Family Besieged*. New York: Basic Books, 1977.

Lawrence, Bruce B. *Defenders of God: The Fundamentalist Revolt against the Modern Age*. San Francisco: Harper & Row, 1989.

Liacopulos, George P., Fr. *Lights of the Modern World: Orthodox Christian Mission and Evangelism in the United States*. Minneapolis, MN: Light & Life Publishing, 2000.

Lossky, Vladimir. *The Mystical Theology of the Eastern Church*. Crestwood, NY: St. Vladimir's Seminary Press, 1976.

Lucas, Phillip Charles. "*Enfants Terribles:* The Challenge of Sectarian Converts to Ethnic Orthodox Churches in the United States." *Nova Religio: The Journal of Alternative and Emergent Religions* 7, no. 2 (2003): 5–23.

———. *The Odyssey of a New Religion: The Holy Order of MANS from New Age to Orthodoxy*. Bloomington: Indiana University Press, 1995.

Luke, Timothy W. "Identity, Meaning and Globalization: Detraditionalization in Postmodern Space-Time Compression." In *Detraditionalization: Critical Reflections on Authority and Identity*, ed. Paul Heelas, Scott Lash, and Paul Morris. Cambridge, MA: Blackwell Publishers, 1996.

Mathewes-Green, Frederica. *At the Corner of East and Now: A Modern Life in Ancient Christian Orthodoxy*. San Francisco: HarperCollins, 1999.

———. *Facing East: A Pilgrim's Journey into the Mysteries of Orthodoxy*. San Francisco: HarperCollins, 1997.

Mayer, Egon. *Love & Tradition: Marriage between Jews and Christians*. New York: Plenum Press, 1985.

McBrien, Richard P. "Vatican Council II." In *The HarperCollins Encyclopedia of Catholicism*, ed. Richard P. McBrien. New York: HarperCollins, 1995.

McGinty, Anna Mansson. *Becoming Muslim: Western Women's Conversions to Islam*. New York: Palgrave Macmillan, 2006.

McGuckin, John Anthony. *The Orthodox Church: An Introduction to Its History, Doctrine, and Spiritual Culture*. Malden, MA: Wiley-Blackwell, 2008.

Meyendorff, John. *Living Tradition: Orthodox Witness in the Contemporary World*. Crestwood, NY: St. Vladimir's Seminary Press, 1978.

———. *The Orthodox Church: Its Past and Its Role in the World Today*. Translated by John Chapin. New York: Pantheon, 1962.

Meyendorff, Paul. *Russia, Ritual, and Reform: The Liturgical Reforms of Nikon in the Seventeenth Century*. Crestwood, NY: St. Vladimir's Seminary Press, 1991.

Miller, Randall M., and Jon L. Wakelyn, eds. *Catholics in the Old South: Essays on Church and Culture*. Macon, GA: Mercer University Press, 1983.

Mitchell, Leonel L. "Christian Initiation: The Reformation Period." In *Made, Not Born: New Perspectives on Christian Initiation and the Catechumenate*. Liturgical Studies from the Murphy Center for Liturgical Reseach. Notre Dame, IN: University of Notre Dame Press, 1976.

Moore, Laurence R. *Selling God: American Religion in the Marketplace of Culture*. New York: Oxford University Press, 1994.

Morris, Paul. "Community beyond Tradition." In *Detraditionalization: Critical Reflections on Authority and Identity*. Cambridge, MA: Blackwell Publishers, 1996.

Morrison, Peter A. *A Demographic Overview of Metropolitan Pittsburgh*. Santa Monica, CA: Rand IP-246, Rand Corporation, 2003.

Murphy Center for Liturgical Research. *Made, Not Born: New Perspectives on Christian Initiation and the Catechumenate*. Notre Dame, IN: University of Notre Dame Press, 1976.

My Big Fat Greek Wedding. Directed by Joel Zwick. Hollywood, CA: Warner Brothers, 2002.

Narayan, Uma, and Julia J. Bartkowiak. "Introduction." In *Having and Raising Children: Unconventional Families, Hard Choices, and the Social Good*, ed. Uma Narayan and Julia J. Bartkowiak. University Park: Pennsylvania State University Press, 1999.

Neitz, Mary Jo. *Charisma and Community: A Study of Religious Commitment within the Charismatic Renewal*. New Brunswick, NJ: Transaction Books, 1987.

Norman, Corrie E., and Don S. Armentrout, eds. *Religion in the Contemporary South: Changes, Continuities, and Contexts*. Knoxville: University of Tennessee Press, 2005.

Obolensky, Dimitri. *The Byzantine Commonwealth: Eastern Europe, 500–1453*. London: Weidenfeld & Nicholson, 1971.

O'Leary, Stephen. "Cyberspace as Sacred Space: Communicating Religion on Computer Networks." *Journal of the American Academy of Religion* 64, no. 4 (Winter 1996): 781–806.

Oliver, John. *Touching Heaven: Discovering Orthodox Christianity on the Island of Varlaam*. Ben Lomond, CA: Conciliar Press, 2004.

O'Loughlin, Thomas. *Celtic Theology: Humanity, World, and God in Early Irish Writings*. New York: Continuum, 2000.

Orsi, Robert. "Everyday Miracles: The Study of Lived Religion." In *Lived Religion in America: Toward a History of Practice*, ed. David D. Hall. Princeton, NJ: Princeton University Press, 1997.

————. *The Madonna of 115th Street: Faith and Community in Italian Harlem, 1880–1950.* 2nd edition. New Haven, CT: Yale University Press, 2002.

Orthodox Church in America. *Come and See! Encountering the Orthodox Church.* Syosset, NY: Department of Religious Education, OCA, 1983.

Otto, Rudolf. *The Idea of the Holy: An Inquiry into the Non-Rational Factor in the Idea of the Divine and Its Relation to the Rational.* Translated by John W. Harvey. New York: Oxford University Press, 1958.

Pace, Enzo. "Religion as Communication: The Changing Shape of Catholicism in Europe." In *Everyday Religion: Observing Modern Religious Lives,* ed. Nancy T. Ammerman. New York: Oxford University Press, 2007.

Pankhurst, Jerry, Victor Roudometof, and Alexander Agadjanian, eds. *Eastern Orthodoxy in a Global Age: Tradition Faces the Twenty-First Century.* Walnut Creek, CA: AltaMira Press, 2005.

Papioannou, George. *From Mars Hill to Manhattan: The Greek Orthodox in America under Patriarch Athenagoras I.* Minneapolis, MN: Light & Life Publishing, 1976.

Patsavos, Lewis J. "A Canonical Response to Intra-Christian and Inter-religious Marriages." In *Intermarriage: Orthodox Perspectives,* ed. Anton C. Vrame. Brookline, MA: Holy Cross Orthodox Press, 1997.

Peck, M. Scott. *The Road Less Traveled: A New Psychology of Love, Traditional Values and Spiritual Growth.* New York: Walker and Company, 1985.

Poe, Marshall. "Moscow, the Third Rome." *Jahrbucher fur Geschichte Osteuropas* 49, no. 3 (2001): 412-429.

Prodromou, Elizabeth H. "Religious Pluralism in Twenty-First-Century America: Problematizing the Implications for Orthodoxy [*sic*] Christianity." *Journal of the American Academy of Religion* 72, no. 3 (September 2004): 733–57.

Queen, Christopher. "Ambedkar, Modernity, and the Hermeneutics of Buddhist Liberation." In *Dr. Ambedkar, Buddhism and Social Change,* ed. A.K. Narain and D.C. Ahir Delhi: B.R. Publishing, 1994.

Rambo, Lewis R. *Understanding Religious Conversion.* New Haven: Yale University Press, 1993.

Rieff, Philip. *The Triumph of the Therapeutic: Uses of Faith after Freud.* New York: Harper & Row, 1966.

Roof, Wade Clark. *Spiritual Marketplace: Baby Boomers and the Remaking of American Religion.* Princeton, NJ: Princeton University Press, 1999.

Rosenthal, Edward C. *The Era of Choice: The Ability to Choose and Its Transformation of Contemporary Life.* Cambridge, MA: MIT Press, 2005.

The Russian Primary Chronicle: Laurentian Text. Translated and edited by Samuel Hazzard Cross and Olgerd P. Shobowitz-Wetzor. Cambridge, MA: The Medieval Academy of America, 1953.

Rutherford, Jonathan, ed. *Identity, Community, and Cultural Difference.* London: Lawrence & Wishart, 1990.

Saloutos, Theodore. *The Greeks in the United States.* Cambridge, MA: Harvard University Press, 1964.

The Sayings of the Desert Fathers: The Alphabetical Collection. Revised edition. Translated by Benedicta Ward. Kalamazoo, MI: Cistercian Publications, 1984.

Schaeffer, Frank. *Dancing Alone: The Quest for Orthodox Faith in an Age of False Religion.* Brookline, MA: Holy Cross Orthodox Press, 1994.

Schmemann, Alexander. *For the Life of the World: Sacraments and Orthodoxy*. 2nd edition. Crestwood, NY: St. Vladimir's Seminary Press, 1997.

Schwartz, Adam. *The Third Spring: G.K. Chesterton, Graham Greene, Christopher Dawson, and David Jones*. Washington, DC: Catholic University of America Press, 2005.

Schweiger, Beth Barton, and Donald G. Mathews, eds. *Religion in the American South: Protestants and Others in History and Culture*. Chapel Hill: University of North Carolina Press, 2004.

The Seven Ecumenical Councils of the Undivided Church: Their Canons and Dogmatic Decrees, Together with the Canons of All the Local Synods Which Have Received Ecumenical Acceptance. Nicene & Post-Nicene Fathers. Edited by Henry R. Percival. Reprint. Grand Rapids, MI: Eerdmans Publishing Company, 1997.

Shevzov, Vera. "Letting the People into Church: Reflections on Orthodoxy and Community in Late Imperial Russia." In *Orthodox Russia: Belief and Practice under the Tsars*, ed. Valerie A. Kivelson and Robert H. Greene. University Park: Pennsylvania State University Press, 2003.

Shore, Bradd. "American Middle-Class Families: Class, Social Reproduction, and Ritual." In *Family Transformed: Religion, Values, and Society in American Life*, ed. Steven M. Tipton and John Witte, Jr. Washington, DC: Georgetown University Press, 2005.

Slagle, Amy. "Imagined Aesthetics: Constructions of Aesthetic Experience in Orthodox Christian Conversion Narratives." In *Aesthetics as a Religious Factor in Eastern and Western Christianity: Selected Papers of the International Conference held at the University of Utrecht, the Netherlands, in June 2004*, ed. Wil van den Bercken and Jonathan Sutton. Leuven, Belgium: Peeters, 2005.

———. "In the Eye of the Beholder: Perspectives on Intermarriage Conversion in Orthodox Christian Parishes in Pittsburgh, Pennsylvania." *Religion and American Culture: A Journal of Interpretation* 20, no. 2 (2010): 233–57.

Snow, David A., and Richard Machalek. "The Convert as a Social Type." In *Sociological Theory*, 259–89. San Francisco: Jossey-Bass, 1983.

Sollors, Werner, ed. *Theories of Ethnicity: A Classical Reader*. Basingstoke: Macmillan, 1996.

Sophrony, Archimandrite. *St. Silouan the Athonite*. Translated by Rosemary Edmonds. Crestwood, NY: St. Vladimir's Seminary Press, 1999.

Sparks, Randy J. *Religion in Mississippi*. Heritage of Mississippi Series. Volume 2. Jackson: University Press of Mississippi, 2001.

Stark, Rodney, and William S. Bainbridge. *The Future of Religion: Secularization, Revival and Cult Formation*. Berkeley: University of California Press, 1985.

———. "Networks of Faith: Interpersonal Bonds and Recruitment in Cults and Sects." *American Journal of Sociology* 85, no. 6 (May 1980).

———. *A Theory of Religion*. New York: Peter Lang, 1987.

Stark, Rodney, and Roger Finke. *The Churching of America, 1776–2005: Winners and Losers in Our Religious Economy*. 2nd edition. New Brunswick, NJ: Rutgers University Press, 2005.

Stevick, Daniel B. "Christian Initiation: Post-Reformation to the Present Era." In *Made, Not Born: New Perspectives on Christian Initiation and the Catechumenate*, Liturgical Studies from the Murphy Center for Liturgical Research. Notre Dame, IN: University of Notre Dame Press, 1976.

Stokoe, Mark, and Very Rev. Leonid Kishkovsky, "The Emerging American Mission: Evangelization." In *Orthodox Christians in North America, 1794-1994*. Orthodox

Church in America website: http://www.oca.org/MVorthchristiansnamericaTOC. asp?SID=1.

——.*Orthodox Christians in North America, 1794–1994.* Syosset, NY: Orthodox Christian Publications Center, 1995.

Swartz, David. "Bridging the Study of Culture and Religion: Pierre Bourdieu's Political Economy of Symbolic Power." *Sociology of Religion* 57 (Spring 1996): 71–85.

Swidler, Ann. "Culture in Action: Symbols and Strategies." *American Sociological Review* 51, no. 2 (April 1986): 273–86.

——. *Talk of Love: How Culture Matters.* Chicago: University of Chicago Press, 2001.

Treadgold, Warren. "The Persistence of Byzantium." *Wilson Quarterly* 22, no. 4 (1998): 66–91.

Turner, Victor. "Symbolism, Morality, Social Structure." In *The Forest of Symbols: Aspects of Ndembu Ritual.* Ithaca, NY: Cornell University Press, 1967.

Tweed, Thomas. *Our Lady of the Exile: Diasporic Religion at a Cuban Catholic Shrine in Miami.* New York: Oxford University Press, 1997.

Tyson, Ruel W., James L. Peacock, and Daniel W. Patterson, eds. *Diversities of Gifts: Field Studies in Southern Religion.* Urbana: University of Illinois Press, 1988.

U.S. Bureau of the Census. *State and County Quickfacts (Allegheny County, Pennsylvania)*, Washington, DC, 2000. Accessed online at http://quickfacts.census.gov/qfd/states/42/42003.html.

Valliere, Paul. "Introduction to the Modern Orthodox Tradition." In *Teachings of Modern Orthodox Christianity on Law, Politics, and Human Nature*, ed. John Witte, Jr., and Frank S. Alexander. New York: Columbia University Press, 2007.

——. *Modern Russian Theology: Bukharev, Soloviev, Bulgakov: Orthodox Theology in a New Key.* Grand Rapids, MI: William B. Eerdmans Publishing Company, 2000.

Viswanathan, Gauri. *Outside the Fold: Conversion, Modernity, and Belief.* Princeton, NJ: Princeton University Press, 1998.

Vrame, Anton C., ed. *Intermarriage: Orthodox Perspectives.* Brookline, MA: Holy Cross Orthodox Press, 1997.

Ward, Karen. "Making Adult Disciples: Rite for Our Times—Adult Baptism." *Christian Century* 116, no. 10 (March 24, 1999): 348–50.

Ware, Kallistos (Bishop). "The Witness of the Orthodox Church in the Twentieth Century." *SOUROZH* 80 (May 2000).

Ware, Timothy. *The Orthodox Church.* 2nd edition. New York: Penguin Books, 1993.

Waters, Mary C. *Ethnic Options: Choosing Identities in America.* Berkeley: University of California Press, 1990.

The Way of a Pilgrim. Translated by Olga Savin. Boston: Shambhala, 1996.

Whitehead, Barbara Dafoe. "The Changing Pathway to Marriage: Trends in Dating, First Unions, and Marriage among Young Adults." In *Family Transformed: Religion, Values, and Society in American Life*, ed. Steven M. Tipton and John Witte, Jr. Washington, DC: Georgetown University Press, 2005.

Whitehead, Barbara Dafoe, and David Popenoe. "Who Wants to Marry a Soulmate?" In *The State of Our Unions 2001.* Piscataway, NJ: National Marriage Project, Rutgers University, 2001.

Whitehead, Harriet. *Renunciation and Reformation: A Study of Conversion in an American Sect.* Ithaca, NY: Cornell University Press, 1987.

Whitesides, Paisios Bukowy. "Ethnics and Evangelicals: Theological Tensions within American Orthodoxy." *St. Vladimir's Theological Quarterly* 41, no. 1 (1997): 19–35.

Wind, James P., and James W. Lewis, eds. *American Congregations.* Volume 1: *Portraits of Twelve Religious Communities.* Chicago: University of Chicago Press, 1994.

——. *American Congregations.* Volume 2: *New Perspectives in the Study of Congregations.* Chicago: University of Chicago Press, 1994.

Witte, John Jr., and Frank S. Alexander, eds. *The Teachings of Modern Orthodox Christianity on Law, Politics, & Human Nature.* New York: Columbia University Press, 2007.

Wuthnow, Robert. *After the Baby Boomers: How Twenty- and Thirty-Somethings Are Shaping the Future of American Religion.* Princeton, NJ: Princeton University Press, 2007.

——. *America and the Challenges of Religious Diversity.* Princeton, NJ: Princeton University Press, 2005.

——. "The Family as Contested Terrain." In *Family Transformed: Religion, Values, and Society in American Life,* ed. Steven M. Tipton and John Witte, Jr. Washington, DC: Georgetown University Press, 2005.

——. *The Restructuring of American Religion: Society and Faith since World War II.* Prince-ton, NJ: Princeton University Press, 1988.

Websites

American Carpatho-Russian Orthodox Diocese of the USA: http://www.acrod.org

The Brotherhood of St. Moses the Black: http://www.mosestheblack.org

Glenmary Research Center, Nashville, TN: http://glenmary.org/GRC (now in Cincinnati, OH)

Greek Orthodox Archdiocese of America: http://goarchh.org

Hartford Institute for Religion Research, Hartford, CT: http://hirr.hartsem.edu

Orthodox Church in America: http://www.oca.org

The Pew Forum on Religion and the Public Life: http://pewforum.org

The Self-Ruled Antiochian Orthodox Christian Archdiocese of North America: http://www.antiochian.org

U.S. Census Bureau: http://www.census.gov

Ukrainian Orthodox Church of the United States of America: http://www.uocofusa.org

Periodicals

Again. Mount Hermon, CA: Evangelical Orthodox Church. 1979–1987.

Again. Ben Lomond, CA: Conciliar Press, a Department of the Antiochian Orthodox Church of North America. 1987–2009.

The Handmaiden. Ben Lomond, CA: Conciliar Press, a Department of the Antiochian Orthodox Church of North America. 1997–2009.

Index

Mathewes-Green, Frederica, 50

Maximus the Confessor, 20, 90, 181n.5

McGuckin, Anthony, 17

Media, 9, 168: electronic, 9, 28, 33, 36, 50–52, 58, 61, 78, 144; print, 9, 48–49, 58, 144; in spiritual marketplace 39–40, 78; television, 40, 52, 78, 123

Methodist/Methodism, 44, 47, 92, 153; United, 164, 165

Meyendorff, Fr. John, 22, 23–24, 49, 90, 91, 116, 129

Mississippi, 3, 15, 24, 61; Orthodoxy in, 33–34; 143; 147–56; Protestantism in, 33, 152–53

Moscow, 111; Patriarchate, 19; as "Third Rome," 19

Multiculturalism, 87, 138–39

Muslim/Islam, 19, 45, 48, 55, 122

My Big Fat Greek Wedding (film), 124

Nazarene, Church of the, 102

Neopatristic theology, 22; importance of Tradition in, 90–91; view of the church in, 116

New Age spiritualities, 165

Newman, Cardinal John Henry, 71, 119

New Religious Movements (NRMs), 11; authority as liberating in, 99; conversion to, 41–42, 53

Nicene-Constantinopolitan Creed, 22, 26, 74

Obolensky, Dimitri, 19

O'Conner, Flannery, 81

The Odyssey of a New Religion (Lucas), 11

Old Believer Schism, 116

Optina Monastery, 79

Orsi, Robert, 12

Orthodox Christianity: as ancient/early church, 7–8, 9–10, 49, 85, 91; architectural features of, 26, 31; authority in, 20–21, 101; compared to Protestantism/Roman Catholicism, 18–21; change resistant, 23, 85, 86, 99; contrasted with American culture, 8–10, 86–88, 92–93; conversions to, 9–11, 25, 65; as cultural "toolkit," 13, 15, 85, 99, 104, 106; in the United States, 8–10, 16–17, 24–25; and

ethnicity, 19, 24–25, 124–42; as morally liberating, 101–3; organization of, 19–21; portrayed as "exotic," 17; ritual life of, 23, 63, 96,105–17; source of self-fulfillment, 85, 86, 98–99, 112–13, 144; "spiritual capital" of, 63, 71–72, 159; and spiritual marketplace, 9–10, 24, 37, 43, 48–49, 53, 63, 83, 72, 85, 126, 143, 161; Tradition in, 8, 21–24, 86, 90–92, 99, 100–101, 129; as "true church," 7, 86–87, 98–100, 121, 158

The Orthodox Church (Ware), 19, 117

Orthodox Church in America (OCA), 32, 52, 89, 132, 139; conversions to, 25, 65; ethnographic research at, 26, 33, 171, 172; formation of, 19; mission efforts of, 33; in Pittsburgh, 26

Otto, Rudolf, 41

Ottoman Turks, 19

Pace, Enzo, 78

Papal infallibility, 22

Paul, Apostle, 41, 129

Peck, M. Scott, 40

Pelikan, Jaroslav, 9

Pentecostal/Pentecostalism, 4, 46, 47, 123, 165

Pew Research Center, 5

Pews: absence of in Orthodox churches, 108, 121; conflicts over, 117, 118, 120; presence of in Orthodox churches, 26, 31

Pittsburgh: demographics of, 164–65; Orthodoxy in, 25–27, 28, 30, 32, 133–34, 145, 156

Pittsburgh Steelers, 9, 160

Pluralism, religious, 4–5, 9, 10, 86, 87, 88, 89, 91, 158

Poland, 19

Polumalu, Troy, 9

Pope, 20, 21, 102

Practice theory, 12

Presbyterian/Presbyterianism, 34, 44, 46, 51, 59, 62, 121, 144, 151, 152, 164, 165, 171, 172

Print media. *See* Media

Prodromou, Elizabeth H., 10

of evangelical Protestantism in, 33; Orthodox presence in, 9, 33, 145–46, 148, 149, 150, 154; racial divisions in, 154–55; religious sensibilities of converts in, 148–54; social/spiritual dichotomy, 152–53

Spiritual capital, 63, 71–72, 126, 159

Spiritual marketplace, the: in America, 5–6, 8, 38–40, 126,158; in converts' backgrounds/childhoods, 43–48, 148; choice in, 5–7, 12, 13, 43–48, 60, 70–71, 83, 158, 161; clerical perspectives on, 58–60; commitment in, 15, 158–59 ; conservative churches in, 6; consumerism in, 87–89; and conversion, 12–13, 38, 43; cradle Orthodox responses to, 126–27; as cultural "toolkit," 13, 14, 85, 130–31, 157, 158; and intermarriage converts, 54, 57–58; Orthodoxy and, 9–10, 24, 37, 43, 53, 63, 83, 85, 126, 143, 161; pluralism in, 3–6, 43–48, 60, 70–71, 87; relativism in, 87, 89; religious seeking in, 12, 43–48, 58–60, 83,116; self-reflexivity in, 43, 39–40, self-reliance in, 7

Starets. See Elders

Stark, Rodney, 6, 53

Strategies of action: and choice, 42; in identity construction, 8, 13, 15, 85, 98, 103,159; in the Orthodox Church, 100–101, 103, 104, 106, 159. *See also* Ritual; Toolkit, culture as

Swidler, Ann, 12, 68, 96, 109

Symeon the New Theologian, 91, 181n.5

Taiwanese-American conversions, 53

Theophan the Recluse, 91, 182n.5

Thomas Aquinas, 20

Tikhon of Zadonsk, 91, 182n.5

Toth, Alexis Fr., 25

Toolkit, culture as, 12–13, 15, 59, 85, 99, 104, 106, 148, 158. *See* Ritual; Strategies of action

Tradition, 15; definitions of, 21–22, 90; as factor in conversions, 59, 85, 86, 90–92, 94, 98–99, 104, 157–58; and human/"little" traditions, 23–24, 110, 129; as liberating, 86, 98–101; and new media, 51; in Orthodox Church, 8, 21–24, 86, 90–92, 99, 100–101, 129; in the spiritual marketplace, 11, 157–58

Transformation, self. *See* Self-fulfillment/growth

"Triumph of the therapeutic," 85

Trinity, 18

Truth: as factor in conversions, 4, 47–48, 60, 91–92, 105, 118, 134,159; as liberating, 99; in Orthodox Church, 7, 8, 85, 86–92, 99, 104, 140; in other churches/religions, 89, 121–22

Turner, Victor, 36

Ukraine, 131, 136

Ukrainian: immigrants, 27; Orthodox Church, 26

Unchurched, the, 80, 92, 165, 171

Unitarian/Unitarianism, 92

Valliere, Paul, 17, 21

The Varieties of Religious Experience (James), 40

Vatican II Council, 6, 22, 23, 89–90, 95, 116, 135, 173n.5

Viswanathan, Gauri, 13, 42

Vladimir, Prince of Kiev, 105, 108

Ware, Bishop Kallistos (Timothy Ware), 19, 20, 33, 49, 117

Waters, Mary, 127

The Way of a Pilgrim, 79

Wayne, John, 138

Whitehead, Barbara Dafoe, 54

Whitehead, Harriet, 42

Whitesides, Paisios Bukowy, 11, 49, 126

Wuthnow, Robert, 46, 54, 96

Lightning Source UK Ltd.
Milton Keynes UK
UKHW011956260123
416025UK00004B/242